Heterodox Economics and Global Emergencies

From the financial crash to the climate emergency and Covid-19, this book demonstrates that recent crises have had unequal impacts, they require a heterodox approach to economics for their understanding, and new ways of thinking are needed to address them. Drawing on a variety of heterodox and radical perspectives and global voices, including those from India, Africa, and South America, this collection explores the causes and impacts of global emergencies from a wide array of viewpoints. The first section outlines how the pandemic has shown up the biases of orthodox thought and policy, particularly its Eurocentric and patriarchal focus on the urban, formal economy. It outlines how adding an international dimension to institutional analysis uncovers systematic inequalities in the responses to emergencies, and how new paradigms can provide better alternatives. The massive interventionism worldwide has led to renewed interest in the global financial system, and also in Marxian approaches to money. The second section of the book therefore considers a range of alternative approaches to the study of finance – from Marx to Minsky – which are currently being revisited. The collection concludes with a suggestion for heterodox economics pedagogy, since changing economics education is vital for future dissemination of real-world ideas. The book will be of interest to a variety of researchers and postgraduate students, and lecturers, especially in the fields of development, health, labour and feminist economics, and also international political economy and heterodox economics.

Ariane Agunsoye is Senior Lecturer in Economics in the Institute of Management Studies, Goldsmiths, University of London, UK.

Thoralf Dassler is Senior Lecturer at the University of Westminster, UK.

Eurydice Fotopoulou is an Economist for the International Monetary Fund (IMF). All views expressed here are of the author and do not necessarily represent the views of the IMF, its Executive Board, or IMF management.

Jon Mulberg is Associate Lecturer in the Faculty of Arts and Social Science at the Open University, UK.

Routledge Frontiers of Political Economy

Economic Theory for the Real World
Victor A. Beker

The Structure and Operation of Modern Economies
Alessandro Romagnoli

Researching Poverty and Austerity
Theoretical Approaches, Methodologies and Policy Applications
Edited by Caroline Moraes, Morven G McEachern and Deirdre O'Loughlin

Nature and Economic Society
A Classical-Keynesian Synthesis
Tony Aspromourgos

Economic Policies of Populist Leaders
A Central and Eastern European Perspective
Edited by István Benczes

Political Economy of the Spanish Miracle
State, Labor and Capital, 1931–1973
Diego Ayala

Heterodox Economics and Global Emergencies
Voices from Around the World
Edited by Ariane Agunsoye, Thoralf Dassler, Eurydice Fotopoulou and Jon Mulberg

For more information about this series, please visit: www.routledge.com/Routledge-Frontiers-of-Political-Economy/book-series/SE0345

Heterodox Economics and Global Emergencies

Voices from Around the World

Edited by Ariane Agunsoye, Thoralf Dassler, Eurydice Fotopoulou and Jon Mulberg

Routledge
Taylor & Francis Group
LONDON AND NEW YORK

First published 2024
by Routledge
4 Park Square, Milton Park, Abingdon, Oxon OX14 4RN

and by Routledge
605 Third Avenue, New York, NY 10158

Routledge is an imprint of the Taylor & Francis Group, an informa business

British Library Cataloguing-in-Publication Data
A catalogue record for this book is available from the British Library

ISBN: 9781032582818 (hbk)
ISBN: 9781032588926 (pbk)
ISBN: 9781003451990 (ebk)

DOI: 10.4324/9781003451990

Typeset in Times New Roman
by Newgen Publishing UK

Contents

List of Contributors *vii*

Introduction: Permacrisis, Overlapping Crises, Inter-crises 1
ARIANE AGUNSOYE AND EURYDICE FOTOPOULOU

SECTION 1
Inequalities and Alternative Approaches **9**

1 Heterodox Economic Policy Outlook: A Proven Boon at the Time of a Global Pandemic 11
MEDHA A. SATHI

2 The Reach of Fiscal Stimulus for Urban Women Informal Sector Workers in Bengaluru during COVID-19 27
R. VIJAYAMBA

3 The Impact of Covid-19 on the Economy of Lower-Income Bogotá Families: An Analysis Using Polanyi's Concept of the Economy as an Instituted Process 40
SONIA CAROLINA LÓPEZ CERÓN

SECTION 2
Finance and the Causes of Crises **57**

4 On the Financial Instability Hypothesis and Its Global Implications Post-Covid-19 59
BARKIN CIHANLI

5 Estimating Economic Surplus in Argentina: The Neoliberal Strategy, Its Crisis and the Neo-Developmentalist Model (1991–2015) 75
LEANDRO MARCELO BONA

6 The Commodity Character of Marx's Theory of Money: An Assessment of the Debate and Open Problems 97
NICOLÁS AGUILA

SECTION 3
Economics Education and Change **117**

7 Qualitative Economics and the Opportunity to Push for Heterodoxy in the Classroom 119
JUAN DAVID PARRA

8 Conclusion: "Crisis of What?" "Crisis for Whom?" 143
JON MULBERG AND THORALF DASSLER

Index *153*

Contributors

Nicolás Aguila is in the Department of Philosophy, Politics, and Economics, Universität Witten/Herdecke.

Ariane Agunsoye is Senior Lecturer in Economics in the Institute of Management Studies, Goldsmiths, University of London.

Leandro Marcelo Bona is in the Latin American Faculty of Social Sciences (FLACSO-Argentina), and the National University of La Plata (Argentina).

Sonia Carolina López Cerón is Assistant Professor at the Pontificia Universidad Javeriana, Bogotá, Colombia.

Barkin Cihanli is in the Economics Department at the University of Missouri-Kansas City.

Thoralf Dassler is Senior Lecturer at the University of Westminster, UK.

Eurydice Fotopoulou is an Economist for the International Monetary Fund (IMF). All views expressed here are of the author and do not necessarily represent the views of the IMF, its Executive Board, or IMF management.

Jon Mulberg is Associate Lecturer in the Faculty of Arts and Social Science at the Open University, UK.

Juan David Parra is Assistant Professor in the Instituto de Estudios en Educación (IESE), Universidad del Norte, Colombia.

Medha A. Sathi works at the Centre for Economic and Social Studies (CESS).

R. Vijayamba is a research fellow at the Centre for Sustainable Employment, Azim Premji University.

Introduction

Permacrisis, Overlapping Crises, Inter-crises

Ariane Agunsoye and Eurydice Fotopoulou

At the moment of writing, in early 2023, the world economic outlook is pretty bleak. There are persistently high levels of inflation across the world, soaring cost of living, unemployment, supply chain disruptions, soaring energy costs, and armed conflicts. In the aftermath of one the most severe global health crises, the spread of Covid-19, overstretched public health provision is only adding to the long list of factors that have aligned to expose the shortcomings of the mainstream economic mode of operation.

The word "crisis" has become ubiquitous this century in colloquial vocabulary,[1] starting with the financial crisis of 2008 which left deep scars in many economies and initiated a doctrine of forced austerity, driven by neoclassical economic orthodoxy. "Crisis" is not in the title of this book, but it is very much in the core of the issues we seek to address. However, it implies a temporary nature of the issues at hand, which is grossly misleading. The issues that our society faces – not limited by geography – have been in the making for decades. Profound economic and social changes of recent decades have left many at a disadvantage, which has only been exposed once a health emergency swept across the world, to show in the most brutal way the shortcomings of capitalism and the misconceived approaches to health based on conventional economic theory and policy.

The term "emergencies", which we have opted for to convey a clear message, indicates that the situation has brought societies at a breaking point and requires urgent action. In fact, it requires a complete reset to explain and resolve the chronic crises described in this volume, which only recently have surfaced in multiple versions in media and popular discourse around us.

This is where the work collected in this volume seeks to make a contribution by focusing more on the urgency of action, the urgency of re-comprehension, and the vision for a sustainable solution. It puts forward the argument that recent overlapping crises require a more radical, heterodox approach to economics for their understanding, and new ways of thinking to address them. By now there is ample evidence of how recent shocks in supply, demand, health, and the environment have had unequal impacts across the world and on different population groups. The collection goes beyond that. It outlines how the pandemic has uncovered once again the biases of orthodox thought and policy, particularly its Eurocentric and

DOI: 10.4324/9781003451990-1

patriarchal focus on the urban, formal, market economy. Further, it demonstrates that we need a heterodox approach to economics for understanding chronic crises and developing new ways of addressing them, with the long-term goal of preventing them by fostering equitable, greener development.

The book examines how ignoring a variety of inequalities such as class, gender, and ethnicity, as well as ignoring the informal economy and alternative rationalities, leads not only to unequal impacts during emergencies but also to an inability to formulate adequate emergency responses. Another goal of the book is to shed more light on the way austerity policies have often led to a healthcare deficit, as well as to deeper economic crises, which, in turn, exacerbated the effects of health shocks throughout the world. These discussions challenge orthodox economics and economic policy worldwide, resulting in the re-emergence of interventionist policies and radical economics. The volume has an international, heterodox, and interdisciplinary perspective and brings to the fore voices from the Global South – where the unequal impact of Covid-19 on society and economy is more manifest – and employs an institutional and critical approach to understanding economics and for devising policy responses to emergencies.

Section 1: Inequalities and Alternative Approaches

The first section of the book starts by emphasizing the systematic inequalities in the responses to emergencies, and how new paradigms can provide better alternatives. The particular focus lies on inequalities based on class, gender, and being part of the informal sector. The first two chapters discuss the responses to the Covid-19 emergencies in India, unveiling the impact of differential approaches. Whilst in the first case heterodox approaches to poverty reduction helped to smoothen the impact of lockdowns on marginalized workers, the second chapter looks at the matter from almost a mirror-opposite view, by showing how the focus on mainstream economic approaches intensifies existing inequalities during emergencies. The third chapter then concludes this section by drawing attention to Colombia, employing insights from Karl Polanyi to show why the institutional setting, despite its limitations, was not challenged as a result of the pandemic.

Numerous countries during the pandemic introduced state support programmes which were more in line with heterodox understandings of fiscal and monetary support than with the orthodox focus on market relations. Drawing a distinction between mainstream and heterodox economic approaches when tackling inequalities, the second chapter of this volume highlights the insufficiency of solutions based on market relations and suggests that a new world is possible by learning from the heterodox approaches that were adopted during the pandemic. For this purpose, the author has chosen to elaborate on a poverty eradication programme of the Indian state Kerala. Here, Sathi argues that while the Indian government neglected the impact of lockdowns on lower income earners, informal sector workers, and migrant workers, the government of Kerala and its particular focus on poverty reduction has helped to lower the impact of Covid-19 lockdowns. Kerala's redistribution programme has been built on heterodox social provisioning approaches seeking to increase social mobility by providing public housing, free medical care, provision of education, and price control on food. This approach to poverty reduction was essential in making sure everyone – including migrant workers and workers in the informal sector – received sufficient help in the form of food, shelter, and money. In contrast, the central government did not provide food or subsidies to migrant workers which led to many migrant families having to walk days to get to their home without sufficient supplies, resulting in many deaths. The success of this programme shows, on the one hand, that a decentralized approach to poverty reduction can be beneficial during emergencies and, on the other hand, the need to develop long-term heterodox approaches to be able to fight the continuous emergencies the world is dealing with.

In a similar theme, Vijayamba is looking into an intersectionality of vulnerability that led to exclusion and intensification of hardship during the pandemic. Whilst gendered and racialized dimensions of the pandemic have been discussed extensively within the frame of the formal market and unpaid work, highlighting how women and/or people from minority groups have been disproportionally affected by unemployment, underemployment, and a rise in unpaid work, there has been lesser focus on the informal sector. This gap is filled by the third chapter. Vijayamba analyses the interplay between Covid-19 fiscal stimulus programmes introduced by the Indian government and their impact on rural female workers in Bengaluru. Highlighting the inadequacy of government subsidies, which not only have ignored the needs of rural female workers but also exacerbated inherent inequalities in the informal sector, the author argues that gendered dimensions within the informal labour market need to be taken into account when planning and implementing emergency responses. Vijayamba unpicks the details of the policies introduced and unveils how these are inadequate for female rural workers working in the informal sector. For instance, because monetary support for female workers depended on the condition of them having a bank account, as part of the frame of the financial inclusion initiative of the government, female workers without a bank account were unable to receive such monetary help. It thus has resulted in no access to sufficient food and income by female rural workers, which was further intensified when/if their husband lost their job too, when considering the household. Consequently, relying on mainstream economic assumptions of financial inclusion initiatives eventually disadvantaged women who did not want to take part in the programme because they were working in the informal sector. The incorporation of the financial inclusion programme within the fiscal stimulus thus had the opposite effect of what financial inclusion initiatives aim to achieve: it intensified financial insecurity in contrast to providing financial security.

An integral part of challenging mainstream approaches to tackle inequalities is discussing alternative theoretical approaches in the context of the pandemic. While the previous two chapters have been instrumental in this by means of empirical discussions, Cerón, in Chapter 3, employs Karl Polanyi's exploration of the interplay between economy and society, and seeks to identify how forms of economic integration, such as market or households, become institutionalized. The author combines a historical analysis with current emergencies, highlighting the impact of the changing institutionalization of the family unit on access to financial support by the government. The author starts with an exploration of the impact of the state, mapping the definition of the family unit throughout time, spanning across colonial times, to the introduction of the welfare state, to the sweeping wave of the neoliberalization of the state welfare provision. During these time periods, the definition of the family has oscillated between accepting single mothers and extended families, and narrower definitions of a family, implying a husband and wife and their children, where the husband is the main breadwinner, and opening up the definition to same-sex couples, single fathers, and non-married couples. These different phases of definition demarcate that a different degree of institutionalization of families has an impact on the support provided by government. Cerón shows how traces from the variety of the institutional label of families can be found in the way Colombia dealt with the impact of Covid-19, and have contributed, alongside an interaction with dimensions of inequalities, to an individualization of coping strategies.

Section 2: Finance and the Causes of Emergencies

Naturally, the ability of each state depends on its ability to finance the public provision of welfare, and this was widely acknowledged during the pandemic. The broad interventions worldwide that mobilized state resources for public health provision and economic support have led to a renewed interest in the global financial system, and among those specifically in Marxian approaches to money. However, the duration and level of economic support and public health provision are largely conditional on public finances. These rely on the institutional setting and the ideology that informs its assumptions. With this consideration in mind, the second section of the book therefore presents a range of alternative approaches to the study of finance – from Minsky to Marx – which are currently being revisited, and are acutely topical, as we are going through a (yet another) period of high inflation.

The section starts by discussing the prominent financial instability hypothesis introduced by a key figure in heterodox economics, Hyman P. Minsky. Minsky unveiled one major flaw of mainstream economic approaches: the financial structure is not essential in the functioning of the economy where money is argued to be neutral. In contrast, Minsky places finance at the centre of the economy, revealing how capitalism has an inherent tendency to financial instability: periods of boom are followed by financial crash. Cihanli takes up Minsky's financial instability hypothesis and explores the interplay between finance and institutional settings, seeking to answer what sources of financial instability are and what does it mean for economic policies, a topic that can determine the ability of a state to prevent crises or act quickly during emergencies. For this purpose, the author first unpicks the key components of the financial instability hypothesis, before showing how insights from the hypothesis can be helpful to understand current global issues. Of particular interest here is the impact of finance on the sovereignty of states, limiting the possibilities of domestic policy space and highlighting the need to re-establish sovereignty, which is of particular importance in developing countries that may have seen their fiscal space squeezed during the pandemic. The chapter closes by making policy suggestions, mainly how Minsky's insights could be used to restructure public and private institutions in a capitalist market economy.

The following chapter develops further the discussion on the type of state governance and its ability to deploy effective economic policy and integrates an empirical lens. Bona explores the Argentinian economy and draws a comparison between times of neoliberal and redistributive policies of the same administration, and its impact on inequalities within the country. Given the turbulent path of exchange rates in Argentina over the last few decades, this chapter can be seen as a case study on public finances and debt management. The example of Argentina would be a useful lesson for countries with similarly high dependencies on international finance as the leniency extended by international donors during the pandemic has drawn to a close. During the neoliberal policy period, tax reductions for wealthier individuals were introduced accompanied by a deregulation of the labour market, alongside diminishing public investment, whereas in the periods of redistributive policy emphasis lay on increasing taxes and tariffs and use the rising public revenue for public investment. To explain the impact of differential policy responses on social wealth and its unequal distribution, the author draws on the concept of economic surplus and suggest methods to measure it, as it can essentially circumscribe the ability of a state to engage in public welfare provision. Economic surplus is defined here as the income from manifold exploitations, reflected in profits, rents, interests and high incomes. Empirical evidence provided in the chapter shows that economic surplus is always higher than needed for social reproduction, yet the policies introduced had an impact on its extent. During the period of neoliberal policies, wealth was mainly channelled towards the social elites, whereas, as expected by heterodox theories of redistribution, periods of redistributive policies have led to countering this tendency. Aside of the income effect, this empirical exploration also suggests that the cost of living increased, which highlights the need to not solely focus on how economic surplus is appropriated, but on how it is generated and what it means. Is it the outcome of productive or unproductive activity? These reflections by Bona are more relevant than ever given the cost of living crisis experienced by numerous countries.

The section then returns to fundamental issues by contemplating the nature of money, which can or cannot allow governments to deal with emergencies, with Aguila's exploration of Marx's theory of money. The author takes up Marx's theory of money and discusses its implications, as well as limitations in the current monetary order, with the consequences those may have in economic emergencies. For this purpose, a distinction is drawn between the Bretton Woods era where the dollar was established as world currency and its convertibility to gold, and the current monetary order where gold convertibility has been phased out. The key question Aguila seeks to answer is then what does the modern, post-Bretton Woods monetary order mean for Marx's theory of money as commodity and as unit of account. To answer this question the author provides a theoretical discussion and explores the social meaning of money as well its physical components. Aguila concludes his discussion on the diametrical views between money as a social entity and as a commodity, by arguing that money provides the solution to the organization of labour and as such it does not have to be a commodity in physical form, but it can be a commodity in ideal form, "establishing the unity of social labour". The question remaining then is what the unit of account in a post-Bretton Woods world can be, if there is no convertibility to gold, having relevance to current debates on cryptocurrencies, with the possible implications this can have on public finances.

Section 3: Education and Change

The collection concludes with a suggestion for heterodox economics pedagogy, since changing economic education is vital for future dissemination of real-world ideas. It is not sufficient to discuss heterodox economics; it is essential to be able to communicate it to broaden economics students' horizons. Hence, the final chapter highlights how recent events have reinforced the need to include pluralistic ideas. Parra outlines how qualitative explorations can be beneficial here to overcome some of economics' limitations. For this purpose, the author first outlines key aspects which are missing in current teachings of economics, including the most recent advances in introducing pluralistic views in the form of the CORE project. Additionally, it introduces an alternative approach to teaching economics which challenges elements of economic reasoning and brings new insights with the help of qualitative research. A case is built on how interviews, observations and/or focus groups can help to inform but simultaneously challenge quantitative studies and therefore being especially essential for heterodox understandings of economic phenomena. For instance, while households' financial decisions are observable in the case of economic indicators such as debt statistics, their underlying causes, for example, in the form of motivations are not evident. To outline its key contributions, Parra draws on auto-ethnographic experiences in designing and delivering a pluralistic methods course, revealing potential complications and strategies employed. Given the continuous emergencies the world economy has experienced, this is a long overdue discussion on the need for increased engagement with not only pluralist theories but also pluralist methodologies.

A volume collecting this research seems a reasonable approach to deal with a broadly skewed understanding of the issues identified. In global and regional context alike, the contributions acknowledge that the way we define institutional units, and their governance can have very tangible effects on people's ability to survive or not in an emergency. Besides this, the type of policy adopted in each case examined in the book, with its underlying ideological priorities, apart from being an exercise in macroeconomic housekeeping, is a reminder of and a study on emergencies that have passed but left deep scars. The contributions invite us to set the record right, by paying attention to the root of emergencies: money, and its function in modern economies. This, in turn, can determine the ability of governments to take effective action to provide public welfare. However, accounting for the function of money is not sufficient. It needs to be complemented by practitioners of economics that have broader intellectual horizons. We aim to contribute to the development of a new generation of economists, and perhaps convince a few more on the way, by offering an alternative, humanity-centric (not individualistic) discourse, with examples of how it can trickle down into pedagogy of economics. We encourage the interested reader to use this book to reassess the common arguments put forward to justify responses to "crises", rather than actively dealing with emergencies.

It would be remiss to claim that this volume covers the entire spectrum of emergencies that modern societies can encounter. We focus on economic crises, via the lens of the most recent pandemic, but this leaves out other emergencies, moral and environmental. The collection is drawn from contributions to the 2020 Association for Heterodox Economics conference "The World Transformed", and several of the papers are from sessions organized by the Young Scholars Initiative (YSI) of the Institute for New Economic Thinking (INET). As a result, it showcases the up-and-coming scholarship of the economists of the future.

We hope that the book will be of interest to a variety of researchers and postgraduate students, and lecturers wishing to widen their syllabus, especially in the fields of development, health, labour and feminist economics, international political economy, and heterodox economics. With this contribution, we address another gap- – that in all these fields we can find a lack of teaching material that combines these topics by showcasing scholarship from the global South.

Note

1 Google trends, from 2004 to 2023. Available at: https://trends.google.com/trends/explore?date=all&geo=GB&q=crisis&hl=en-GB. Accessed 02/02/2023.

Section 1

Inequalities and Alternative Approaches

1 Heterodox Economic Policy Outlook

A Proven Boon at the Time of a Global Pandemic

Medha A. Sathi

Introduction

One of the major differences between orthodox economics and heterodox economics is their definition of governance. While the orthodox definition of governance stresses the process of contract initiations, negotiations, and adaptions in the market, heterodox economics defines governance as the process of crafting and putting into effect legislations and regulations to create stability in the market (Palay, 1984; Baskoy, 2012; Jo, Chester and D'Ippoliti, 2018). It can be said that while the orthodoxy is concerned about markets and rational choice, heterodoxy is a counter-disciplinary approach that values pluralism in its approach as well as policies. Heterodox economic policies are primarily concerned with the process of social provisioning and it advocates various economic and social activities in a socio-historical milieu, that includes paid and unpaid, market and non-market activities carried out by human beings to sustain their survival and reproduction (Jo, Chester and D'Ippoliti, 2018). In this context, this chapter discusses a survival story from a southern state of India with a policy history that has made a significant difference in successfully fighting the global pandemic.

On 31 December 2019, China reported a cluster of cases of pneumonia in Wuhan in its Hubei Province, which can be marked as the beginning of the change the world was going to witness. A novel coronavirus was eventually identified, named SARS-CoV-2, which started spreading all over the world. On 11 March 2020, the World Health Organization declared the disease COVID-19 caused by the virus SARS-CoV-2 as a pandemic as the morbidity and death toll were increasing uncontrollably. Many countries went into lockdown, banned international and domestic travel, took students out of schools, and had their economy stuck. On 24 March 2020 government of India declared its first part of a nationwide lockdown limiting the movement of 1.3 billion people, which included informal sector workers that constitute more than 8% of India's economy. The lockdown was criticized widely for the lack of preparation across the nation. The migrant laborers – who are about 40 million (Census, 2011) – were not provided any mode of transportation to go back to their respective homes and were forced to walk thousands of miles (the Government has no official accounts of the current number of migrant laborers in India; the Finance Minister mentioned the number of migrants could be 80 to

DOI: 10.4324/9781003451990-3

110 million). These migrant laborer families that included women and children had to walk back homes with limited food and supplies for days and many lost their lives during this tragic journey. Unemployment in India rose from 6.7% on 15 March to 26% in April, one month into the lockdown. According to estimates, 140 million people lost employment and more than 45% of Indian households witnessed an income drop compared to the previous year. Though all of these demanded immediate state intervention with extraordinary policy response, any sense of equanimity and responsibility on the part of the government was missing toward its citizens and most importantly toward its working poor (Kannan, 2020).

On the other hand, a few Indian states, especially several southern Indian States, were noteworthily responsible toward their citizens and it was seen that the policy response was timely and beneficial. States like Tamil Nadu and Kerala tackled food security problems during the lockdown and assured every ration card holder received what was necessary for surviving the lockdown through the public distribution system. Tamil Nadu state government provided free rations including pulses and cooking oil for free to migrant laborers. Through the 'Amma Canteen',[1] cooked food was delivered to the elderly and destitute. Kerala, a state that has always been celebrated worldwide because of its alternative development model, with remarkable accomplishments in human development (which is often termed as the 'Kerala model of development'), has also proved with its policy response to be a model in COVID-19 resilience.

Kerala, with an area of 38,863 sq. km with 33.3 million people, is one of the geographically smallest states in India. It is not a very industrialized state and nearly half of its population depended on agriculture as its main income source. Nevertheless, Kerala ranks first in the Human Development Index and life expectancy compared to other Indian states (Census, 2011). The state has very significant in and out-migration (Jalan and Sen, 2020), and the remittances from these out-migrant Keralites form one-third of Kerala's gross domestic product (Krishnan, 1994). But such high rates of migration were also a huge challenge as the state had to deal with many of them returning to the state during COVID-19.

As we had mentioned before, Kerala is known for its 'Kerala model of development', which has its base in the theory of 'public action' (Drèze and Sen, 1989) that prioritized health and education (Parayil, 1996; V′eron, 2001). The keystone to this model of development is said to be in its redistributive policies. The redistributive policies that took place in the 1950s onwards included land reforms, public housing, free and inexpensive medical care, expanded educational services, price control on food and necessities, and other policies that promoted social mobility among the marginalized groups (Franke and Chasin, 1994). All these social provisioning heterodox economic policies have made it a globally acclaimed model of development even though it may have failed to create many industries in the state. One of the major characteristics of the 'Kerala model of development' is that Kerala state has 35%–40% of its annual spending given to local government bodies (Kadiyala, 2004; Venugopalan, Bastian and Viswanathan, 2021). It also seems that the local bodies in Kerala have been very much involved in implementing its policies through public participation in one way or the other. Roy and Dave (2020) claim that the Kerala model of COVID-19 relief is built on sound principles of governance that have had historical precedence. They were able to make use of the benefits of the political system and social institutions because of the decentralized form of government. In particular, the approximately 60 lakh[2] self-help groups (SHG) initially created to focus on livelihood generation and also look at concerns of women's empowerment and their participation in development activities were an important part of crisis management. He suggests the importance of people and government coming together, which can result in a substantial improvement in welfare.

Kerala became India's first state to report a case of COVID-19, as on the 30 January 2020 a student studying in Wuhan returned home, and from then Kerala has been showing exceptional stories of fighting the virus, reducing death tolls and infection rate compared to most of the other states in India even by taking care of the migrant laborers (Roy and Dave, 2020). The state ensured everyone obtained their basic requirements of food and shelter – including migrant workers, whom they call 'guest workers'. Kerala provided its citizens with free rice and food grains and grocery kits of essential items to cope with the lockdown. It guaranteed aid of Rs.1,000 to any below poverty-line ration card holders and laborers. Despite being the first hotspot in India for COVID-19, it contained the virus better than many other states in India by employing a number of frugal innovations to combat the virus and the difficulties caused by its spread for life and livelihoods of its people (Sarkar, 2021). The innovations include campaigning against the spread of the virus, installing corona care centers, appropriate resource mobilization, safe and fast testing, proper tracing, giving proper quarantine facilities and so forth. Similar to its governance model, Kerala's model in fighting COVID-19 attracted the world's attention (Faleiro, 2020; Sarkar, 2021). Kerala saw its policies that focused on improvements in primary health, poverty eradication, and welfare with strong local governments become an added strength during the fight against the pandemic. Its long-term investment in local governments has helped in confronting the pandemic (Isaac and Sadanandan, 2020) and such long-term policies are very important along with the quick response policies in the face of a pandemic (Dutta and Fischer, 2021). Also Kerala's biggest poverty eradication program 'Kudumbashree' proved to be an indispensable resource in the face of the COVID-19 fight of Kerala. As mentioned above, Kerala's local governments have been found to be working with the participation of the public and Kudumbashree is one such organization that works with the local bodies of the state. The literature suggests that Kerala's decentralized response system which includes the State government, local government, Kudumbashree, public health system, and social capital helped the state to control the pandemic (Chathukulam and Tharamangalam, 2021). This chapter tries to analyze how Kudumbashree has helped Kerala in the face of the COVID-19 fight. The chapter also tries to give a way forward for Kudumbashree that can help the state in its exit strategy in building its economy post-pandemic or in the 'new normal'. The study tries to document and review the activities of Kudumbashree with the help of secondary data sources which include published literature on Kudumbashree, the official website of Kudumbashree, newspaper reports, and several other resources.

Kudumbashree

'Kudumbashree' was set up in1997, by the State Poverty Eradication Mission of the Government of Kerala. The name 'Kudumbashree' literally means 'prosperity of family'. It is essentially a community network that covers the entire State of Kerala comprising women's SHGs under the theme of poverty eradication and women empowerment. In the face of the COVID-19 fight as the state was in lock-down, Kudumbashree started 1,144 community kitchens that serve 2.8 lakh food packets a day. The grocery kits provided by the state government were distributed in cloth bags produced by Kudumbashree and a lot more activities similar to this that helped the COVID-19 fight were carried out which will be analyzed later in this chapter. It is worth mentioning that Kudumbashree's activities had also helped Kerala to fight the flood it has faced in 2018.

Kudumbashree has been a subject of study since its introduction and the stories of its success have been a topic of interest for years. A lot of literature studies how Kerala has been successful in alleviating poverty through the Kudumbashree mission and how it has worked as a tool for women empowerment. The literature identifies Kudumbashree as one of the best poverty eradication practices globally (Devika and Thampi, 2007). Panackal, Singh and Hamsa, (2017) in their empirical study find out that there is a positive impact on social and family empowerment after becoming a part of SHGs (Kudumbashree). As a result, self-employment, income, volatility, and education are strengthened and supported. When viewed within constructs of empowerment, capability poverty, citizenship, and participation in democratic processes, such SHGs and the community development processes that go along with them can be seen to make a modest but significant contribution to larger transformations of oppressive structures. Anand (2005) studies the innovative governance of Kerala and points out that Kerala has had the sharpest reduction in poverty through community participation in the poverty eradication program and numerous other people-centered development techniques. Ali and George (2019) say that in terms of empowerment, Kudumbashree has enhanced women's ability for decision-making. Kudumbashree has played a vital role in improving the bargaining capacity of women which contributes toward a reduction in gender inequality. Kudumbashree women have also been involved actively during the post-recovery activities of the biggest flood that Kerala had faced in the last 100 years (Anandan, 2018). It is important to mention that Kudumbashree has given the poor women in the state a strong institutionalized presence (Williams and Gurtoo, 2011; Dutta and Fischer, 2021).

Kudumbashree was set in the context of the people's plan movement. The people's plan campaign was in itself the idea of restructuring the role of the state by democratizing it, which was essentially done by the devolution of the state budget's 35%–40% of total planned outlay to the local bodies (Mannathukkaren, 2010)., Kudumbashree is a result of the bottom-up planning and decentralization to eradicate poverty and empower women in the state of Kerala. The mission statement of Kudumbashree is:

> To eradicate absolute poverty in ten years through concerted community action under the leadership of Local Self Governments, by facilitating organization of the poor combining self-help with demand led convergence of available services and resources to tackle the multiple dimensions and manifestations of poverty, holistically.
>
> (State Poverty Eradication Mission, 1996)

After two decades, it has been proved to be a great success in achieving its aim and beyond. Kudumbashree is connected to the development activities of the local government, and it has been acting as an effective tool to execute various development goals of social and economic development. These activities are carried out through three levels of community-based organizations of women that is, at the neighborhood level: neighborhood groups (NHGs), area level: area development societies, and panchayat/municipality level: Community Development Societies. Any women irrespective of social or economic status are welcome to join the group which ensures wide participation. It has various projects under several names that aim at different strategies, such as destitute rehabilitation, capability development, thrift, and microcredit, financial inclusion, crisis management, tribal development, urban and rural development, and promoting gender equality and social visibility. The program has 44.91 lakh members and covers more than 50% of the households in Kerala.

Kudumbashree in COVID-19 Resilience

Kudumbashree has been an inevitable part of Kerala's strong COVID-19 resilience. The relief and rehabilitation activities of Kudumbashree in the Kerala flood in 2018 are worth mentioning here. It impressively contributed toward rebuilding Kerala after the devastating floods it faced in 2018. In the extraordinary times of a pandemic and lockdown, when Kerala and its resilience is a celebrated model, Kudumbashree has played a significant role that has to be equally celebrated. The state's long-term investment in local government and feminization of poverty eradication programs at the grassroots level has built into a great resilience force which had complete public trust which was really important for its smooth functioning (Dutta and Fischer, 2021). Kudumbashree has been part of the implementing process of many COVID-19 policies of the government of Kerala, and we would understand in this session why it would have been nearly impossible for the local government to carry out its COVID-19 combating activities without the support of Kudumbashree. Here we try to bring Kudumbashree's COVID-19 activities[3] into six broad categories ('the six Cs'): Converging, Connecting, Caring, Creating, Capability enhancing, and Continuing. We shall discuss each of these categories in turn.

Converging

Lockdown was rather a difficult time where there were no secure essential services and citizens were left with fewer or no choices, and it was the state's duty to ensure such services. During the lockdown, Kerala ensured that nobody should go hungry or be pushed toward starvation in the state. Kudumbashree worked with the state to make the provision of such essential services a success. Along with the free ration and essential supplies through the public distribution system, community kitchens were open all over the state: 1144 community kitchens were started with the help of local self-government which was worked out by Kudumbashree. Out of these, 379 have been started as budget hotels called 'Janakeeya hotels' (meaning people's hotels) of Kudumbashree. It has also established takeaway counters in 13 places to meet the needs of drivers. As the government decided to distribute grocery kits to its citizens, Kudumbashree volunteers prepared 87 lakh grocery kits in 54 warehouses that were distributed to the people. Kudumbashree has a project for women farmers through joint liability groups (JLGs). Though the COVID-19 lockdown had affected the JLGs, more than 16,268 JLGs across the state have stood together and donated around 115.94 metric tonnes of agricultural commodities for the community kitchens. Pieces of evidence from the literature suggest that compared to individual farming, community farming has fared better outcomes (Agarwal, 2021). One of the pillars on which Kudumbashree based its COVID-19 reaction was the convergence of agricultural livelihoods and food assistance initiatives (Agarwal, 2021). Kerala being a consumer state was concerned about its food sustainability at this time of a pandemic, and so the government has introduced a scheme called 'Subhiksha Keralam', which aims at large-scale production of rice, fruits, vegetables, tubers, grains, and legumes as part of achieving self-sufficiency. This has also been taken as a short-term activity plan for Kudumbashree members. We have mentioned before the excellence of local governance in Kerala which was found to be actively working with public participation. At the time of COVID-19, when the implementation process of policies is difficult, Kudumbashree being an existing team of efficacy in the state has stepped up to be a very useful tool. When in immediate need at such a critical time, Kudumbashree became the 'women power' which the state was able to rely on. The convergence of Kudumbashree with the state resulted in better outcomes of COVID-19 support to the public.

Connecting

The lockdown disconnects people, and communication is an important key to ensuring an effective response from people to contain the pandemic. Kudumbashree through their NHGs made it possible to spread the message of 'breaking the chain' of the COVID-19 spread. Kudumbashree has formed 1.9 lakh social media groups with 22 lakh NHG members to educate them and their families about government instructions regarding protocols to stay safe and reduce community spreading. Kudumbashree also conducted various programs for the elderly and children to keep them engaged during the lockdown respecting the guidelines of lockdown protocols. It is to be noted that the long-term investment in literacy and education of women eased this advanced communication at the time of COVID-19 (Agarwal, 2021). The government of Kerala's success in facilitating Phatic labor that created a stable social infrastructure over the years (Elyachar, 2010; Ajay, 2019) has really paid off in connecting people for passing critical information in lockdowns. Phatic labor signifies the labor of women that creates an efficient social infrastructure by producing and maintaining communication channels (Elyachar, 2010). Kudumbashree, through the above-mentioned connecting activities, improved the communication process during the pandemic which aided equitable information flow. As they work at the ground level, people without access to much technology were still able to be included in the awareness campaign through Kudumbashree. Equal access to information has been ensured by Kudumbashree.

Creating

The economy is hindered and the production process is a challenge during a pandemic. There was a huge demand for masks and sanitizers at the time of lockdown, and instead of depending on other sources, Kerala found the solution in Kudumbashree. Kudumbashree has prepared and sold more than 47.75 lakh cotton masks through around 306 tailoring units and has prepared more than 6.3 thousand liters of sanitizers with 21 microenterprises. Also, they had started to make face shields and protective gears that are to be used by the healthcare workers. Likewise, Kudumbashree has found the scarcity of necessary products and turned that into an opportunity that benefits economically by serving the needs of the state. An economy can only function when the production process is on the move. Even when there was a lockdown and livelihoods were hit because of it, Kudumbashree women found new opportunities to enhance their livelihood. This livelihood not only helped them but also helped to meet the immediate demands of the market – creating products that are important for the survival of the economy as well as the survival of the people stuck in a pandemic and Kudumbashree has successfully taken care of both.

Caring

When the world is going through unusual times, it affects the mental and physical well-being of everyone who has to go through that. There are 1.54 lakh destitute families in Kerala with1.14 lakh elderly members (above 60 years who are under vulnerable population). To reach out to them, Kudumbashree has entitled 2,176 resource persons who contact them every five days and enquire about their health and other needs, and ensure they get food and health care (this is done in convergence with UNICEF). Kudumbashree, through its 360 community counselors, also provided counseling and mental support to those who were suffering because of various issues in lockdown. It also conducted a campaign to reduce the mental strain of persons who had to suffer domestic abuse during lockdown to send a message to them saying they are not alone in this. They also provided food and related services to people under observation in corona care centers. Working with the Kudumbashree has led to the development of a close-knit care ethic that is centered on the prevention and control of disease through interpersonal relationships (Dutta and Fischer, 2021). From this, we could say that Kudumbashree has also been successful in performing the best in the care economy which is one of the most important areas when it comes to a health emergency.

Capability Enhancing

One of the most important factors to consider is an exit strategy to ensure economic empowerment of the people, as many had lost jobs, and have come back from foreign courtiers losing their jobs. The government has declared many loan schemes to solve the economic and employment problems of these people. Since there is already a network created by Kudumbashree, the scheme has become easy to execute. Kudumbashree NHGs were ensured to be given interest-free loans according to each one's demand. This would improve access to credit for people who need it.

Continuing

Any resilience will not be complete if the negative effects of the disaster on existing programs are not properly taken care of. Kudumbashree is active in skill training programs that come under 'Deen dayal Upadhyay Yojana' under the ministry of rural development, Government of India, in which there are 6,999 students undergoing training in 167 courses. Kudumbashree has successfully ensured the continuation of the courses through online. Similarly, Kudumbashree is striving to continue other ongoing schemes. Also, resilience has to be continued to make sure the survival of the people post-pandemic. Kudumbashree has been supervised and conducted systematically by the state which will ensure the continuation of the schemes that it has started to combat the pandemic-driven socioeconomic issues.

Kudumbashree as a Model in Crisis and Resilience

The results of activities of Kudumbashree in Kerala during the COVID-19 lockdown prove that community participation, localization, and cooperation are key to fighting any crisis. The heterodox path of development leads to a stronger resilient state in the face of any crisis. An active and powerful local government, with community participation engaging in social action, has made the COVID-19 fight of Kerala more confident. This intervention of Kudumbashree is very significant globally as the pandemic has shown the significance of people's participation in governance. Such interventions can be a model for many states to improve their crisis management and improve resilience toward any kind of crisis they encounter.

The model that can be derived from the activities of Kudumbashree can be illustrated as in Figure 1.1. The fast and wide reach of the policies by the government has been made possible by the six Cs of Kudumbashree which can be claimed as a powerful model of people-centric crisis management.

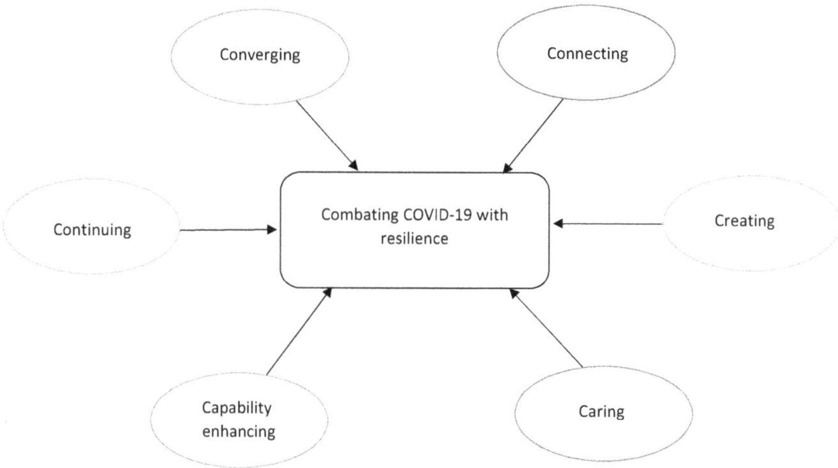

Figure 1.1 Combating COVID-19 with resilience.

Kudumbashree's fight against COVID-19 through the methods of converging, connecting, creating, caring, capability enhancing, and continuing can be adopted as a model for crisis management. Converging means bringing together the community and the state and working to meet the immediate needs of the society in crisis. Connecting is to reach everyone to create awareness. Creating means creating economic opportunities from the crisis and improving entrepreneurship. Caring is giving support to the vulnerable population in need. Capability enhancing is the economic empowerment of people by providing credit support. Continuing means focusing on already existing schemes, overcoming the challenges, and also ensuring the continuation of the activities. As mentioned before, it was years of systematic governance which have made this possible now; this Kudumbashree model of resilience is a potential developmental model toward a humanitarian development path.

As a result of COVID-19, it is estimated that 437 million women and girls will be living in extreme poverty along with another 47 million new poor women because of the pandemic, and such feminized poverty eradication policies are more than significant at this time (Shamsuddin, 2021). Kerala's long-term investment in institutions and women (Agarwal, 2021) has to be stressed and should be taken forward as a model. Women-centric interconnected networks of local institutions with government support need to be built to face the challenges that follow COVID-19 (Agarwal, 2021). Kerala with strong community-level resilience which has proven to complement the technological responses in handling the pandemic has a big role in reducing the spread of COVID-19 (Singh et al., 2012; Sarkar, 2021). Empowerment of women is not only economic empowerment or autonomy but induces social changes which involve the willingness of women to participate in the process of changing their communities for good with their strong agency (Mosedale, 2005; Calas, Smircich and Bourne, 2009; Venugopalan, Bastian and Viswanathan, 2021). Kudumbashree is essentially the institutionalization of social capital that has been created by the state. This chapter adds to the literature that says that social capital is not only necessary but also sufficient for the containment of a pandemic (Jalan and Sen, 2020; Chathukulam and Tharamangalam, 2021). As we know, a pandemic is a life-altering phenomenon for most people and to be involved in combating such a difficult situation is a challenge but also improves the confidence of those who are involved in it, as the Kudumbashree model has been found to bring new purpose in many women's life (Shamsuddin, 2021).

Kerala is a state which has swiftly and decisively acted to keep its death rates and infection rate down. The state successfully flattened the COVID-19 curve in two waves it had to face. We have seen that Kudumbashree with its extensive activities has played a major role in this. Kerala could do this not because it sprang into action immediately, but because of the path of the development process for years leading up to it. Decades of investment in universal health care along with devolution of government which give power and responsibility to the local government which has proved to be a powerful tool in the resilience of the COVID-19 pandemic. Kerala's relief package of two billion rupees was directed toward the activities of local government as well. Kudumbashree has proven to be the backbone of effective local governance in the state at the time of the pandemic.

Comparing the States

As Kudumbashree is also based on Sustainable Development Goals (SDGs), it has been a tool for Kerala for achieving them to a larger extent. Kerala ranked first among other states of India in the Sustainable Development index of 2019. A composite score of SDGs was computed in the range of 0–100 for each state based on its level of performance in achieving the goals. The scores were divided into four: Aspirant, Performer, Front runner, and Achiever for 0 to 49, 50–64 to 99, and 100, respectively. Kerala had scored 70 which makes it a front runner. To compare different states in COVID-19 resilience, their respective SDG scores and the average of doubling days of the number of cases of COVID-19 are taken (as a proxy for COVID-19 resilience) (see Figure 1.2). Twelve states are taken for this comparison, six states with the highest number of cases and six with the lowest number of cases as on 27 April 2020.

There is a positive correlation between average doubling days of COVID-19 cases and the SDG score of the states with a correlation coefficient of 0.59. From this, we could understand that states which have been trying to move in a heterodox people-centric development path have been safer in the COVID-19 fight if we take the average doubling days as a proxy for resilience. Gregory (2005) stresses that the importance of democratic decentralization with equal participation of women creates an alternative paradigm for sustainable development. Kudumbashree and its activities fit right into the UN SDGs of no poverty, gender equality, reduce inequalities, and responsible consumption and production (UNDP, 2015). According to

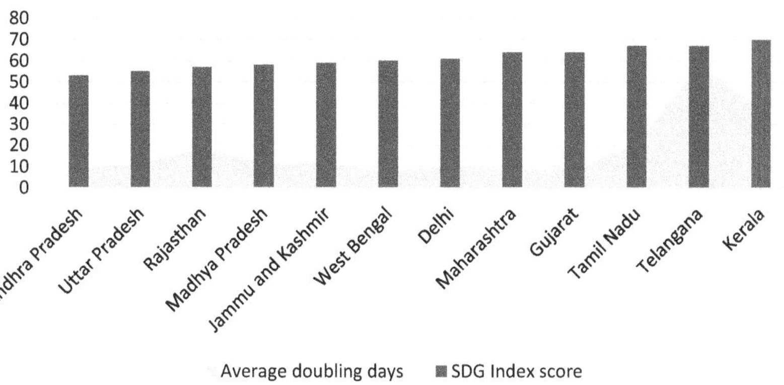

Figure 1.2 Comparison between average doubling days of COVID-19 cases and SDG Index.

the United Nations Development Programme (UNDP), 736 million people still lived on less than US$1.90 a day as at 2015, and progress in eradicating poverty is found to be uneven as women are less paid, are less educated, and own less property (UNDP, 2015). To achieve SDG 1 more equitably, women have to be given more preference, and Kudumbashree is right on the mission. Kudumbashree helps in many ways to improve the livelihood and income of women in marginalized sections of the society which is contributing toward SDG 1. When equal opportunities are ensured, that contributes toward SDG 5 of gender equality. Equal opportunities for women will be achieved in many ways and one way is when there are more women in public as leaders and Kudumbashree with no doubt is achieving that goal. Kudumbashree helps enhance the capabilities of women who did not have access to education or skill development. Kudumbashree with its many schemes opens up a world of opportunities for women which adds to the gender equality goal of UNDP. SDG 10 is to reduce inequalities and as mentioned earlier, Kudumbashree targets the upliftment of marginalized sector women and provides opportunities to empower them. Though it appears that Kudumbashree might not be reaching fully to those women who live in the environmental margins of the state (Tribal women and Fisherfolk women), it has its potential to improve and work toward achieving SDG 10. Lastly, SDG 12 of responsible consumption and production is being achieved through Kudumbashree schemes. Their close work with local government and the general public can bring awareness towards efficient management of our resources and waste. Responsible and environment-friendly production practices seem to be included in the practice of Kudumbashree and if they continue to improve on them, it would add to the achievement of SDG 10. The SDGs are more close to the heterodox policies as opposed to the mainstream accumulative ones and it promotes in achieving gender equality and poverty eradication with social changes in communities (Venugopalan, Bastian and Viswanathan, 2021). So it is high time for the states to focus on SDGs as a base for their governance policies which would improve their resilience toward any crisis.

The Way Forward

Any crisis is an opportunity to improve. Kudumbashree has shown that the feminization of the development process has been the backbone of crisis management and poverty eradication in the state of Kerala. Kerala as a consumer state could go into a food crisis unless correct measures are taken to improve farming and food production and attain self-sufficiency through an expansion of JLG-based group farming. The study by Agarwal (2012) remarks that a large percentage of unpaid workers are women who work on family farms. She rightly points out that the feminization of agriculture has inherent value and may be helpful in addressing the global food shortage, a view which has been confirmed by the aforementioned JLGs. Kudumbashree which has a vast reach and community strength can work as microenterprises understanding the demand of the global market. It could improve the scope of Kudumbashree's production units that produce various products that have high demand in the market. This can add toward the exit strategy of the state. Inspired by Kudumbashree, its model can be applied in other states as a model of crisis management as well as for attaining SDGs, which are to be prioritized for better and egalitarian development.

It is often claimed that neoliberal globalization and liberal capitalism have not been found to be effective in containing a pandemic as the United States, the greatest power in the world, has been shown to be the worst at doing so, and policies based on such leaderships may not be successful for the new normal (Chathukulam and Tharamangalam, 2021), and instead social provisioning and more heterodoxically inclined policies would save the life and livelihood of people in crisis. The best weapon to fight uncontrolled neoliberal capitalist globalization is localization, and such a measure in Kerala, through Kudumbashree, has been helping the state effectively tackle one crisis after another, from floods to health emergencies (Kannan, 2020). Neoliberalism is based on the premise that government intervention only makes things worse for everyone, even for the poor, by attempting to promote economic development or social welfare (Bockman, 2013). But clearly, the activities of Kudumbashree has proved otherwise. It is said that neoliberalism limits people's access to 'social cure' that increases their well-being (Becker, Hartwich and Haslam, 2021) and Kudumbashree, which is a heterodox economic policy outcome, has contributed well toward the 'social cure' that was necessary in the time of the pandemic.

UNDP indicates that inequalities will tend to increase post-COVID-19 and improving the capabilities and focusing on human development has become difficult as well as inevitable. Strategies that create access to income generation, education, and so on, might reduce the human development losses caused because of COVID-19. Failing to address basic capabilities in response to the COVID-19 crisis could even reverse the convergence. Kudumbashree has often been hailed as an accessible gateway to public life for the poorest women although evidence suggests that it has not been a completely feministic empowerment, and Kudumbashree should witness more feminist mobilization making it more democratic in nature (Devika, 2016). Kudumbashree has the potential to be a model, and it should improve its horizons by understanding its own strengths and weakness. Improving its democratic nature and inclusion of women in the environmental margins of the state as well could be a way forward for Kudumbashree. States could follow the model of Kudumbashree in its anti-poverty measures which is essentially proven to be a success. Feminization of development process could be a solution for the unequal state of the world we currently live. Such development could lead to improvements in gender equality and overall well-being of the society.

Conclusion

Localization, community participation, and feminization of the development process are proven boons in fighting the challenges caused by the pandemic. Kudumbashree has proven to be one of the biggest strengths of Kerala model development. Though there are challenges, its commitment and competence have set an example for other states. With the activities that can be sorted into the six Cs model: Converging, Connecting, Caring, Creating, Capability enhancing, and Continuing. Kudumbashree has shown that an alternative path is not implausible. It has also been seen that there is a positive correlation between the level of SGD index and COVID-19 resilience. The larger the focus on attaining the SDGs, the larger the capability of combating the pandemic with resilience. Instead of focusing on an accumulative development path, only moving toward a heterodox path of development can promise a safe, secure, and decent life at the time of any crisis.

This successful poverty eradication mission is one example of how heterodox economic policies, which allow the state to maintain the flow of goods and services necessary to meet the demands of individuals who engage in its activities (Gruchy, 1987), can help secure the livelihood of people in the face of any disaster that they face. The vision of heterodox economic policies can be brought under the arena of the social provisioning process (Jo, Chester and D'Ippoliti, 2018) and Kudumbashree fits into that policy arena. Kudumbashree is the perfect example of the feminization of poverty eradication policies and it seems to be successful in dealing with the potential 'entitlement failure' (Fine, 1997) during the pandemic. Kudumbashree has been very successful in tackling the food security issues that came with the lockdown. The most important duty of the state when the crisis happens is to protect its citizens, and, for example, without Kudumbashree it would have been impossible for the state of Kerala to run so many community kitchens and essential commodity production units. Therefore, Kudumbashree's model of crisis management is an inevitable tool to avoid any kind of entitlement failures during any crisis. Essentially, social inclusion, longtime investment in feminization of crisis management, and social capital building have been found to be the success of Kerala model which have improved the collective resilience of the people of Kerala. So to improve collective well-being, governments should move more toward social provisioning policies that is being proven to be a strong tool to combat the issues in any kind of emergency situations.

Notes

1 'Amma Canteen' also known as 'Amma Unavagam' is a state-run canteen that is a food subsidization program run by the Government of Tamil Nadu in India.
2 A lakh is 100,000.
3 The information about the COVID-19 activities of Kudumbashree has been taken from the website (Kudumbashree, 2022) as well as newspaper reports.

References

Agarwal, B. (2012) 'Food Security, Productivity, and Gender Inequality', IEG Working Paper No. 320. www.binaagarwal.com/downloads/apapers/Food%20security,%20productivity,%20gender%20inequality.pdf

Agarwal, B. (2021) 'Livelihoods in COVID times: Gendered perils and new pathways in India', *World Development*, 139(3). Elsevier. doi: 10.1016/j.worlddev.2020.105312

Ajay, A. (2019) *Women's Sociality and the Potential of Kudumbashree as a Social Infrastructure Insights from a Village in Kasargod District Anamika Ajay*. https://cds.edu/wp-content/uploads/2014/10/RULSG-Kudumbashree07.pdf

Ali, H. M. and George, L. S. (2019) 'A qualitative analysis of the impact of Kudumbashree and MGNREGA on the lives of women belonging to a coastal community in Kerala', *Journal of Family Medicine and Primary Care*, 8(9), pp. 2832–2836. doi: 10.4103/jfmpc.jfmpc

Anand, J. S. (2005) 'Innovative approaches in governance: The Kerala Experience', pp. 1–11. Available at: napsipag.org/pdf/Kerala_Experience.pdf

Anandan, S. (2018) 'Kerala floods: Kudumbashree women play big role in clean-up', *The Hindu*, 28 August. Available at: www.thehindu.com/news/national/kerala/kudumbasree-collects-5-cr-for-flood-relief/article24801984.ece (Accessed: 25 July 2022).

Baskoy, T. (2012) 'Market Governance', in King, J. (ed.) *Companion of Post-Keynisian Economics*. 2nd edn. Cheltanham: Edward Elgar, pp. 387–392.

Becker, J. C., Hartwich, L. and Haslam, A. S. (2021) 'Neoliberalism can reduce well-being by promoting a sense of social disconnection, competition, and loneliness', *British Journal of Social Psychology*, 60, pp. 947–965.

Bockman, J. (2013) 'Neoliberalism', *Contexts*, 12(3), pp. 14–15. doi: 10.1177/1536504213499873

Calas, M. B., Smircich, L. and Bourne, K. A. (2009) 'Extending the boundaries: Reframing "entrepreneurship as social change" through feminist perspectives', *Academy of Management Review*, 34, pp. 552–569.

Census (2011) *Census*. https://censusindia.gov.in/census.website/

Chathukulam, J. and Tharamangalam, J. (2021) 'The Kerala model in the time of COVID19: Rethinking state, society and democracy', *World Development*, 137(105207). doi: 10.1016/j.worlddev.2020.105207

Devika, J. (2016) 'The " Kudumbashree Woman " and the Kerala Model Woman: Women and Politics in Contemporary Kerala'. doi: 10.1177/0971521516656077

Devika, J. and Thampi, B. V. (2007) 'Between "empowerment" and "liberation": The Kudumbashree initiative in Kerala', *Journal of Gender Studies*, 14, pp. 33–59.

Drèze, J. and Sen, A. (1989) *Hunger and Public Action*, New York: Oxford University Press. doi: 10.1080/08109029108631968

Dutta, A. and Fischer, H. W. (2021) 'The local governance of COVID-19: Disease prevention and social security in rural India', *World Development*, 138(105234). doi: 10.1016/j.worlddev.2020.105234

Elyachar, J. (2010) 'Phatic labor, infrastructure, and the question of empowerment in Cairo', *American Ethnologist*, 37(3), pp. 452–464. doi: 10.1111/j.1548-1425.2010.01265.x

Faleiro, S. (2020) *What the world can learn from Kerala about how to fight COVID-19*, MIT Technology Review. Available at: www.technologyreview.com/2020/04/13/999313/kerala-fight-COVID-19-india-coronavirus

Fine, B. (1997) 'Entitlement failure?', *Development and Change*, 28(4), pp. 617–647. doi: 10.1111/1467-7660.00058

Franke, R. W. and Chasin, B. H. (1994) *Kerala: Development through Radical Reform*. San Francisco: in collaboration with the Institute for Food and Development Policy.

Gambhir, A., Singh, S., Duckworth, S. and Sotiropoulos, A. (2012) *Frugal Innovation: Learning from Social Entrepreneurs in India*. London: Serco Institute State Poverty Eradication Mission (1996) *State Poverty Eradication Mission*. www.kudumbashree.org

Gregory, S. (2005) *Sustainable Livelihood and Grass-roots Empowerment*. Thiruvananthapuram: Centre for Development Studies..

Gruchy, A. G. (1987) *The Reconstruction of Economics: An Analysis of the Fundamentals of Institutional Economics*. London: Greenwood Press.

Isaac, T. and Sadanandan, R. (2020) 'COVID-19, public health system and local governance in Kerala', *Economic & Political Weekly*, 55(21), p. 11.

Jalan, J. and Sen, A. (2020) 'Containing a pandemic with public actions and public trust: The Kerala story', *Indian Economic Review*, 55, pp. 105–124. doi: 10.1007/s41775-020-00087-1

Jo, T.-H., Chester, L. and D'Ippoliti, C. (2018) *The Routledge Handbook of Heterodox Economics. Theorizing, Analyzing, and Transforming Capitalism*. London: Taylor & Francis.

Kadiyala, S. (2004) *Scaling up Kudumbashree Collective Action for Poverty Alleviation and women's Empowerment*. Washington, DC: International Food Policy Research Institute.

Kannan, K. (2020) 'COVID-19 lockdown: Protecting the poor means keeping the Indian economy afloat', *Economic & Political Weekly (Online)*, (April), pp. 1–6.

Krishnan, T. N. (1994) 'Foreign Remittance, Consumption and Income', paper presented at the International Congress on Kerala Studies, AKG Centre for Research and Studies, Thiruvananthapuram.

Kudumbashree (2022) *Kudumbashree*. Available at: www.kudumbashree.org/

Mannathukkaren, N. (2010) 'The "poverty" of political society: Partha Chatterjee and the people's plan campaign in Kerala, India', *Third World Quarterly*, 31(2), pp. 295–314. doi: 10.1080/01436591003712007

Mosedale, S. (2005) 'Assessing women's empowerment: Towards a conceptual framework', *Journal of International Development*, 17, pp. 243–257.

Palay, T. (1984) 'Competitive institutional economics: The governance of rail freight contracting', *Journal of Legal Studies*, 13(2), pp. 265–287.

Panackal, N., Singh, A. and Hamsa, S. (2017) 'Kudumbashree and women empowerment in Kerala: An overview and theoretical framework', *Indian Journal of Commerce & Management Studies*, VIII(1), pp. 16–21. doi: 10.18843/ijcms/v8i1/02

Parayil, G. (1996) 'The "Kerala model" of development: Development and sustainability in the third world', *Third World Quarterly*, 17(5), pp. 941–958.

Roy, A. and Dave, S. K. (2020) 'When people and governments come together: Analysing Kerala's response to the COVID-19 pandemic', *Economic & Political Weekly*, (April), pp. 1–7.

Sarkar, S. (2021) 'Breaking the chain: Governmental frugal innovation in Kerala to combat the COVID-19 pandemic', *Government Information Quarterly*, 38(101549). doi: 10.1016/j.giq.2020.101549

Shamsuddin, A. (2021) *How a women's organization became 'chief architects' of the COVID-19 response in Southern India: From poverty to power*. Available at: https://oxfamblogs.org/fp2p/how-a-womens-organization-became-chief-architects-of-the-covid-19-response-in-southern-india/ (Accessed: 3 May 2021).

UNDP (2015) *Sustainable Development Goals* | United Nations Development Programme. Available at: www.undp.org/sustainable-development-goals?utm_source=EN&utm_medium=GSR&utm_content=US_UNDP_PaidSearch_Brand_English&utm_campaign=CENTRAL&c_src=CENTRAL&c_src2=GSR&gclid=Cj0KCQjw54iXBhCXARIsADWpsG-t01N2iIaNCwIsjXCG234aOAFrSE-3z9RW4n7YriMJEaYFXOmjc_ (Accessed: 28 July 2022).

Venugopalan, M., Bastian, B. L. and Viswanathan, P. K. (2021) 'The role of multi-actor engagement for women's empowerment and entrepreneurship in Kerala, India', *Administrative Sciences*, 11(31). doi: 10.3390/admsci11010031

V′eron, R. (2001) 'The "new" Kerala model: Lessons for sustainable development', *World Development*, 29(4), pp. 601–617.

Williams, C. C. and Gurtoo, A. (2011) 'Evaluating women entrepreneurs in the informal sector: Some evidence from India', *Journal of Developmental Entrepreneurship*, 16(03), pp. 351–369.

2 The Reach of Fiscal Stimulus for Urban Women Informal Sector Workers in Bengaluru during COVID-19

R. Vijayamba

Introduction

The COVID-19 pandemic has affected India's economy in several ways. The Government of India imposed an abrupt nationwide lockdown on March 22, 2020. The pandemic hit the poor and marginalized sections of the urban economy deeply. Around 90 per cent of India's workforce is informally employed. The absence of secure jobs and long-term social security benefits characterize informal wage employment (Kesar & Abraham, 2020). They were struggling before the COVID-19 pandemic, which is now intensified. A major share of the urban workforce has lost their earnings and employment (WIEGO, 2020; APU, 2020).

The effect of the lockdown has been disproportionate to the women in the informal economy. During such a crisis, women lose their jobs and incomes immediately. Rapid assessment surveys by UN Women's Regional Office for Asia and the Pacific across countries showed that female informal workers were more likely to lose their jobs than men (UN WOMEN, 2020). With the most stringent measures of lockdown and almost 90 per cent of the informal workforce that disproportionately has women, India risks the livelihoods of female informal workers (ILO, 2020).

Bengaluru provides a typical case of an Indian city with a burgeoning service sector. Post-liberalization, the service sector in Bengaluru attracted massive scale migration, particularly for low-end jobs. Amid the attention garnered by information technology, the low-end service and manufacturing sectors are the largest employers in the city.

Research findings of the studies by many scholars and organizations discuss the worrying aspects of loss in employment and earnings from the pandemic (APU, 2020; SWAN, 2020; Afridi, Dhillon & Roy 2020; NCAER, 2020; Jan Sahas, 2020). There was an immediate fall in consumption levels, and the Governments of the State and the Centre announced a fiscal stimulus to boost the levels of consumption in the economy.

The Government of India announced a fiscal stimulus of INR 1.7 lakh crore during April 2020 and INR 20 lakh crore during May 2020 for the economy during the pandemic. The fiscal stimulus mainly composed of distribution of food grains through the Public Distribution System and direct cash transfers to the beneficiaries' accounts. The Central Government distributes rations to the Antyodaya

DOI: 10.4324/9781003451990-4

Anna Yojana households and Priority Households that cover 800 million people.[1] These households are eligible to receive 5 kg of food grains per person per month, respectively, at INR 3/kg for rice, INR 2/kg for wheat, and INR 1/kg of coarse cereals. As part of the fiscal stimulus, it said that INR 500 shall be provided to all female Jan Dhan account holders for the next three months.[2]

The State mentioned that it shall provide 5 kg of wheat/rice per person and 1 kg of pulses per household per month for the next three months. The Government of Karnataka announced free rations for two months for the beneficiaries of the Public Distribution System and the distribution of excess milk from the Karnataka Milk Federation in slum areas. It also announced a transfer of INR 1500 to the registered construction workers. Many scholars have argued that the overall stimulus is less than one per cent of the country's gross domestic product and highly inadequate for an unprecedented crisis like the COVID-19 pandemic (Nagaraj & Kapoor, 2020; Mander, Ghosh & Patnaik, 2020).

The studies on the loss of employment and earnings present a grim picture of urban informal workers. The motivation to study urban female informal workers is as follows. Among the urban informal workers, women, in particular, have lost their work. The sectors that have faced high job loss due to COVID-19 employ more women. International Labour Organization's predicted job loss impact due to COVID-19 shows that the impact on construction is medium, and it has 7 per cent of the global female workforce. The impact of job loss for manufacturing is high, and it has 39 per cent of women's share globally (ILO, 2020). Women generally bear the burden of providing food and financial security to their families during a pandemic (UN WOMEN, 2020; Kabeer, 2020). The urban female informal workers lack a source of safety net to rely on during such emergencies. Most of them do not own any land, house, or a formal source of credit. Unlike rural women, they usually live far away from their families and communities to rely on any support.

The objectives of the study are to understand if the urban female informal workers received the food and financial security measures offered as part of the fiscal stimulus package. The different categories of urban female informal workers include garment workers, construction workers, and domestic helpers. The study investigates the various aspects of the livelihood crisis faced by urban female informal workers due to inadequate food and financial security. It is based on personal, telephonic interviews and insights from other surveys conducted during this period.

The study finds that domestic workers availed of free food rations, but it was insufficient. The construction workers and the garment workers did not receive food rations. Concerning financial security, most of the respondents did not have Jan Dhan accounts, and only one respondent in the study received a cash transfer. Domestic helpers and garment workers struggled to pay rents and utility bills during the lockdown period. The urban female informal workers resorted to informal credit to tide over this phase. Therefore, the inadequate food and financial measures coupled with poor working conditions have threatened the livelihoods of the urban female informal workers.

Post-COVID Studies in Urban India

Surveys conducted during this period confirm that there is a massive loss of employment in Karnataka. The study by Azim Premji University showed that 76 per cent of the workers lost work in urban areas. Almost three out of four respondents lost their jobs in urban Karnataka. Casual workers and self-employed workers were the worst hit with eight in ten losing their jobs (APU, 2020). Women were disproportionately affected and had lesser chances of returning to the workforce. Around 47 per cent of women lost jobs and did not return to work by the end of 2020, whereas 7 per cent of the men lost jobs and did not return (APU, 2021).

A few studies found that many segments of the population did not receive their wages and salaries to meet the usual household expenditures. A survey by the Alternative Law Forum and Garments Mahila Karmikara Munnade on 82 garment workers in four districts of Karnataka (Bengaluru, Ramanagara, Mandya, and Mysore) mentioned that 63 per cent of the workers did not receive any salary for April 2020 and 17 per cent of the workers received less than half of their salaries for April 2020 (Garments Mahila Karmikara Munnade & Alternative Law Forum, 2020). A study by Stranded Workers Action Network (SWAN) on 11,159 persons in various States showed that 78 per cent of casual workers did not receive any payment at all during the period of lockdown. Their sample mainly consisted of daily wage/construction workers, drivers, and domestic helpers (SWAN, 2020). Afridi, Dhillon and Roy (2020) studied 413 households in industrial areas of Delhi and showed that 91 per cent of the men could not work during the lockdown. Among them, 85 per cent of them did not earn any income and half of them (53 per cent) did not receive full salary. A study by the National Council of Applied Economic Research (NCAER) on 1750 households in Delhi also showed that the lockdown affected the incomes of 72 per cent of casual workers significantly (NCAER, 2020). A study by the Domestic Workers Sector Skill Council on domestic workers in eight States found that 85 per cent of the domestic workers were not paid for the lockdown period (Newsclick, 2020).

These surveys point to the minimal reach of the fiscal stimulus. A survey by Jan Sahas on 3196 construction workers from North and Central India reported that 14 per cent of laborers did not have ration cards, and 17 per cent did not have bank accounts (Jan Sahas, 2020). These were some of the problems for the effective reach of the fiscal stimulus. The study by the Alternative Law Forum and Garments Mahila Karmikara Munnade found that 51 per cent of the workers did not receive free rations, and 60 per cent did not receive subsidized rations (Garments Mahila Karmikara Munnade & Alternative Law Forum, 2020). According to Afridi, Dhillon and Roy (2020), around 50 per cent of the respondents had no access to food, and provision of groceries by the State formed the major assistance for 89 per cent of the respondents. The survey by NCAER said 43 per cent of the households received food rations, and only 19 per cent received cash transfers (NCAER, 2020). The survey by Azim Premji University (APU, 2020) showed that 71 per cent of the Karnataka urban households procured rations. Only 27 per cent of them received at least one cash transfer.

There lies an argument for a universal public distribution system with more rations for six months, cash transfers of INR 7000 for two months and ensuring urban employment guarantee programs (APU, 2020). The study by SWAN showed that 62 per cent of the respondents did not receive rations in Karnataka. Therefore they argue for doubling the rations for three months and distributing INR 7000 per month to poor households (SWAN, 2020). Scholars at Ashoka University support a cash transfer of INR 6000 per family with ration cards in urban areas (based on poverty estimates by Rangarajan committee) (Borah et al., 2020).

Data and Methods

The study uses both secondary and primary sources of data. It uses the Periodic Labor Force Survey (PLFS) of 2017–18 by the National Statistical Office to analyze urban female work participation across industries using National Industrial Classification code 2008 in Karnataka. The official source on employment indicated that the urban female workers mainly worked in garment industries and construction. Primary data were collected from urban female informal workers in Bengaluru, Karnataka, across caste and age groups. The different categories of urban female informal workers included garment workers, construction workers, and domestic helpers. The workers were interviewed using a semi-structured schedule and based on purposive sampling. The interviews were mostly conducted by telephone, and a few interviews with construction workers were based on visiting the working sites. The data were collected during May 2020. While the findings from primary data are based on purposive sampling and cannot be generalized or representative, the study also includes observations from other surveys conducted during this period that show similar results.

Results

Findings from the Periodic Labor Force Survey

Nature of Urban Female Work Force in Karnataka

The urban female work participation rate in 2017–18 was 16.8 per cent in Karnataka. Table 2.1 shows that the manufacturing sector was the largest employer and employed 28 per cent of Karnataka's urban female workforce. Education and industry of wholesale and retail trade employed 14 per cent and 11 per cent of the urban female workforce, respectively. But the important category of workers that got affected by the pandemic were the construction workers and those who did service-based work (e.g., domestic helpers). Construction and service activities each employed 3 per cent of the urban female workforce.

Further, the division of manufacturing into subsectors in Table 2.2 brings out that almost 54 per cent of the urban female workforce in manufacturing was employed in the manufacturing of textiles and wearing apparel.

Table 2.1 Distribution of urban female workforce by industry for all ages, Karnataka (in per cent)

Description of industry	
Agriculture, forestry, and fishing	11.1
Manufacturing	28.1
Construction	3.1
Wholesale and retail trade; repair of motor vehicles and motorcycles	11.6
Education	14.1
Human health and social work activities	5.3
Other service activities	3.8
Activities of households as employers; undifferentiated goods and services	6.9
Others	16.0
	100.0

Source: Author's calculations from PLFS (2017–18).

Note: The category of Others included mining, electricity, water supply, transportation, information and communication, food services, real estate, scientific and technical activities, administrative services, arts, and entertainment.

Table 2.2 Distribution of urban female workforce in manufacturing for all ages, Karnataka (in per cent)

Description of industry in manufacturing sector	
Manufacture of food products	6.8
Manufacture of tobacco products	21.1
Manufacture of textiles	11.0
Manufacture of wearing apparel	42.8
Manufacture of rubber and plastic products	2.7
Other manufacturing	15.6
	100.0

Source: Author's calculations from PLFS (2017–18).

Note: The category of Other manufacturing included manufacturing beverages, leather products, furniture, paper, chemical products, rubber, basic metals, and electrical equipment.

The disaggregation of construction into subsectors showed that the construction of buildings engaged 87 per cent of the urban female workers in the construction sector in Karnataka. Civil engineering involved 12 per cent of them.

The macro trend for India showed similar results. Manufacturing industry was the largest employer and employed 25 per cent of the urban female workforce. In the manufacturing industry, the garment industry employed almost 53 per cent of the urban female workforce. The division of construction into subsectors showed that the construction of buildings employed 69 per cent, civil engineering engaged 24 per cent, and specialized construction activities employed 7 per cent of the urban female workforce in the construction sector.

The distribution of urban female workforce in manufacturing of textiles across different forms of labor indicated that 41 per cent of them worked in self-employed household enterprises as helpers in Karnataka. Another 41 per cent of them worked as casual laborers. The distribution of urban female workforce in manufacturing of wearing apparel showed that more than half of them, around 52 per cent, worked as salaried workers. The macro trend for India showed that a majority of the workers in the manufacturing of textiles and wearing apparel worked as self-employed workers in household enterprises. The distribution of female workers in the construction of buildings across different forms of labor pointed out that a majority of them, that is, 85 per cent of them, were casual laborers in Karnataka and was similar to the India trend.

The lack of social security benefits and job contracts characterizes the female workers in the manufacturing and construction sectors in Karnataka. Around 29 per cent of the female workers in the manufacturing of wearing apparel were eligible for PF/pension, and 25 per cent of them were eligible for maternity benefits in Karnataka. None of the workers had written job contracts. Almost 75 per cent of the workers were not eligible for paid leave. Almost all the workers in the construction of buildings did not have a written job contract, and 75 per cent of them were not eligible for any social security benefits.

Findings from Primary Data

Socioeconomic Profile of the Respondents

The domestic helpers in the study were between the ages of 30–40. They came from less privileged social groups of the society, such as Scheduled Tribes. Some of them did not have formal years of schooling, whereas few had obtained 9–10 years of schooling. They lived in nuclear families with their spouses and one to two kids. Their spouses worked as daily laborers in construction sites or grocery shops, and a few worked as cab drivers. The daily laborers did not have a fixed salary and got INR 300–350 a day based on the availability of work. The income earned by these women was extremely crucial in running the households. The domestic helpers worked in three to four houses and earned around INR 2000–2500 per house. Their monthly income ranged between INR 7000 and INR 8000.

The construction workers in the study were between the ages of 25 and 40 years. They migrated for work from different parts of Tamil Nadu and North Karnataka. Some of these women had not obtained any schooling, while few young women below 30 years of age had completed ten years of schooling. The construction workers lived in the sheds close to their working sites. They got around 24–25 days of work a month and were paid INR 350 per day, and the men got INR 400–450 per day.

The garment workers were between the ages of 25 and 30 years and had completed five to ten years of schooling. The garment workers worked around 7.5 hours daily and had hourly targets of about 60–70 pieces. They earned INR 9000–9500 per month, and INR 800–1000 was deducted for social security benefits. Their husbands worked in small services, as workers in canteen, iron man, plumber, and so on, and their salaries ranged between INR 12000 and INR 13000 a month.

Food Security

The domestic helpers availed food rations regularly before the lockdown. The food grains were distributed based on the number of family members enrolled in the ration card. Each member aged 10 years and above was entitled to 6–7 kg of food grains. They got rice grains for free and sometimes pulses, soap, and salt based on the availability. Few of them paid out of their pockets to buy pulses and cooking oil. The quality of the food rations was not consistent.

During the lockdown, all the domestic helpers received rations. In the first round, their families got 20–35 kg of rice grains depending on the number of members enrolled and 4 kg of *atta*.[3] In the second round of distribution of food grains, they availed 1 kg of pulse along with rice grains. The food rations were a necessity for them during the lockdown. However, they felt that the items covered and the quantity given were insufficient to feed their family. A domestic helper named Nalini expressed:[4]

> My family is surviving through the food rations we got. 20 kg of rice is not sufficient to feed my two children and my husband for a month. I can't manage to cook three meals a day with only 20 kg of rice and now have ended up having 5 kg of rice left. We have to spend on our own to buy any other groceries. I have no option but to cook *ganji*[5] for our survival now.

A domestic worker got 0.5 liters of milk for a month. There were a few instances of distribution of cooked food by the city corporation office. However, these women preferred distribution of food grains over cooked food to meet the requirements of young kids at home.

No domestic workers received any help from the neighbors or community in the locality. A domestic worker, Rama, said:

> People look down on us if we stand in a queue to avail free milk. We feel ashamed. Even after waiting for an hour or two, I have not got it. They distributed to only a few known ones. So, I have decided to manage with whatever few things I have and not ask anyone for help.

The construction workers did not get rations, and their families in native places availed it. It was challenging to manage two meals a day with no work and wages for 50 days continuously. The construction workers managed to feed themselves and their kids with cooked food given by their owners or some volunteer groups in the localities. A construction worker named Gowri said: 'We have lived on the food offered by some humble people. They get cooked food to these sites and distribute it. On some days, I get it once, and some days I get it twice.'

These women struggled hard to feed their kids during the pandemic. Gowri said: ‘I could not get free milk packets distributed by the office also. Someone collected four packets and gave one packet to feed my kid.’ Bagyamma, a construction worker, said: ‘I request the street vendor to give me some vegetables to feed my kids, and later I give INR 4 or 5. Sometimes I get the leftover rotten vegetables.’ Some other construction workers ate less to feed their kids.

The garment workers did not have ration cards. Some of them had it in their native places and shared the food grains distributed to their families every month. Otherwise, they purchased groceries from fair price shops at a lower price. During the lockdown, few garment workers got food rations that consisted of 5 kg rice grains, 0.5 liters of oil, 0.5 kg sugar and 1 kg toor dal even without a ration card. But it was not sufficient to manage three meals a day for their families. Some of them purchased food grains from the ration shops and had an agreement to pay later. They consumed fewer quantities of food because of the increased prices of vegetables.

Financial Security

Few domestic helpers had Jan Dhan accounts in their names, and only one among them received INR 500 during the lockdown. They survived on the money given to them by their employers. Very few houses paid domestic helpers their salaries for both months (March and April 2020), and most of them paid them only for March 2020. The lack of regular flow of income brought immense anxiety among these workers. A domestic worker, Laxmi, said: ‘My husband has no work for the last 3–4 months. The house runs on my income. I don’t know when I can go back to work. I am anxious about the payment of rent and loans.’ Another domestic worker, Lata, said: ‘I spend money carefully in these difficult times. Before, if I purchased fruits or vegetables for INR 40 for my kids, now I restrict myself to INR 20.’ The domestic workers in the study stayed in rented houses. The monthly rent ranged from INR 4500 to INR 6000. They negotiated to pay the rent after three months.

The construction workers did not have Jan Dhan accounts, and very few workers who had accounts did not receive cash transfers from the government. They had not registered themselves as construction workers. Some of them tried to create an account and get the money but could not do it. Savita, a construction worker, said:

> I wanted to get INR 500 and went to the office to create an account. They asked me to get my identity cards (Aadhar and Pan). When I took it, they asked me to come again, and this happened two times. After that, I did not go.

The construction workers did not get work for 50 days and were not paid wages for the same period. They received money in the range of INR 1000–2000 per family to manage their expenses and food rations by their owners. However, they were unclear about the terms of repayment. Naga, a construction worker, mentioned: ‘The owner has asked to repay the money. But we told him we could not go back and got stuck here during the lockdown. How can we pay? We should see what will happen.’

The garment workers did not have Jan Dhan accounts, and they had bank accounts through the factories they worked. They received half of their salaries during the first month of the lockdown and were uncertain about it during the second month. It was extremely challenging to pay the rent, loans, and utility bills. A garment worker, Asha, said:

> I had to pay INR 1000 per week to the SHG for the loan taken. I am pressurized to repay. I told them I have no source of income to pay now, and only those who have kept money can pay it.

The factories of a few garment workers resumed operations after the second week of May 2020, but some of them were still unsure of their work. So they were trying to join factories that had started working.

Discussion and Way Forward

This paper aimed to analyze the reach of the food and financial stimulus to the urban female informal workers in Bengaluru during COVID-19 pandemic. The findings from the secondary sources of data on employment revealed that a major share of the urban female workforce worked in garment industries. Some of them worked in the construction sector. The socioeconomic characteristics of workers in construction sector emphasized that a large number of them belonged to socially disadvantaged groups with no formal schooling. A predominant share of the workers in the garment and construction sectors had no social security benefits, written job contracts, and paid leaves.

The lack of social protection made their livelihoods more vulnerable during the pandemic because of the abrupt lockdown. The findings from the primary data point out these aspects. The distribution of food rations enabled the domestic workers in this study to manage two meals a day. Yet the items distributed were insufficient, and there was an immediate need to include essential groceries (sugar, oil, salt, pulses). The construction workers had not received any food rations distributed by the State during the lockdown. They depended on the food distributed by others and were uncertain of getting food. Garment workers in the study purchased food rations from the fair price shops at low prices and did not receive free food rations. So the distribution of food grains through public distribution system was beneficial, but it did not reach all, particularly the construction workers stranded in cities. This study emphasizes the existing argument of the universal public distribution system with broader coverage of essential items.

Concerning financial security, the reach of Jan Dhan accounts was very poor, and the amount given was extremely negligible. All the domestic workers had accounts, and only one of them received INR 500. The construction workers and garment workers in this study did not have Jan Dhan accounts at all. The urban female informal workers had difficulty in managing their monthly expenses during the lockdown. The domestic workers and garment workers could not pay rent and negotiated for an extension with their owners. All the construction workers in the study borrowed money from their employers and were uncertain about repayment terms. There was an urgent need for higher cash transfers, at least an amount between INR 5000 and INR 6000 per family for three months. The mentioned cash transfers did not reach women because of lack of bank accounts and the inability to travel distances to withdraw money (APU, 2020; Borah et al., 2020; SWAN, 2020). Cash transfers need to include more beneficiaries through ration cards and house listings used in the latest socioeconomic surveys to identify the poor.

The pandemic further threatened the livelihoods of poor domestic helpers. Their 'touch heavy jobs' were at risk even after a few relaxations of the lockdown. In many cities, people perceived that domestic helpers carried the infection. Ironically, digital media endorsed this through advertisements for electronic appliances in the kitchen and promoted sacking them out of work (Scroll, 2020; Newsclick, 2020). In fact, this misconception increased the burden of unpaid and care work of many women working from home.

The sudden layoffs by the factories resulted in protests by garment workers demanding their wages and jobs in a few districts of Karnataka (Madaik, 2020). Similarly, domestic workers' unions also protested the sudden layoffs and the denial of their employers to employ them post-lockdown in Bengaluru and other big cities (Menon, 2020). With this existing problem, employers need to be more aware of not laying off female employees to ensure better participation of women in the labor markets.

Uttar Pradesh, Madhya Pradesh, Himachal Pradesh, and Gujarat decided to relax labor laws. They have proposed raising working hours to 12 hours per day and not providing for overtime pay. Following this, Karnataka also notified to exempt factories from Sections 51 and 54 of the Factories Act and raising working hours from 8 to 10 hours a day during May 2020 and later withdrew the notification due to pressure from the working classes (Garment Mahila Karmikara Munnade & Alternative Law Forum, 2020). This move would exploit female garment workers' labor significantly. Various such measures to increase production and profits of the industries post lockdown has triggered policy discussions for gender-sensitive policies.

Scholars have argued for gender-centric policies in mitigating this crisis (Bhattacharya, 2020; Deshpande, 2020; Grown & Paramo, 2020; Joy, 2020; Mukherjee, 2020; IMF, 2021). The provision of food by poor women workers forms an irreplaceable part of social reproduction and remains undervalued. The imposition of sudden lockdown impacted the financial security that, in turn, posed a heavy burden on the food security of these households. The shortage of food in the household forces responsibility for solutions onto women. Women and young girls often get the least food during such times (Agarwal, 2022). The urban female informal workers did not have an opportunity to voice out the challenges of providing food and financial security during the pandemic and therefore remained unheard in the policies.

Women's loss of employment has manifold implications that are not discussed adequately. Some of these are immediate, while others are medium and long-term effects and are not visible immediately (Agarwal, 2022). Among the expected outcomes, the loss of jobs resulting in reduced savings, the sale of jewelry and small animals owned by women, and an increase in informal borrowings are sequential effects. An indirect impact is reduced food security for women, which may result in poor nutritional intake for a long period. Few studies have discussed the negative effects on women's dietary diversity.

This study extends the existing argument that there should be a distinct outlook of policies for rural and urban women. In ensuring food and financial security to the urban female informal workers, the results support the provision of a universal public distribution system, cash transfers collated through various registrations, and an urban employment guarantee program.

Acknowledgment

I am grateful to Prajwal N. for helping me conduct the interviews and Niyati S. for her comments and suggestions.

Notes

1 Antyodaya Anna Yojana and Priority Households are sponsored schemes by the Government of India to provide highly subsidized food to the poorest families.
2 Pradhan Mantri Jan Dhan Yojana is a financial inclusion program of the Government of India that aims to expand and make affordable access to financial services such as bank accounts, remittances, credit, insurance, and pensions.
3 Atta refers to wheat flour.
4 The names of the respondents are changed to maintain anonymity.
5 Ganji refers to a semiliquid soft food made by boiling rice in water.

References

Afridi, F., Dhillon, A. & Roy, S., 2020. *How has Covid-19 crisis affected the urban poor? Findings from a phone survey – I.* Ideas for India. [Online] Available at: www.ideasforindia.in/topics/poverty-inequality/how-has-covid-19-crisis-affected-the-urban-poor-findings-from-a-phone-survey.html

Agarwal, B., 2022. *Imperatives of recognizing the complexities: Gendered impacts and responses to Covid-19 in India, Economia Politica* 39 (1): 31–53. [Online] Available at: https://doi.org/10.1007/s40888-021-00242-8

Azim Premji University (APU), 2020. *Azim Premji University COVID19 Livelihoods Survey: Release of Early Findings*. Bangalore: Azim Premji University.

Azim Premji University (APU), 2021. *State of Working India 2021: One Year of Covid 19, Centre for Sustainable Employment*. Bangalore: Azim Premji University.

Bhattacharya, T., 2020. *Social Reproduction Theory and why we need to make sense of the COVID-19 crisis*. [Online] Available at: www.tithibhattacharya.net/new-blog

Borah, A., Das, S., Dasgupta, A., Deshpande, A., Mahajan, K., Ramaswami, B., Saha,A. & Sharma, A., 2020. *The Coronavirus Pandemic: Are We Ready for the Long Haul?* Sonipat: Asoka University.

Deshpande, A., 2020. *Protecting Women Is Missing from Pandemic Management Measures in India.* [Online] Available at: https://flipboard.com/@quartz

Garment Mahila Karmikara Munnade & Alternative Law Forum , 2020. *Garment Workers, Covid 19 Pandemic and the Lockdown – A Report from South Karnataka,* Garments Mahila Karmikara Munnade and Alternative Law Forum.

Grown, C. & Paramo, C. S., 2020. *The coronavirus is not gender-blind, nor should we be.* [Online] Available at: https://blogs.worldbank.org/voices/coronavirus-not-gender-blind-nor-should-we-be

International Labour Organization (ILO), 2020. *COVID-19 and the world of work.* Second edition. Geneva: International Labour Organization.

International Monetary Fund (IMF), 2021. *Gender Equality and COVID-19: Policies and Institutions for Mitigating the Crisis.* Fiscal Affairs, International Monetary Fund. [Online] Available at: https://www.imf.org/-/media/Files/Publications/covid19-special-notes/en-special-series-on-covid-19-gender-equality-and-covid-19.ashx

Jan Sahas, 2020. *Voices of the Invisible Citizens: A Rapid Assessment on the Impact of COVID-19 Lockdown on Internal Migrant Workers*. New Delhi: Jan Sahas.

Joy, S., 2020. *Coronavirus Crisis: No lockdown for domestic violence.* Deccan Herald. [Online] Available at: www.deccanherald.com/specials/insight/coronavirus-crisis-no-lockdown-for-domestic-violence-829941.html

Kabeer, N., 2020. *Labour market inequalities are exacerbated by COVID-19,* LSE School of Public Policy. [Online] Available at: https://blogs.lse.ac.uk/covid19/2020/05/18/naila-kabeer-labour-market-inequalities-are-exacerbated-by-covid-19/

Kesar, S. & Abraham, R., 2020. *Interview: The State of Labour and COVID-19.* Catharsis. Available at: www.catharsismagazine.com/post/interview-the-state-of-labour-and-covid-19

Madaik, D., 2020. *1,300 Garment Factory Workers Lose Their Jobs Overnight in Karnataka Amid COVID-19 Pandemic.* The Logical Indian. [Online] Available at: https://thelogicalindian.com/news/1300-garment-factory-workers-lose-their-jobs-overnight-in-karnataka-21541

Mander, H., Ghosh, J. & Patnaik, P., 2020. *A plan to revive a broken economy,* The Hindu. [Online] Available at: www.thehindu.com/opinion/lead/a-plan-to-revive-a-broken-economy/article31577261.ece

Menon, G., 2020. *Domestic workers to protest loss of jobs, wages during lockdown.* Citizen Matters. [Online] Available at: https://bengaluru.citizenmatters.in/bengaluru-domestic-workers-job-loss-no-wages-covid-19-lockdown-dwru-46617

Mukherjee, I., 2020. *Social distancing from house help is exposing the sexism in Indian families*, scroll. [Online] Available at: https://scroll.in/article/957299/social-distancing-from-house-help-is-exposing-the-sexism-in-indian-families

Nagaraj, R. & Kapoor, R., 2020. *Provide income support, restore jobs,* The Hindu. [Online] Available at: www.thehindu.com/opinion/lead/provide-income-support-restore-jobs/article31577278.ece

National Council of Applied Economic Research (NCAER), 2020. *Delhi NCR Corona virus Telephone Survey Round 2.* NCAER National Data Innovation Centre. [Online] Available at: www.ncaer.org/event/round-2-ncaers-delhi-ncr-coronavirus-telephone-survey

Newsclick, 2020. *85% Domestic Workers Not Paid During Lockdown, says Survey.* Newsclick. [Online] Available at: www.newsclick.in/85%25-Domestic-Workers-Not-Paid-Lockdown-Survey

Scroll, 2020. *Covid-19: Kent RO withdraws ad against house helps kneading dough, issues apology.* Scroll. [Online] Available at: https://scroll.in/latest/963124/covid-19-kent-ro-withdraws-ad-against-house-helps-kneading-dough-issues-apology

SWAN, 2020. *32 Days and Counting: COVID-19 Lockdown, Migrant Workers, and the Inadequacy of Welfare Measures in India.* Stranded Workers Action Network. [Online] Available at: https://ruralindiaonline.org/en/library/resource/32-days-and-counting-covid-19-lockdown-migrant-workers-and-the-inadequacy-of-welfare-measures-in-india/

UN WOMEN, 2020. *Surveys show that COVID-19 has gendered effects in Asia and the Pacific.* [Online] Available at: https://data.unwomen.org/resources/surveys-show-covid-19-has-gendered-effects-asia-and-pacific

WIEGO, 2020. *Impact of public health measures on informal workers livelihoods and health.* WIEGO. [Online] Available at: www.wiego.org/resources/impact-public-health-measures-informal-workers-livelihoods-rapid-assessment

3 The impact of Covid-19 on the economy of lower-income Bogotá families

An analysis using Polanyi's concept of the economy as an instituted process

Sonia Carolina López Cerón

The institutionalization of Colombia's economy and Covid-19

The Covid-19 pandemic has been a historical moment where it is possible to observe causal mechanisms such as inequality – in income, wealth, land, education, gender relations, health service access and environmental conditions – operating more openly within particular economies. In the case of Latin America, and in particular Colombia, the pandemic does not appear to be challenging the institutionalized economy. This chapter explores this observation with an approach informed by Polanyi's concept of economy as an instituted process. It also includes an understanding of a stratified reality where the institutionalization of the economy results from the interplay of causal mechanisms operating from the structural and cultural dimensions. This approach analyzes the specific mechanisms that explain the possibility for adjustment, or not, of the social system (Archer, 1995), which in this case is the economy of lower income Bogotá families.

The present analysis aims to give insights into explaining the impact of Covid-19 on lower income Bogotá families and the persistence of the pre-pandemic institutionalization of the economy. The chapter begins by outlining Polanyi's concept of the economy as an instituted process. Then it discusses how the Colombian family and economy have developed historically alongside public policies at the national level and in Bogota. After this, the analysis focuses on mechanisms of inequalities (of income, environmental, educational and gender relations) from the structural dimension, and administrative corruption from the cultural dimension. The data used are secondary and have been collected from mayoralty, academic sources and national and international newspapers.

Polanyi's economy as instituted process

Polanyi's critique of economic liberalism (Despain, 2011, p. 278) and his contributions to the study of the substantive and formal meanings of the economy are reasons to consider his works and to start building upon them. The substantive meaning of the economy recognizes the facts while the formal meaning

DOI: 10.4324/9781003451990-5

recognizes the logic (Polanyi, 1957, p. 243). In this way, facts and logic are both equally necessary components for the explanation of the economy. The facts of the economy are a variety of forms of economic integration. The logic can or cannot include the variety of forms of economic integration. Polanyi proposed three forms of economic integration, one of them belonging to the logic of the market, and two more which were absent in the dominant theory of economics of his time.

Polanyi proposes that there are exchanges that are not necessarily linked to gains, or as he states in *The Great Transformation*, not related with the economic market (Polanyi, 1944, p. 57). He characterizes behavior within four principles: reciprocity, redistribution, market and householding (Polanyi, 1944, pp. 49–57), and later in his work renames these as the forms of economic integration. This classification was the result of his analysis of anthropological research, archaeological evidence and historical studies of different societies. Polanyi analyzed specific social systems in particular times and places. They were the cases of the Trobiand Islanders of Western Melanesia, the kingdom of Hammurabi in Babylonia, in particular, the New Kingdom of Egypt, ancient China, the empire of the Incas, in the kingdoms of India and in feudal systems in Africa (Polanyi, 1944, p. 50). Polanyi opens space for the study of institutions that are not necessarily related with or dominated by a logic of scarcity of means and rational (interpreted as maximizing of self-interest) behavior.

Polanyi's concept of economy as an instituted process is a contribution for institutional analysis in economics. This concept offers a holistic and dynamic understanding of the economy. The economy as an instituted process includes the possibility of observing the economy, from its substantive meaning, and understanding that economy by analyzing the process that has happened for the economy to be what it is, which includes the impact of the formal meaning of the economy. The economy required a process to be institutionalized in specific ways.

His contribution attempts to identify the institutionalization processes of the different forms of economic integration. With this aim, Polanyi establishes their corresponding patterns of institutionalization that he later goes on to describe as "supporting structures". Each of the forms of economic integration should have a supporting structure to become a form of economic integration. They are symmetry for reciprocity, centricity for redistribution and a market (with a price system) for exchange. These supporting structures have a historical institutionalization process. The analysis of this institutionalization process is the source of understanding the development of an economy.

In this chapter, I go on to use Polanyi's contribution to analyze the economy of the family as an instituted process. I propose a historical institutional analysis of the economy of the lower income families in Bogotá which offers an explanation for the impact of Covid-19. The historical trajectory of the structural and cultural mechanisms impacting the economy of the lower income families in Bogotá contributes to the academic debate. It is an initial and partial analysis for the explanation of the economy of the family in a specific moment and context. This analysis accepts further analysis which offers challenge or support.

The Colombian family and its economy

The work of Gutiérrez (1967; 1973; 1986; 1999a; 1999b) contributes to the understanding of the Colombian family. Based upon historical documents such as contemporaneous diaries of Catholic missionaries, she analyzes the family as an institution and considers its evolution since the fourteenth century. Her analysis is from an anthropological and historical perspective.

Gutiérrez proposes an analytical division of the historical evolution of policies relating to the family, which is useful to illustrate the historical root of the Colombian family's forms of economic integration. The first period is the precolonial and colonial period from colonization sixteenth century until Colombian independence (1819). During this period there were a variety of precolonial and colonial families and since colonization there is support for the ideal nuclear Catholic family. Gutiérrez shows that even when the ideal nuclear Catholic family had the support of the crown and legal authority and was in complementarity with the accepted religion of the time, a variety of family types still prevailed. There was a variety of family formations of indigenous communities and the development of other formations resulting from the evolution of the colonization process. Gutiérrez names this period 'Hispanic acculturative domination' (Dominación aculturativa hispánica). The second period for Gutiérrez is the consolidation of 'criollos' (descendants of the Spanish born in Colombia) from 1819–1952. Based on a survey and interviews carried out in 1951, Gutiérrez (1967) highlights that the predominant legal family in rural and urban Colombia is the nuclear family (85% of the rural couples and 89% of the urban couples, respectively), married through the Catholic ritual. Her analysis identifies the forms of social control for sanctioning nonlegal family types; this was a social sanction that included the punishment by or support of the landowners and providers of working opportunities (Gutiérrez, 1996, p. 52).

Gutiérrez also highlights how the Catholic religion, as part of the acculturation process, contributed to the strength of the nuclear Catholic family as the desired one. The nuclear Catholic family was considered as the legal union. However, she identifies three non-legal family formations: single motherhood, free union and concubinage. She also identifies the characteristics of each formation according to the type of relation between the mother and father, same-class or interclass. These non-legal families were met with social, moral and economic sanctions, depending on the position of the couple in the social pyramid. The descendants of these non-legal unions occupied a specific place in the established social order, always in a lower level than legal descendants or descendants of a legal family. The custom operated outside of the legal system because there was no legal parental obligation. For example, with inheritance, if the father wanted to give any rights to a son or daughter born from a non-legal family, he had to give these before his death (Gutiérrez, 1996, pp. 54–56).

Concubinage, the institution that was mentioned as a group elaboration in the colonization period, has a particular underlying reason in cases where the man belongs to an upper social class, which, during the colonization period was the

Spanish colonizer, afterwards the criollo (the descendant of Spanish people born in Colombia) and until the mid-twenties, the landowner. Between the reasons, one was an underlying one related with the upward mobility in terms of classification in the social pyramid. The sociocultural acceptance of this institution derived from a source of accepted single motherhood. But in some regions in Colombia and particularly in populations recognized in the lower parts of the social pyramid, single motherhood was accepted so long as the single mother offered her work to meet the needs of the child or children and gave extra for the extended family.

Gutiérrez highlights the role of the extended family. An extended family of this period of time is composed of the sum of nuclear families; however, the center is the nuclear family composed by the grandparents. Another form of extended family is when there are non-legal unions, such as single motherhood. The extended family acts as a mediator between the constituting families (characterized by consanguinity) and external society. In general, the norms of extended families are based upon solidarity and cooperation between the members (Gutiérrez, 1996, p. 101). Reciprocity, either based on free giving or none, characterizes economic relations within the extended family.

During this first period there is the consolidation of the nuclear Catholic family complemented by the extended family as the most relevant social unit across the country. This supported the social evolution of reciprocity as an important form of economic integration. It would later be one of the ways in which families received or gave support to other kinship members during the pandemic.

The second period, the mid-twentieth century, is characterized by the beginning of the development of welfare policies. Looking for the end of violence caused by radical intolerance of the two political parties, these two parties made an agreement, 'the National Front' (Frente Nacional). The agreement stated that each political party would cede the presidency to the opposite party during four consecutive presidential periods. After this period there was the consolidation of the national democratically elected government. Subsequent governments worked on national planning. Law Cecilia in 1968 created the Colombian national family welfare institute (Instituto nacional de bienestar familiar – ICBF). This law was inspired by the idea of a welfare state which should be responsible for the care of children, where it can exercise control over parents and reduce the birth rate. The institute was designed with the idea of guaranteeing the father's responsibility within the nuclear family. Family was understood in a conservative way, constituted by a husband and wife with their descendants. The aim of the law Cecilia was the support of the nuclear family that should prevail over other possible forms (Puyana, 2012, p. 217).

The Colombian State introduced public policies based on redistribution with a focus on lower income families. From a political-macro level, it is the introduction of this form of economic integration in the economy of the Colombian family. Welfare policies such as Law Cecilia responded to the contextual evolution of the previously consolidated nuclear family. Lower income families were the target group of welfare programs. During the pandemic, the state designed targeted programs to support lower income families, at the local and national level.

Redistribution from the state was developed during this second period and it is still operating during the pandemic. The form has been through targeted programs.

The third period begins in the last decade of the twentieth century. There is an important tension at the beginning of this decade. The planning of President Cesar Gaviria's government (1990–1994) focused on the openness of Colombia to international trade, accompanied by reduction of public expenditure and a package of neoliberal policies. The relaxation of terms of employment was included in these policies (Law 50 of 1990); taxation on consumption was increased and put forward as the main source of income for the state, instead of rent taxation (Law 49 of 1990); public companies of transport, social security and telecommunications were privatized (Law 1 of 1990) and the health and social security system was reformed (Law 100 of 1993) giving space to private companies to offer these services. In front of these policies was the national constitution of 1991, which was oriented towards a social integration far from these neoliberal policies (Orjuela, 2000, pp. 110–111; Díaz Londoño, 2009, pp. 210–211).

During this third period, there was political support for the development of market exchanges. The governments of the time followed the trend of openness to international trade and flexibilization of working conditions. This flexibilization of working conditions had an evolution that is observable in the high levels of informal employment. People in the informal economy struggled during the pandemic due to the lockdown. Responses to this struggle came from reciprocity and from redistribution from the state. Some donations were made by corporations.

In the 1990s, there was a conjunction of the welfare policies of international institutions, such as the Inter-American Development Bank (IDB) and the World Bank, with a package of welfare policies for lower income households which was implemented by the Colombian government. The conjunction was with the national constitution board. This national constitution's definition of family was as a fundamental institution of society constituted by the marriage of a man and a woman (Colombian National Constitution, 1991). This definition was challenged by 'de facto unions' – families constituted by stepparents and homosexual couples. A court judged in the defense of these families, including them as a possibility for constituting a family. For this reason, these families have access to the same rights as families of heterosexual couples and reconstituted families (families in which children have a biological mother or father who does not belong to the present family). It is also the case for extended families and same-sex partners. The latter were recognized as families by the constitutional court only in 2011 (Prieto, 2015). In 2013, a state council verdict in respect to the lawsuit of a child against the national penitentiary and prison institute deemed that the family could be constituted by:

> a father and a daughter, *or*;
> a single mother with her son or daughter, *or*;
> a free and voluntary decision of a woman and a man to live in a conjugal union, *or*;

the free and voluntary decision of same sex persons professing their love to each other and wish for a conjugal life.

(Puyana, 2013)

From the end of the 2000s there has been a development of juridical protections for the family. There is a law for the protection of family houses against foreclosure and Law 1361 (2009) for the development of public policies for the integral support and strengthening of the family. This law included the creation of the observatory of the family, which was supposed to be part of the National Planning Department, an administrative unit of the national government. The law supports the traditional nuclear form of family and does not recognize single parent families or homosexual couples (Puyana, 2012, p. 217).

An important law passed in 2010 is Law 1413, in which the economy of care is included in national economic accounts. This law looks for measurement of the contribution of women's home caring activities to the national economy and the economic and social development of Colombia (Puyana, 2012, p. 220).

In 2016, the ministry of health and social protection in the national government issued a policy for the support and strengthening of the family which has novelty in relation to Donati´s categorization of family policies. In the policy, family members as individuals and rights holders are included alongside the family (understood in a plural way) as a social subject (Donati, 2011). An important point is that even though the policy tries to open space for families' political participation in family policy design, the agency of the family and its members are understood in Sen´s sense; the government must develop capacities in families and this focuses on the individual level.

This is also the case in Law 1857 (16 July 2017), which modifies Law 1361 of 2009, adding extended family members to the 'family' and including specific activities that can contribute to support of the family by formal employers, telecommunication companies and television providers:

> The duty of the State is to provide families and its members with tools to potentiate its affective, economic, cultural, solidarity resources and criteria of democratic authority in the way that programs for the attention of family and its members give priority to their union and the activation of resources for its functioning as a protector tool par excellence of their members.
>
> (Law 1857, 2017)

This plan has not yet been executed; how it will be implemented is open for further analysis.

The development of public policy focused on regulation and protection to lower income households can be analyzed as the evolution of a capitalist mode of production. Colombian governments followed the trend of designing neoliberal policies and as a consequence of its implementation, the support from the State was necessary to help families and households to cope with the struggles of these policies.

Bogotá's local policies

Local family policies in Bogotá have been partially developed. During the mayoralty of Garzón, in 2006, a public policy for the family was developed that looked to guarantee the rights of the family, respect its diversity and support democratization within the family group. This proposal was not fully implemented, it being the end of Garzón's period as mayor (2004–2007), though the following mayor, Moreno (2008–2011), continued the policy (Puyana, 2012, p. 222). The mayor following Moreno, Petro (2012–2015), also worked with parents as users of public nurseries.

The concept of family in the public document published by Garzon´s government was the following:

> Social organizations, historically built, constituted by persons who recognised and are recognised by the diversity of their structures, arrangements, forms, relationships, roles and subjectivities; which are constituted by two or more members of different or same sex, with or without daughters or sons. The union of these persons are for blood-link, affinity, adoption or for affection in which emotional support, constant living or house sharing links are established and they are collective subjects of rights.
>
> (Secretaría Distrital de Integración Social, 2017, p. 43)

In this policy, the economic dimension of the family is reduced to the market and redistribution. The family is the main provider of the workforce and is also a consumer unit. Family is reduced in its economic dimension to market exchange (Secretaría Distrital de Integración Social, 2017, p. 83) excluding reciprocity. In respect to redistribution, it is related to the right of the family for economic security, which is understood as the mechanism for the family to reach its objectives and develop capacities.

The historical root of inequality

From the structural dimension a significant causal mechanism operating in the economy of the Colombian family is inequality. There are a number of dimensions of inequality, income, education, environmental and gender relations, and the focus firstly is on income inequality due to its relevance during Covid-19 contingency. Income inequality has a link with informal employment, vulnerability and unemployment. These factors made it difficult to implement the lockdown. People without a proper labor contract can lose their income easily, such as people working in the gig economy who had to go out to search for daily income.

Colombian inequality is historical and has its roots in the colonization process. This process spread the seeds of the social and economic stratification of society, based upon the attempt of monopolizing the relation of wealth and power, which in the context of La Nueva Granada meant power over the natural resources of the discovered land. This vested interest which started in the sixteenth century has been strengthened by directional guidance providing, as an outcome, the reproduction of an unequal distribution of material resources and rights among the inhabitants of what is nowadays known as Colombia. The privileged collectivity was first the Aragón and Castilla Crown; later on Creoles were included, who became privileged landowners; then liberal traders joined the latter during the nineteenth century, and the Catholic Church, which has been continuously present with different representations and changing supporting positions, depending on which group has the monopoly of power and wealth. These groups have shared this vested interest, and they keep a privileged position.

The monopoly of power was absolute and through different institutions it was sustained for almost three centuries during the colonization period. A mixture of material resources and cultural reinforcement, cruelty, violence, exclusion based upon race and lineage facilitated by law (Jaramillo Sierra, 2013) created a conjunction of stability in the structural realm and stability in the cultural domain. The scenario has been the reproduction of oppression. Upper income families have preserved a relatively privileged position. Meanwhile, middle income and lower income families belong to an underprivileged position. They have been penalized for any attempt of collective organization and rewarded by their resilient capacity to deal with the system configuration.

Elites have developed a capacity for adaptation to contingent situations. During the history of Colombia there have been external influences. However, the external impacts have been mediated by 'well established dominant groups', the privileged elites, through a reformulation of policies (Archer, 1995, p. 243). During the 1990s, a new openness to free trade confronted local industry with external manufacturers, the government increased taxes on staple foodstuffs and, in some periods, a total prohibition on imports of these goods, sacrificing the nutrition of lower income families (Kalmanovitz, 2017, p. 399).

The goal has been to strengthen their (elites) bargaining power to guide national political and economic decisions. Nowadays, this vested interest is still fed into a paradoxical social representative democratic state, which, in the name of adaptation, has facilitated the development of the capacity to absorb social actors into the hegemonic historical configuration.

In Colombia the combination of the forms of economic relations can change over time; meanwhile the conjunction of stability in the material and cultural domain is kept and the privileged position of elites, in terms of the family, upper income families, is facilitated and protected. Any combination of forms of economic relations, which does not constitute a concerted action able to reshape the structural-cultural system configuration, is welcome.

Different governments have supported the development of the market economy as a place in which families offer themselves as the workforce and are consumers of the products produced by companies. The last efforts of the government, both central (Política Pública Nacional de Apoyo y Fortalecimiento a las Familias, 2016) and local (Política pública para las familias de Bogotá, 2011–2015) in the case of Bogotá, still show the idea of the economy as the market economy, with reciprocity remaining invisible as part of the economy. However, the introduction of the economy of care is a first step, even when it is measured in the same way as a commodity of the market economy.

These inequalities have developed over time and have deepened in such a way that Colombia is currently among the countries with the greatest inequality in income and wealth. Additionally, in the social mobility index, 21 generations are needed to ascend from one level to another in Colombia (Table 3.1). With respect to the Covid-19 pandemic, these inequalities, which have historical preexistences, act as structural causal mechanisms that increase the vulnerability of people within lower income groups.

In Bogotá, there is a geographical and administrative unit which is the locality. There are 20 localities; 19 of those are urban and 1 is rural. Table 3.2 shows the coronavirus cases per locality in Bogotá for 27 July 2020. The localities with higher numbers of coronavirus cases have more houses classified in the lower income levels. In Colombia, we have the socioeconomic strata system which classifies households. The household classification goes from 1 (lowest income households)

Table 3.1 Gini index: Colombia, Brazil, Ecuador and Perú

	Period	*Mean Gini coefficient*	*Variation*[a]
Colombia	2001–2020	53.2%	3.9%
Brazil-PNADC	2012–2020	52.5%	2.9%
Ecuador	2007–2020	47.0%	5.1%
Peru	2000–2020	47.0%	5.1%
Central America	2000–2020	52.7%	2.2%

Source: Adapted from World Bank, 02 February 2023.

Note

[a] Coefficient of variation.

Table 3.2 Covid-19 positive cases per locality in Bogotá 27 July 2020

Positive Covid cases 27/07/2020			
Localidad	*Total*	*Localidad*	*Total*
1. Usaquén	2683	11. Suba	2683
2. Chapinero	1169	12. Barrios Unidos	1169
3. Santa Fe	1434	13. Teusaquillo	1434
4. San Cristóbal	2937	14. Los Mártires	2937
5. Usme	2400	15. Antonio Nariño	2400
6. Tunjuelito	1625	16. Puente Aranda	1625
7. Bosa	5517	17. Candelaria	5517
8. Kennedy	9124	18. Rafael Uribe Uribe	9124
9. Fontibón	2211	19. Ciudad Bolívar	2211
10. Engativá	4308	20. Sumapaz	4308

Source: Adapted from data from Bogotá's mayoralty (Alcaldía de Bogotá, 2020).

Table 3.3 Covid-19 positive cases per locality in Bogotá accumulated 2 January 2023

Positive Covid cases 25/01/2023			
Locality	*F*	*M*	*Total*
1. Usaquén	90646	73967	164613
2. Chapinero	33262	29884	63146
3. Santa Fe	16985	15791	32776
4. San Cristóbal	38259	31708	69967
5. Usme	32466	26251	58717
6. Tunjuelito	20742	17937	38679
7. Bosa	68296	56784	125080
8. Kennedy	123326	101573	224899
9. Fontibón	53607	43910	97517
10. Engativá	112146	92876	205022
11. Suba	160412	129780	290192
12. Barrios Unidos	23705	19831	43536
13. Teusaquillo	29535	25155	54690
14. Los Mártires	12297	11521	23818
15. Antonio Nariño	13100	11056	24156
16. Puente Aranda	36029	31843	67872
17. Candelaria	5237	5003	10240
18. Rafael Uribe Uribe	43648	37519	81167
19. Ciudad Bolívar	55269	45730	100999
20. Sumapaz	80	69	149
TOTAL	**969047**	**808188**	**1777235**

Source: Adapted from data from Observatorio de Bogotá, SALUDATA.

to 6 (highest income households). The first three localities having the highest number of positive cases are Kennedy, Suba and Bosa. These localities have a high proportion of houses classified in strata 2 and 3. The fourth locality is Ciudad Bolivar, which has 61% of households classified in strata 1.

Table 3.3 shows the accumulated coronavirus positive cases per locality in Bogotá for 2 January 2023. As can be seen in Table 3.3, the regions of Suba and Kennedy have accumulated the highest number of positive coronavirus cases in Bogotá. For this period, the third locality is Engativá, which has a similar socio-economic classification to Suba and Kennedy with a high proportion of houses classified in strata 2 and 3.

Colombia has been either the most unequal country in Latin America or the second in the world during the period 2009–2016 (Hellerstein, 2012). Colombia's levels of inequality has been above those of countries such as South Africa. In 2019, 20% of the higher income households get ten times the income of the 20% in the bottom income households. An important aspect to highlight is the relation between household income vulnerability due to the contingency and informality in employment.

Informal working is high in Colombia. In the case of Bogotá, 24% of the workers do not have a formal working contract and their income is 23% of total workers' income in Bogotá. A classification of economic sectors, according to their vulnerability during the crisis and the possibility of remote work, found that the sectors with lower levels of vulnerability are the ones in which it is possible to work remotely (Eslava and Isaacs, 2020). Eslava and Isaacs (2020) find a direct relation between sectors in which there are more workers without formal contract and vulnerability. These authors also find that in lower income households there is more participation in their income from activities in which there are higher levels of working without a formal contract. Finally, another important relation to highlight is between qualification level and working in more vulnerable sectors. Lower education levels are related with higher participation in sectors with higher levels of vulnerability. Persons with higher levels of education are more likely to be working in an activity classified with lower level of vulnerability. Meanwhile a person with an undergraduate degree is more likely to be working remotely which means to be part of a sector with lower level of vulnerability.

The Gini coefficient in Bogotá was 0.5145 in 2019, and 0.5941 in 2020. This variation due to possible job and income losses over the income of houses during the pandemic will position Colombia in a similar level of inequality of income calculated to the one faced at the beginning of the twentieth century (Group of Macroeconomics, 2020).

In response to the impact of the pandemic economic crisis, the national government developed targeted cash programs. One of them is Ingreso Solidario, solidarity income, which includes a large number of vulnerable people. The transfer was US$130 per month. The government used the previous programs and expanded the number of beneficiaries through the use of the SISBEN survey. The SISBEN survey has been used to locate older adults with low or no income. At the local level Bogotá's government also developed targeted programs of subsidies. One of these programs is the program of cash food transfers, Bogotá solidaria en casa. This program used the gig economy survey from the National Institute of Statistics (DANE) from 2018. Non-registered workers can submit an application. A group of senators from different political parties are proposing to replace Duque's government program with an 'emergency basic rent'. It is in procedures in the congress. This program is looking to increase the money transfer to make it equal to a minimum wage.

Gender inequality is an important aspect to include in the analysis. Gender violence increased during Covid-19 pandemic. Between March to May, 34 cases of femicide were reported, three more than the ones in the previous year during the same period. Phone calls to the purple line, which is a line for reducing gender violence, increased from 942 phone calls per week before the pandemic to 3,105 per week during the lockdown. And there is an increase of 80% of claims regarding intra-household violence.

Women were in a disadvantaged position since before the pandemic. In Colombia, women's income is 12% less than men. Regarding work and the attributes of the work, there were more men who had a job and also a job with formal contract (OIT, 2021, pp. 17–18). Women develop 76% of nonpaid care home activities. Also, within the professional health care activities such as being a nurse, 80% are women, and 92% of bacteriologists are women, meaning that they are exposed in a higher level to Covid-19. It is also usual that women have to find a way to generate income when there is a loss in the family income. Covid-19 cases affected more women than men, according to the data from Bogotá's mayoralty. Finally, the recuperation of formal jobs was slower for women than for men (ibid.).

Regarding environmental inequality, the monitoring of air pollution levels shows that air quality is better in the upper income localities, such as Chapinero and Usaquén, than in localities such as Ciudad Bolivar, Bosa and Kennedy. Most of the households are lower income in the latter localities. They are exposed to high levels of air pollution and respiratory illnesses and diseases as a consequence (Daza et al., 2021).

From the cultural dimension: administrative corruption

Administrative corruption is persistent in public contracts. This practice has been more profitable than drug trafficking. There is no market competition and actors can avoid being punished. Bogotá has the highest risk of being discovered. The Observatory of taxes of Pontificia Universidad Javeriana (Observatorio fiscal, 2020) concluded from an analysis of public documents and declarations of the ministry of finance and public credit that there is a lack of transparency about the budget for pandemic programs and how it is spent. From the total amount of budget during the pandemic, which is 11% of GDP, this Observatory could follow 1.70% of the total amount of the budget.

Responses from the people

At the beginning of the pandemic the responses from the people were mainly at the individual level. There were no collective actions taken. Colombia has a historical tradition of repression to collective action. The Obsevatorio de lademocracia (2020) found there is a decrease in levels of trust in others from 30% in March to 12% in May. The decrease happens in strata six and in strata 1; however there is a higher level of trust in strata six. The decrease has an impact on collective care methods and also makes it more difficult to find a possible collective answer.

From the political level, a group of senators from the political center and left proposed the development of universal basic income. This group presented the project for the creation of the universal basic income to replace Duque's (Colombia's actual president) program. This program is looking to increase the monetary transfers to make it equal to Colombian minimum wage, which is US$250 per month. There was a tension between the national government and progressive senators regarding the state budget for redistributive policies. The government discarded a tax progressive reform and the vice president declared that people want everything for free. Meanwhile, progressive representatives presented a proposal of redistribution as a mechanism to transfer state resources to satisfy the needs of the citizens.

The situation changed and people restarted social protests in the streets. These social protests were happening before the pandemic and stopped with the lock-down. They started again as a reaction to the tax reform that Duque's government proposed. The tax reform proposed to lower the threshold at which salaries were taxed and to expand the value added tax to other staples. The 'estallido social' started on 28 April 2021. There were demonstrations and mass street protests in the main cities and also in rural areas. Colombian middle- and lower income people were struggling with the Covid-19 pandemic impact and with the responses from the government. They could not accept the tax reform which would deepen inequalities. The government had to withdraw the reform. The protests and demonstrations continued until June 2021.

Repression of demonstrations and social protest is historical in Colombia and there was no exception during this period. There are reports of social protests in Colombia since 1956. There has been criminalization of social protest, by using claims of infiltration of illegal armed groups in the social protests and through gaps in the law for responses from police and military forces (Saldarriaga, 2021). The Human Rights Watch report of 2022 about the Colombian events of 2021 stated: 'Police officers repeatedly and arbitrarily dispersed peaceful demonstrations and used excessive, often brutal, force, including live ammunition and gender-based violence'. At the moment there is a project for including the people belonging to the 'Primera línea'[1] who are in jail to the social peace processes as speakers for peace.

Conclusions

This analysis of the impact of Covid-19 using Polanyi's concept of the economy as an instituted process brings attention to these three points: first, the Covid-19 contingency has so far deepened preexisting inequalities and responses from the government have been unable to prevent this. Second, the data available show that responses from lower income families remain at the individual level, making it harder to challenge preexisting inequalities. A reduction in trust in others impacts the possible emergence of solidarity, which contributes to the individualization of coping strategies that have remained at the family level. Third, collective action was unable to push the government towards bigger redistributive programs, which could meet lower income families' needs during the pandemic. Collective action through the social protest and demonstrations in the streets impacted the government by forcing the withdrawal of the tax reform, which would have further deepened inequalities.

Note

1 Primera línea is a group that participated in the protests and demonstrations with the objective to protect the social protest.

Bibliography

Alcaldía de Bogotá (2020). Cifras de coronavirus (COVID-19) en Bogotá. Available at: https://bogota.gov.co/mi-ciudad/salud/coronavirus/cifras-de-coronavirus-covid-19-en-bogota (Accessed: 21 January 2023).

Alfaro, L., Becerra, O. and Eslava, M. (2020). EMEs and COVID-19 Shutting Down in a World of Informal and Tiny Firms. Available at: https://economia.uniandes.edu.co/components/com_booklibrary/ebooks/dcede2020-19.pdf (Accessed: 27 July 2020).

Archer, M. S. (1995). *Realist Social Theory: The Morphogenetic Approach.* Cambridge: Cambridge University Press.

CINEP (2020). Base de datos de luchas sociales (BDLS) en Colombia. Available at: www.cinep.org.co/base-de-datos-luchas-sociales/ (Accessed: 21 January 2023).

Constitución Política de Colombia. (1991). Available at: http://www.constitucioncolombia.com/historia.php (Accessed: 25 July 2020).

Daza, V., León D. and Rubiano Galvis, S. (2021). La desigualdad que respiramos: Políticas de calidad del aire, pobreza y desigualdad en Bogotá, 2010–2020. Dejusticia. Available at: www.dejusticia.org/publication/la-desigualdad-que-respiramos-politicas-de-calidad-del-aire-pobreza-y-desigualdad-en-bogota-2010-2020/ (Accessed: 25 July 2020).

Despain, H. (2011). 'Karl Polanyi's Metacritique of the Liberal Creed', *Journal of Critical Realism*, 10:3, pp. 277–302. Available at: DOI: 10.1558/jcr.v10i3.277

Díaz Londoño, J.A. (2009) Estado social de derecho y neoliberalismo en colombia: studio del cambio social a finales del siglo XX. In antropología social. No. 11, Enero - Diciembre 2009, pp. 205–228. Available at: https://revistasojs.ucaldas.edu.co/index.php/virajes/article/view/828 (Accessed: 2 September 2023).

Donati, P. (2011). *Relational Sociology: A New Paradigm for the Social Sciences.* Abingdon: Routledge.

Eslava, M. and Isaacs, M. (2020). Vulnerabilidad del empleo a la emergencia de COVID19 en Bogotá. OBSERVATORIO DE COYUNTURA ECONÓMICA Y SOCIAL. Facultad de Economía, Universidad de Los Andes. Version updated 07 May 2020. Available at: https://economia.uniandes.edu.co/images/archivos/pdfs/CEDE/Observatorio-coyuntura/Gráficos_Empleos_-_Bogotá_-07042020.pdf. (Accessed: 25 July 2020).

González, J. I. (2017). En Bogotá y en Colombia vuelve a aumentar la pobreza. Revista Razón pública. November 2017. Bogotá, Colombia. Available at: www.razonpublica.com/index.php/econom-y-sociedad-temas-29/10699-en-bogotá-y-en-colombia-vuelve-a-aumentar-la-pobreza.html (Accessed: 25 July 2020).

Groups of Macroeconomics (2020). Efectos en pobreza y desigualdad del Covid-19 en Colombia: un retroceso de dos décadas. 18 May 2020. Centro de Estudios sobre Desarrollo Económico (CEDE). Faculty of economics, University of Los Andes. Bogotá, Colombia. Available at: https://economia.uniandes.edu.co/components/com_booklibrary/ebooks/BM%2020.pdf (Accessed: 27 July 2020).

Gutiérrez, V. (1967). *La familia en Colombia Trasfondo histórico* (The Family in Colombia Historical Background). Ministerio de Cultura Editorial Universidad de Antioquia segunda edición 1997.

——— (1973). Tradicionalismo y familia en Colombia. Asociación Colombiana de Facultades de Medicina. Bogotá, Colombia.

——— (1986). Reseña: La familia de hecho en Colombia constitución, características y consecuencias socio-jurídicas. In Boletín 56 Museo del oro. No. 15. https://publicaciones.banrepcultural.org/index.php/bmo/article/view/7300

——— (1996). Familia y cultura en Colombia. Medellín Universidad de Antioquia.

——— (1999a). Familia ayer y hoy. Conference published in Familia, género y antropología. Desafíos y Transformaciones. Ed. Tovar, P. Instituto colombiano de antropología e historia- Icanh-. Family from yesterday and today.

——— (1999b). Estructura, función y cambio de la familia en Colombia. Segunda edición. Editorial Universidad de Antioquia. Medellín, Colombia.

Hellerstein, E. (2012). Inequality Catching up with Colombia, *Berkeley Review of Latin American Studies*, fall 2012. Available at: https://clas.berkeley.edu/research/inequality-catching-colombia (Accessed: 25 July 2020).

Jaramillo, I. C. (2013). Derecho y familia en Colombia: Historias de raza, género y propiedad (1540-1980). 1st ed. 346 p. Universidad de los Andes, Colombia. Available at: www.jstor.org/stable/10.7440/j.ctt19x3h4h (Accessed: 2 September 2023).

Kalmanovitz, S. (2017). *Obra selecta.* Bogotá, Colombia: Penguin Random House Editorial.

LAWS LEY 1857 de 2017 (Julio 26) El Congreso de la República de Colombia.

LEY 1361 de 2009 (Diciembre 3) Diario Oficial No. 47.552 de 3 de diciembre de 2009 CONGRESO DE LA REPÚBLICA: Por medio de la cual se crea la Ley de Protección Integral a la Familia.

LEY 1413 de 2010 (Noviembre 11) 'Por medio de la cual se regula la inclusión de la economía del cuidado en el sistema de cuentas nacionales con el objeto de medir la contribución de la mujer al desarrollo económico y social del país y como herramienta fundamental para la definición e implementación de políticas públicas'. Available at: www.dane.gov.co/files/acerca/Normatividad/Ley1413_2010.pdf (Accessed: 25 January 2023).

Observatorio de Bogotá, SALUDATA. Open data Mayoralty of Bogotá. 6 July. Available at: https://bogota.gov.co/mi-ciudad/salud/coronavirus/cifras-de-coronavirus-covid-19-en-bogota. (Accessed: 25 January 2023).

Observatorio de la democracia (2020). Desconfianza en los demás avanza con cada día de aislamiento, Universidad de los Andes. Available at: https://uniandes.edu.co/es/noticias/sociologia/desconfianza-en-los-demas-avanza-con-cada-dia-de-aislamiento (Accessed: 24 July 2020).

Observatorio fiscal (2020) Pontificia Universidad Javeriana. Octubre 26. Available: https://www.ofiscal.org/_files/ugd/e33cdb_3523d0d4abb8498e879edf7893ad03ed.pdf (Accessed: 26 October 2020)

OIT (2021). Impacto de la COVID-19 sobre el mercado de trabajo colombiano y recomendaciones para la reactivación económica Colombia: OIT / Oficina de la OIT para los Países Andinos, 2021. 36 p. Available at: www.ilo.org/wcmsp5/groups/public/---americas/---ro-lima/---sro-lima/documents/publication/wcms_775897.pdf (Accessed: 21 January 2023).

Orjuela, L. J. (2000). 'La debilidad del estado colombiano en tiempos del neoliberalismo y el conflicto armado'. Versión ampliada de un artículo que el autor publicó en el número 1 de la Revista de Ciencias Sociales de la Facultad de Ciencias Sociales de la Universidad de los Andes y que fue presentada como ponencia en el taller de investigación sobre "Conflictos civiles en Colombia: el reto de lograr la paz y la reconciliación", realizado en la Universidad de Princeton, New Jersey, USA, el 22 de septiembre de 2000. Available at: https://revistas.uniandes.edu.co/doi/pdf/10.7440/colombiaint49-50.2000.05 (Accessed: 25 July 2020).

Polanyi, K. (1944). *The Great Transformation: The Political and Economic Origin of Our Time*. 2nd ed. Boston: Beacon Press.

——— (1957). 'Economy as an instituted process'. In K. Polanyi, C. M. Arensberg and H. W. Pearson (Eds.). *Trade and Market in the Early Empires: Economies in History and Theory*. Glencoe, IL: Free Press, pp. 243–269.

Política Pública Nacional de Apoyo y Fortalecimiento a las Familias (2016). Oficina de Promoción Social, Dirección de Promoción y Prevención. Ministerio de Salud y Protección Social. Bogotá, D.C. Colombia 2016. Available at: www.minsalud.gov.co/sites/rid/Lists/BibliotecaDigital/RIDE/DE/PES/politica-apoyo-apoyo-fortalecimiento-familias.pdf (Accessed: 25 July 2020).

Prieto, M. C. (2015). *Evolución del concepto de familia en Colombia: Una mirada juridisprudencial*. Medellín, Colombia: Tesis Universidad Santo Tomás.

Puyana, Y. (2012). 'Las Políticas de familia en Colombia: Entre la orientación asistencial y la democrática'. *En Revista Latinoamericana de Estudios de Familia* 4: 210–226.

——— (2013). 'Familias colombianas: diversidad, normas y realidad social'. *En Revista Razón Pública*. 28 July. . Available at: https://razonpublica.com/familias-colombianas-diversidad-normas-y-realidad-social/ (Accessed: 25 July 2020).

Saldarriaga, M. (2020). 'La criminalización de la protesta social en Colombia es histórica', Cero sesenta, Universidad de los Andes. Available at: https://cerosetenta.uniandes.edu.co/la-criminalizacion-de-la-protesta-social-en-colombia-es-historica1/. (Accessed: 22 January 2023).

Secretaría Distrital de Integración Social (2017). Política Pública para las Familias de Bogotá 2011–2025. Available at: https://old.integracionsocial.gov.co/anexos/documentos/2015politicaspublicas/06012016_Politica_Publica_para_las_Familias_de_Bogota_2011-2025.pdf (Accessed: 25 July 2020).

World Report (2022). *Human Rights Watch*. Chapter Colombia. Available at: www.hrw.org/world-report/2022/country-chapters/colombia. (Accessed: 22 January 2023).

Section 2

Finance and the Causes of Crises

4 On the Financial Instability Hypothesis and Its Global Implications Post-Covid-19

Barkin Cihanli

The framework of Financial Instability Hypothesis (FIH) consists of a holistic approach to the changes within the capitalist economy of the United States and the evolution of the financial structure of the economy. Hyman Minsky always emphasized the importance of finance in the capitalist system and described the finance as a constantly evolving mechanism that creates inherent stability for the economy. Minsky also proposed policy solutions to mitigate the instability caused by the financial innovation and evolution. He considered the institutions within the capitalist system as the most fundamental elements in regard to providing stability to the innately unstable system. This chapter considers the source of the inherent instability in the capitalist market economy, the roles and responsibilities of the institutions in a market economy, the relationship between the evolutionary process of the finance and the evolutionary process of institutions in a market economy and the policy implications of the FIH for the international financial system. The chapter will attempt to address these research questions by analyzing and evaluating the FIH in regard to the financial instability and the institutions, and will also address the policy solutions proposed by Minsky in regard to the restructuring and the reform of the public and private institutions within the system. In light of Minsky's proposals and their implications, the goal of this chapter is to argue that the FIH is a holistic approach, because it emphasizes the dynamic role of and changes in the institutions of the system together with the theory of investment, finance and unemployment along with the analysis of the capitalist economy of the United States. The reformation and the restructuring of the institutions must take into account the role of and modifications in institutions and the theory of investment, finance and the unemployment for the purpose of the attainment and the maintenance of full employment so as to mitigate the instability of the system, because Minsky's proposals of mitigating the innate instability of the capitalist system rest on the idea of reforming the public and private financial institutions and sector and fighting the poverty and unemployment. These proposals also have several important implications for the international financial system.

The issues of economic instability and financial reform are significant to address, because the current pandemic of Covid-19 has exposed the vulnerability of the American and thus the global financial system. The pending global financial

DOI: 10.4324/9781003451990-7

and economic crises after the end of the pandemic call for severe institutional reform and restructuring of the austerity mindset right now so that the effects of the post-Covid-19 financial/economic crisis could be prevented or mitigated. A major starting point is the reformation of economic thought with respect to the relationship between investment, finance and unemployment and the almost half-a-century impact of austerity policies on the investment, finance and unemployment.

This chapter will consist of three parts. The first part will provide an outline of the framework of the FIH as it pertains to the role and evolution of institutions, the investment and finance and the unemployment in the system. The second part will consist of the policy proposals by Minsky for the restructuring and reform of the institutions to eliminate unemployment and mitigate the innate instability of the international financial system. This part will also attempt to show the necessity to discard the institution of austerity and its corresponding policies and their negative impacts. The last part will provide conclusions and the lessons we could learn from the FIH framework and Minsky's proposals in the context of the reformation and restructuring of the post-Covid-19 global financial system.

Minsky and the Financial Instability Hypothesis

The origins of the FIH seemed to date back to the influence of Joseph Schumpeter and John Maynard Keynes on Hyman Minsky's intellectual development. Schumpeter's work on the Business Cycle Theories regarded business cycles as natural processes throughout the evolutionary path of capitalism. Additionally, Schumpeter categorized three types of cycles: Kitchen (inventory and investment cycles), Juglar (investment cycles with monetary or financial elements) and Kondratiev (major technological innovations see Delli Gatti et al. 1994, 2). The notion of cycles as natural, evolutionary processes of capitalism formed the backbone of the FIH as Hyman Minsky framed it. Minsky was particularly interested in what Schumpeter would call Juglar cycles, because Minsky believed that capitalism was a financial system (Minsky 1993, 145; see also Minsky 1994c, 5). Hence, a thorough analysis of a capitalist market economy must include an analysis of the financial industry and its relationship with the real output, investment and employment determination in an economy since the financial/banking sector has two primary roles: provider of means of payments and the director of real resources into the capital development of economy (Minsky 1994b, 1). As a result of the influence of Schumpeter and Keynes, Minsky put forward the FIH which fundamentally incorporates the investment theory of business cycles and the financial theory of investment for capitalist economies from Keynes' 1936 General Theory (Minsky 1993, 17; see also Minsky 1994c, 5).

The foundation of the FIH rests on the notion of non-neutrality of money and finance by Keynes (Minsky 1994c, 5). Specifically, the modifications in monetary and financial institutions determine the evolutionary pathway of the economy throughout the time (Minsky 1993, 17; see also Minsky 1994b, 2). Minsky stated that money is an integral part of the system as it plays a significant role in the determination of prices of current output and capital assets (Minsky 1994c, 6; see also

Minsky 1993, 17). Through the investment theory, the money and the finance create a number of wave-like chain events which generate an impact on the real variables of the economy. As a result, this impact could result in 'incoherent behavior as a natural outcome of the interactions between flows of income and the payment of flows due to financial commitments' (Minsky 1993, 17). Minsky perceived this as a fundamental property of a capitalist economy (Minsky 1993, 17).

Minsky viewed the payment commitments as products of the ways of financing investment and creating positions in capital assets whose prices depend on the expected profits or expected income that these capital assets would generate. These expected incomes are determined by the aggregate demand of the products produced by these capital assets. These gross capital incomes could be more than enough, just enough or inadequate to fulfill and validate the financial commitments that were undertaken to made the investment. On the whole, if there appear to be lots of people who default on their payments, then this could generate series of debt crises and eventually debt deflations. This notion of debt deflation became incorporated into the FIH due to the influence of Irving Fisher's Debt Deflation Theory of Great Depressions. In order for debt deflation to occur, there has to be 'over indebtedness' in the economy by households, firms and individuals. This over indebtedness stems from the changes in the financing of investment and capital assets as the economy experiences growth. The changes in financing practices result from the modifications in institutions, innovations and inventions of financial instruments. The inclusion of institutions, innovations and uncertainty happened in the context of the Great Depression, as Keynes and Fisher were largely influenced by the Great Depression of 1929 (Minsky 1993, 1819).

The specific focus of Minsky in terms of the institutions within the financial sector centered on the banks. He attributed two key roles to banks in a modern capitalist economy: 'the supply of the means of payments and the channeling of resources into the capital development of the economy' (Minsky 1993, 16). However, there was another bank that Minsky put the most emphasis on the Federal Reserve Bank. The Fed was the product of the panic of 1907, and its establishment served to prevent potential financial crises in the future. Even though the government was expected to be the referee in the banking game in which its responsibilities include, but are not limited to, supervision, regulation and examination of the banks. The U.S. Treasury and the Federal Reserve Bank failed to execute their responsibilities during the period of 1929–1933 (Minsky 1993, 16, 19). As a consequence, the banking and financial legislation of that era concentrated on the reforming of the financial structure of the economy so as to prevent the likelihood of such a crisis from happening ever again (Minsky 1993, 19).

Minsky observed that the financial sector in the United States became increasingly sophisticated with the innovative techniques and strategies of the industry to minimize losses and maximize profits (Minsky 1994a, 3; see also Minsky 1993, 5). This was reflected in his framework of stages of capitalism in which he defined the evolutionary process of capitalism throughout different stages (Minsky 1993, 4). Firstly, the United States had commercial capitalism in which households owned small stock of capital assets. The notion of the separation of finance and the production process was another defining characteristic of this stage. Additionally, financial institutions and the banking existed for the financing of commerce and the related activities.

During the nineteenth century, the commercial capitalism gave way to finance capitalism which included, but was not limited to, the development of canals, railways and utilities together with the manufacturing industry. The key defining characteristics of this stage were the importation of capital goods and the external finance of the projects along with the development of financial houses and creditors to Europe (Minsky 1993, 147–148).

Finance capitalism came to an abrupt end when the Great Depression of 1929 hit the United States and the global economy. The subsequent reforms such as the Glass-Steagall Act and the constructive government deficits enabled the industrial organizations to get rid of their debts. Virtually everyone possessed government debt, and during the recovery, wartime household savings developed massive numbers of small holdings of stocks. In other words, firms were free of stockholder control. Due to the trend of household ownership of firms and corporations, this stage was also called the People's Capitalism. (Minsky 1993, 148)

People's capitalism transformed into money manager capitalism as households started to own interests in pension funds, mutual funds and annuity liabilities of insurance companies. The managers had huge influence on what and how the finance is allocated. Huge mutual and pension funds emerged. The most famous examples included Teachers Insurance and Annuity Fund and College Equity Retirement Fund. The emergence of mutual and pension funds created new layers of financial intermediations. In the beginning, pension funds were ultra-conservative in their investments (only government and top-rated private bonds). The stagflation of the late 70s and 80s made them seekers of short-term total returns (income plus net asset value change). As this trend became the norm, the notions of risk changed. The modern 'finance theory' justified the investment on less than investment grade securities as long as a fund had a diversified portfolio of both assets. Money manager capitalism became a casino capitalism which was characterized mainly by the pursuit of short-term performance and ingenuity of managers (Minsky 1993, 148–149).

The state pension funds increased the supply and demand of equity base for leveraged buyouts and high-yield junk bonds. The result was systemic indebtedness and debt deflation anticipated by Fisher in the 1930s. However, Minsky strongly cautioned that the rise of money manager capitalism had little to do with deregulation. Alternatively, the Fed under Volcker failed its duty to protect the equity base of banks and the thrifts by allowing the rise of interest rates. This crushed the asset values and cash flow patterns (Minsky 1993, 150). The exploitation of zero equity and the slack supervision allowed banks and savings and loan associations to engage in leveraged buyouts (investing on junk bonds or providing bridge financing). Yet the institutional innovation and the evolution were not limited to the emergence and the rise of the mutual and pension funds. (Minsky 1993, 149–150)

Simultaneously, there appeared to be a strong threat by electronic funds and credit cards against commercial banks. Minsky emphasized that the significance of the vender's discount depends on the success of the credit card. According to him, the check system was never profitable for banks, because it required a subsidy to cover its costs. The traditional analysis found 3.5 to 4 percent cost to deposits by checks. When the relationship banking was the norm, the banks could bear this burden. The check system relies on income from assets and other fees to cover some partial costs. As a consequence, the emergence of money market funds made banks realize their need to retain deposits through meeting the market. Banks could not compete with money market funds if they cannot profit from the check system. Minsky suggested that this could be done via replacing checks with debit cards, maintaining a venders discount on debit card payments and fully priced checks (Minsky 1993, 150–151). Moreover, the invention of derivatives and the changing executive structure of the financial firms and corporations in the mid-1990s quickly became a concern of Minsky as he pointed out that similar scenarios triggered the financial meltdown and the debt deflation of the 1929 (Minsky 1994a, 3–4). Overall, the emergence of credit card happened due to technical innovation in computation and statistical analysis of large samples of data. There had been other changes in the financial system, but the most important ones were the emergence of new layers of intermediation, and the developments in the payments mechanism. Overall, the evolutionary stages of capitalism demonstrated the evolution of the financial institutions, business models and practices and norms. The evolution of these financial institutions had generated a series of problems that Minsky strongly cautioned against. (Minsky 1993, 151) However we need to consider the underlying theory of investment and finance that paved the way for the evolution of the financial institutions.

The main elements of the investment and finance theory within the FIH stem from Keynes's General Theory Chapters 3 to 6, Irving Fisher's theory of debt deflation and the writings of Henry Simons (Minsky 2008, 192; see also Minsky and Vaughan 1990, 24 and Minsky 1988, 5; Minsky 1994a, 7). The main argument within the theory of investment and finance is that 'Instability is determined by mechanisms within the system, not outside it; our economy is not unstable because it is shocked by oil, wars, or monetary surprises, but because of its nature' (Minsky 2008, 192). Neoclassical synthesis and the orthodox Keynesians such as Hicks, Hansen and Samuelson ignored the fundamental elements of the General Theory, that 'Capitalist market mechanisms cannot lead to a sustained, stable price, full-employment equilibrium. Serious business cycles are due to financial attributes that are essential to capitalism' (Minsky 2008, 194; see also Minsky and Vaughan 1990, 24; Minsky 1993, 7; Minsky 1994a, 1). FIH is in sharp contrast to neoclassical synthesis which suggests that ceteris paribus, decentralized market mechanism will attain a self-sustaining, stable-price, full-employment equilibrium (Minsky 2008, 192). Overall, the investment and finance theory within the FIH also takes the role and the evolution of institutions, usages and policies into account in regard to the financial properties of capitalism: The 'adaptability and the instability of capitalism' results from the financial structure of capitalism (Corporate Capitalism) (Minsky 2008, 196; see also Minsky 1988, 17–18).

The investment and finance theory under the FIH regard the capitalist economy as a financial system (Minsky 2008, 192; see also Minsky 1989, 27). Capitalist economy include capital assets which leave a residue of financial instruments which have prices. Capital assets and debt instruments turn cash flows into current prices. Investment leads to the production of capital assets. The price of investment is equal to the income that capital asset is anticipated to generate. In turn, the expected income of capital assets influences the demand price of investment output (Minsky 2008, 191–200). Thus, the price of capital and financial assets is determined by cash flows and capitalization rate. If capital assets yield adequate income, the past debts are validated. If not, the debt and capital asset price deflation could reduce investment demand. Additionally, Minsky put forward the existence of two sets of prices: current output and capital asset (Minsky 2008, 200; see also Minsky and Vaughan 1990, 25). According to him, these prices depend upon different variables in different markets, but they are related (Minsky 2008, 200–201; see also Minsky 1988, 14).

The theory also states that in the capitalist system, profits both drive businesses and validate past decisions and future expectations. Minsky's assumptions within his theory of investment and finance hold that workers consume all of their wages, while capitalists save all of their profits. Furthermore, profits equal investment (Minsky 2008, 191). Financing influences the prices of capital assets, the effective demand for investment and the supply price of investment outputs (Minsky 2008, 207). Hence, investment is the fundamental element of the direction of the economy; the government budget, the behavior of consumption and the path of money wages are supplementary. Ultimately, profits, capital-asset prices, financial market situation and investment determine the financial (in)stability (Minsky 2008, 191).

Business investment could be characterized as spending money for the production of goods as inputs of other production processes that are anticipated to earn revenues. This could be divided into two: internal and external financing. Minsky stated that a decision to invest is based on the conditions of liability. Cash flow commitments, present-value calculations and liquid-asset holdings lead to developments in financial markets and institutions, and influence the behavior and the viability of economic units (Minsky 2008, 192).

At this point, it would be useful if one considers the investment and finance theory of FIH in comparison with Patinkin Resolution of the neoclassical synthesis which advocates the path to full employment through normal market processes. Initially, an exogenous money variable influences consumption out of income which leads to an increase in the price-level-deflated value of money balance. This, in turn, results in an increase in demand for consumer goods and thus more employment. As a consequence, Friedman argues that this resolution proves that capitalist market system is not flawed; the path to full employment equilibrium is compatible with the market system under the neoclassical synthesis. On the other hand, Minsky believed that the story did not end once the economy reaches the full employment equilibrium. The Patinkin Resolution fails to acknowledge the influence of bankruptcy on asset prices and financing of investment. It also fails to explain the transitory state beyond full employment. Once full employment is attained and maintained, it leads to a speculative boom beyond full employment. Patinkin process might lead the economy out of a stagnation, but not to an equilibrium. Market mechanism could bring the economy to full employment which contains endogenous disequilibrating forces (Minsky 2008, 196–197).

Borrowing and lending on the margins of safety creates money. Money supply is influenced by the debt commitments. The demand for capital assets result from their expected profitability. Due to the inherent speculative element, there appears to be larger debt financing due to the optimism of the full employment and beyond. This tends to coincide with the financialization and financial innovation which result in higher price for assets and higher demand price for current investment, because more external financing is available for investment. The subsequent higher investment and higher profits generate an investment boom and inflation (Minsky 2008, 198–199). These endogenous disequilibrating forces play a key role in the periods of expansion. This 'period of tranquility', as Joan Robinson put it, tended to be interrupted by investment booms, inflations, financial and monetary crises and debt deflations (Minsky 2008, 197; Minsky 1994a, 2–3, 6). Thus, Minsky attempted to define an underemployment equilibrium which is 'transitory state following a debt deflation and a deep depression' (Minsky 2008, 197).

In another avenue, market reactions to unemployment would be to lower wages and prices. Lower money wages and prices result in low profits and cash flows. This simply means no validation of past debt, depending on the ratio of internal to external finance which could ultimately pave the way for debt deflation and bankruptcy (Minsky 2008, 197–8).

On a more detailed account, the determination of capital asset prices forms the backbone of the theory of investment and finance theory of the FIH. In this framework, capital assets yield quasi rents which are simply gross profits. Furthermore, quasi rents could be transformed into prices of capital assets which determine the supply price of investment good for that good to be produced. Financial assets are also similar to capital assets. They involve capitalizations of the future cash flows and contain elements of uncertainty. Prices of capital and financial assets also rely on cash flows and market conditions. The higher the quantity of money, the higher the capital and financial asset prices. This, in turn, leads to higher price of capital assets due to higher returns and capitalization rate and higher borrowing at favorable rates. As a consequence there appears to be an increase in consumption and investment (Minsky 2008, 200–204). These forces lead the economy into a speculative boom.

There are three sources of finance: cash and financial assets on hand, internal funds and external funds. Aggregate internal funds are not adequate to finance gross investment because of the outflow of business debts, dividends, interests, repayment of principal on debts and executive labor costs. Internal funds are supplemented with external funds. External funds are determined by expected revenues and the financing of capital assets. Balance sheets have a mix of internal and external funds. Production-financing is short-term. Permanent financing includes bonds, mortgages, equity issues and corporate retained earnings. Prices of capital assets and market conditions create a demand function of investment. Labor costs and short-term interest rates create a supply function of investment. Under this framework, financing affects the effective demand for investment. The decision to invest relies on uncertainty. Uncertainty depends on history and conventions (and also innovation). A history of success could reduce the margin of safety, while a history of failure could do the opposite (Minsky 2008, 205–207).

Large government deficit and current account surplus on the balance of payments are necessary for the internal funds to be utilized in investment (Minsky 2008, 212). If the internal funds are not adequate, then the external funds could be borrowed. However, an increase in borrowers' risk due to increase in external financing reduces the demand price of capital assets (Minsky 2008, 212–213). Lenders' risk is a function of interest rates and covenants and codicils. These are dependent on negotiations and uncertainty. Investment will happen until the point of the intersection of the borrowers and lenders' risk. Yet this point is an implicit price that is never observed. The curvature of borrowers and lenders' risk will depend on their expectations and past successes. Investment is also determined by the anticipated cash flows, because the investment is a function of quasi rents. If cash flows are not enough then external financing is necessary. If there are more profits than expected, the improvement in the flow of internal funds will implicitly increase the price of capital assets and borrowers' willingness to finance externally (Minsky 2008, 212–216). However, the availability of investment is not the only thing that determines the investment.

Short-term interest rate influences the supply price of output (Minsky 2008, 217; see also Minsky and Vaughan 1990, 26). Partially completed investment could create an inelastic demand for finance. The rising inelastic demand will result in an increase in supply prices unless they are infinitely elastic. The cost of financing increases after the favorable conditions have been maintained over time. The supply of finance could become very inelastic due to policies and endogenous forces of banking and financial system. This could increase the short-term interest rates quickly and dramatically which in turn leads to rapid increases in long-term interest rates, and thus decrease in prices of stocks and bonds. These could have adverse effects on the demand price for capital assets and the supply price of investment (Minsky 2008, 217–218). Overall, the investment and finance theory within the FIH demonstrates the evolutionary processes within the financial institutions, public and private sector to pinpoint the changes that create the instability for the capitalist economy of the United States. However, the instability generated by the evolutionary changes in financial institutions, behavior and the structure of public and private sector and the labor market was not the only problem that the American economy was experiencing?

FIH-Informed Policy Proposals

According to Minsky, one of the biggest problems that the capitalist economies was facing in the mid-1990s was unemployment. Unemployment appeared to occupy a prominent role within the FIH, because Minsky believed that the attainment and the maintenance of tight full employment could mitigate the instability of the capitalist system. Minsky also complained that the monetary and fiscal authorities were unjustifiably tolerating persistently high unemployment at the expense of their fight against inflation. One of the fundamental problems of the system was the perception of the unemployed as being flawed, and not the market system. As a result, Minsky's proposals for the elimination of the unemployment aimed not only to change the behavior of people, but also to change the system. Hence, the ultimate goal was the attainment and maintenance of 'tight full employment' and the modification of institutions so that inflation and old practices were tamed. Minsky defined tight full employment as a phenomenon 'when a broad cross-section of occupations, industries, and locations, employers at going wage and salaries, would prefer to employ more workers than they in fact do' (Minsky 1965, 1–5). In order to understand the significance of the commitment to tight full employment, one needs to unpack Minsky's perspective of the labor markets in the United States.

Minsky defined the labor market tightness as the combination of cohesive relative wages and the prominence of trade unions. He also categorized the labor market into two sets of industries: high and low-wage industries. The high-wage industries include highly selective, skilled and trained labor with infinitely elastic labor supply at the going wage, whereas the low-wage industries were characterized by the upward-sloping supply curve, but the position depends upon the number of workers employed by the high-wage industries. When the employment in the high-wage industries increases, the supply curve of workers in the low-wage industries shifts to the left. When the employment in the high-wage industries decreases, the supply curve of workers in the low-wage industries shifts to the right. If the demand for high-wage workers increases, the supply curve of low-wage workers shifts to the left. Thus, wages fall and employment rises in the low-wage industry. The same scenario happens if aggregate demand increases. The changes in the low-wage industry rely on the reaction of labor force participation to higher wages and improved job availability. At the end of the day, low-wage workers' wages would rise, while high-wage workers' wages would remain constant (Minsky 1965, 3–8). On the basis of this framework of the labor markets and the tight full employment, Minsky put forward a series of intermediate policy objectives to eliminate poverty and unemployment.

The intermediate policy objectives aimed to constrain the rise of wages in high-wage industries while facilitate the rise of wages in low-wage industries; keep the price levels in high-wage industries constant or let them rise at a lower rate than the labor productivity in the high-wage industries; increase the price levels in the low-wage industries at the same or higher rates of labor productivity. Minsky warned that there could be transitional inflation, but once the tight full employment is maintained, this would cease. He also denied that the American society and the government had to choose between inflation and poverty. According to him, inflation would happen if you believe in it. In other words, there was a psychological component to the occurrence of inflation. As a result, he stated that not all inflations were bad (Minsky 1965, 9–11). Apart from the intermediate policy objectives, Minsky had a holistic approach to the fight against poverty.

His program against the poverty was extensive and attempted to address the institutional structure of the labor markets, government sector and educational sector. Initially, he required a clear definition of full employment as tight full employment together with the inclusion of a relative income policy. He advocated for the creation of a more homogenous and fluid labor force to prevent transitional inflation (labor aggregate demand exceeds aggregate supply). Furthermore, job training, job relocation, substitution of labor and so on could make the labor force more homogenous and fluid. He stressed the significance of the necessity to increase spending on education to break the cycle of poverty and on specific programs designed to help high school dropouts. He also supported the resurrection of programs similar to WPA, NYA and CCC from the New Deal era, yet warned that public works programs could be inefficient because they provide jobs for already-well-off workers. He advised the establishment of a wage support law with the national minimum wage. Moreover, he called for the collaboration of federal, state and local governments to design and submit projects and employ workers according to their needs. Eventually, he desired to institute transitionary policies such as the protection of the high-wage workers for their capital losses during the transitional period, subsidized employment opportunities for the poor and ill-trained, and improvements in transfer payments like children's allowances and universal medical care for everyone without means tests (Minsky 1965, 18–24).

Minsky's reformation proposals also have several implications for the international financial system. The current international trading framework from the terms of trade perspective could enhance our understanding of the 'parallel trends between the policies of full utilization of resources in a developed country and of full mobilization of domestic resources in a developing country' (Kregel 2004, 289). The dynamics of terms of trade simply results in a 'transfer of productivity in primary commodities sector to consumers in developed countries' at the expense of the suppression of real wage growth and internal demand for 'domestically produced goods in developing countries'. As a consequence this suppresses the growth of internal demand necessary for domestic industrialization (Kregel 2004, 289). This implies the necessity of some form and extent of state intervention in developing countries to alter the terms of trade to favor the domestic industrialization.

In the context of globalization, and the erosion of financial sovereignty, there appears to be unstable global dynamics which limit the domestic policy space for developing countries. In the contemporary world, the fundamental difficulty comes down to the 'reconciliation of global integration with divergent national policy objectives' (Kregel 2019, 3). Kregel attributes the existence and maintenance of the global imbalances to the 'absence of an international adjustment mechanism, or as a clearing union as recommended by Keynes' which could promote 'full utilization of global resources' (Kregel 2010, 3; see also Kregel 2008, 2). These imbalances were also a result of asymmetrical production and industrialization structures between industrialized and developing countries (Kregel 2008, 2). Kregel noted that several developing countries adopted domestic industrialization policies based on export-led growth so as to 'avoid the IMF conditionality or an adjustment to their external flows through financial crisis' (Kregel 2010, 7; see also, Kregel 2008, 7). However, this development strategy is in direct contrast to 'any automatic or coordinated adjustment policy' and 'global full employment policy' since it results in 'unsustainable policies' overall (Kregel 2010, 7, see Kregel 2008, 5, 9). Since these strategies necessitate global imbalances, stability of the international reserve currency cannot be maintained and any attempt to eliminate global imbalances could enervate the export-led development strategies (Kregel 2010, 8).

In addition to Minsky's proposals for the reformation of the financial systems, Kregel proposed 'domestic demand-led development strategies' which could be supplemented by capital flows for developing countries (Kregel 2010, 8). This also necessitates the reformation of the international financial system on the basis of the Keynesian proposal of a clearinghouse mechanism in which 'bancor surpluses could, within certain limits, automatically be lent to deficit countries' instead of being hoarded by national central banks (Kregel 2019, 3; see also Kregel 2008, 10). 'This adjustment mechanism could have domestic limits on aggregate debits and credits and penalties for exceeding the limits' (Kregel 2019, 3). Eventually, this mechanism serves to provide adequate national policy space in the context of an 'integrated global or regional system' and simultaneously recover the 'stabilizing role of capital flows' (Kregel 2019 3).

In lieu of Kregel's emphasis on both domestic demand-led industrialization and Keynesian clearinghouse proposal, national self-sufficiency plays a significant role for developing countries to regain their financial sovereignty. In his lecture titled 'National Self-Sufficiency' in 1933, John Maynard Keynes warned that economic internationalism maintained the international peace through '… the capture of foreign trade, and the penetration of a country's economic structure by resources and the influence of foreign capitalists …' (Keynes 1933). However, he pointed out that this global system generated an 'ownership-operation' structure that damaged the 'relations among men' since foreign capitalists tended to lack a sense of responsibility toward citizens of countries in which they chose to invest their capital. Even though Keynes admitted that a certain level of international specialization and comparative advantage was necessary, he had become doubtful about the consequences of the loss of economic national self-sufficiency. Therefore, Keynes advised: '… let goods be homespun whenever it is reasonably and conveniently possible, and above all, let finance be primarily national …'. He believed that 'a greater degree of national self-sufficiency and economic isolation' could maintain global peace and stability among countries, because this would enable countries to be 'free from interference from economic changes elsewhere' and focus on their own 'ideal social republic'. Ultimately, Keynes regarded the 'policy of an increased national self-sufficiency as an ideal itself, but as directed to the creation of an environment in which other ideals (political sovereignty) can be safely and conveniently pursued' (Keynes 1933).

We now turn to the policy implications of FIH for the global financial system in the context of domestic demand-led industrialization and clearinghouse mechanism proposals, which could result in a two-dimensional approach to the issue of reformation and restructuring of the global financial system. Firstly, the international financial organizations like the IMF and the World Bank have failed to address the transformation of development issue into sovereign debt problem. This failure has put countless developing countries into vicious cycles of economic stagnation and debt. The resolution of this economic issue could bring social and political stability to developing countries suffering from the impacts of the structural adjustment policies that serve as the modern tools of colonialism. The international financial organizations like the IMF and the World Bank led by the financially sovereign countries must pay attention to the evidence that these structural adjustment policies, such as the reduction in government spending, privatization, deregulation of trade and financial institutions, have not been working. They therefore need to be either restructured or abandoned thoroughly. For example, the Seattle Conference convened by the World Trade Organization in 1994 to discuss the multilateral trade negotiations failed to address the issue of developed countries' imposition of trade liberalization on the developing countries (Drabenstott 2001, 1).

Another area that requires global readjustment is the global financial and commodity markets which are subject to minimum regulation and supervision, if any at all. The current system is designed in a way to promote chronic commodity shortages and global commodity price distortions which results in unstable economic and political conditions. This instability promotes unexpected price fluctuations, unforeseeable markets and unreliable trade flows from which the developing countries tend to suffer relatively more than the developed countries due to their structural economic weaknesses. Kregel's proposal of a Keynesian clearing union mechanism for financial and capital flows could be extended to include commodity flows in order to eliminate global imbalances in national self-sufficiency in food and energy production. This clearinghouse mechanism could also be established both inter- and intra-regionally to encourage South-South trade among developing nations. If implemented within a specific country, it could improve the terms of trade, distribute productivity gains more evenly and foster a balanced growth approach among different sectors. The financially sovereign countries/regions with commodity and energy surpluses must, within certain limits, transfer their surpluses to financially non-sovereign (or less sovereign) countries/regions by means of grants, aids and/or foreign direct investment.

However, the developing/financially less or non-sovereign countries need to address the issue of domestic financial reform. The national economic and financial reform strategies for developing countries must be established on the basis of the attainment of financial sovereignty. In other words, this issue could be framed on the basis of the strengthening of domestic economic and financial structure. This will address the root causes of structural problems in developing countries and strengthen the structure of their economies on the path to development. Firstly, developing country governments must not be allowed by both their citizens and international supervisory and regulatory mechanisms to issue IOUs denominated in foreign currency (Tymoigne and Wray 2013, 40). This must include domestic financial institutions which should be regulated and supervised to prohibit or limit their issuance of foreign currency-denominated liabilities (Tymoigne and Wray 2013, 50). This argument relies on the notion that sovereign currency creates more policy space, so issuing debts denominated in foreign currencies must be subject to stricter international and domestic regulation and supervision (Tymoigne and Wray 2013, 40–41).

Some countries might have limited real and external financial resources so their policy space could be highly constrained, as their only resources could be unskilled labor and unproductive land, and/or their government currency might not be accepted externally (Tymoigne and Wray 2013, 42). In such cases, foreign direct investment and aid via the above-mentioned clearinghouse mechanism become fundamental. However, the maximum utilization of labor force for specific public purposes like infrastructure-building and public projects could still be viable options with the existing limited external and domestic physical and financial resources (Tymoigne and Wray 2013, 42–43). The strategies of export-led growth and import substitution could be amended toward the production of high-value-added manufacturing and service goods rather than agricultural cash crops (Kaboub and Aliriza 2019). The accumulation of capital and technology required for the production of high-value-added services and commodities could be via the above-mentioned clearing union proposal. The balance of payments constraint could be mitigated to generate more domestic policy space via Kregel's domestic demand-led industrialization strategy based on the Keynesian sense of national self-sufficiency. This is why the circulation of domestically produced goods and services within the developing countries is fundamental.

Another important element of financial sovereignty is the determination of exchange rate regime. The higher sensitivity to fluctuations in exchange rates could induce a government to peg its currency (Tymoigne and Wray 2013, 43). This changes the spectrum of policy space available to a government:

> A crawling peg provides some policy space that varies according to the exchange rate band. A currency board, the last step before completely giving up monetary sovereignty ('dollarization'), provides almost no policy space and so makes it difficult for a government to set its own policy agenda.
>
> (Tymoigne and Wray 2013, 43)

The determination of exchange rate regime could be tailored for specific trade and economic structure of each country to vary along the spectrum of full financial sovereignty to different degrees of financial sovereignty.

More broadly, these proposals are in concert with Keynes and Minsky that unemployment, arbitrary distribution of income, price instability and financial instability are primary challenges to all market economies which necessitate some degree of government involvement for resolution. Therefore, the government must take direct actions continuously over a cycle, 'by putting in place structural macroeconomic programs that directly manage the labor force, pricing mechanisms, and investment projects, and constantly monitoring financial developments'. The permanent and structural nature of these programs could immunize them from the political cycle and considerations to a certain degree. This aims to eliminate 'problems of lags, credibility, and time inconsistency'.

On the other hand, this does not necessarily mean a blind application of a rule since discretion must be cautiously applied based on the institutional framework of each public program. The Job Guarantee program relies on permanent and structural nature with discretion if needed. Yet a unified commitment to global full employment policy could be supplemented with 'capital controls for developing economies, credit controls, socialization of investment and the management of wage and interest rates'.

Additionally, instead of promoting fine-tuning policies, the role of a 'rightly distributed' demand along with the right level of aggregate demand attempt to mitigate the innate instability of market mechanisms (Tymoigne and Wray 2013, 44–5). Most importantly, increasing aggregate demand in order to reach full employment delinks full employment from economic growth. Similarly, Job Guarantee spending is not a 'perfect substitute' for private spending. Instead, the Job Guarantee targeted spending aims to improve the structure and flexibility of the labor market by developing a group of 'employable labor while simultaneously ensuring continuous employment of those ready and willing to work'. The increase in taxes in concert with government Job Guarantee spending is discretionary based on inflation pressures. The implementation of institutional automatic stabilizers could ensure the dampening of inflationary pressures in developing countries. The degree of decentralization of Job Guarantee could rely on 'principles of democratic governance, transparency, and accountability'.

Overall, the Job Guarantee program is a 'rightly distributed' spending program in which government spending is targeted exactly toward those who want to work. This cannot put direct pressure on wages and prices since the workers in the program were part of disguised unemployment and could still be available for private sector employers 'at a small mark-up over the Job Guarantee program wage – the minimum wage'. In essence, the Job Guarantee will decrease recruiting and hiring costs due to the existence of an employable group of people. If anything, this could decrease inflation pressures. As a consequence, the anti-inflationary adjustments to spending is likely to happen among the employed instead of leading to unemployment and poverty.

With respect to financial stability, interest rate manipulations have limited effectiveness and can, in fact, lead to instability. Instead, governments in developing countries could engage in hedge financing via the establishment of a financial sector which prioritizes long-term recurring relationships, and the regulation and supervision of financial innovations based on safe financial products. Creditworthy loans and direct credit controls are fundamental in taming speculative behaviors, or to more generally fighting inflation pressures and asset bubbles. These practices could be more effective than interest rate increases to decrease lending to speculators (Tymoigne and Wray 2013, 44–49).

Conclusion

The argument that the FIH is a holistic approach, which contains, but is not limited to, the role of and changes in the institutions of the system together with the theory of investment, finance and unemployment could be supported by means of the analysis of the capitalist economy of the United States and the global financial system. As a result, the reformation and the restructuring of the international financial institutions need to take the role of and modifications in institutions and the theory of investment, finance and the unemployment into account for the purpose of the attainment and the maintenance of full employment and the mitigation of the instability of the system. The issues of economic and financial instability are significant to address, because the concepts of investment, finance and unemployment could not be separated from global capitalism and Minsky's proposals of mitigating the innate instability of the international capitalist system rest on the idea of reforming the public and private international financial institutions and sector and fighting the poverty and unemployment.

References

Delli Gatti, D., Gallegati, M., and Minsky, H. P., 1994, 'Financial Institutions, Economic Policy and the Dynamic Behavior of the Economy.' *Hyman P. Minsky Archive.* Paper 75.

Drabenstott, R. M., 2001, 'Introduction,' Food and Agriculture Committee of National Policy Association Policy Brief, Agricultural Trade Negotiations and the Developing Countries after Seattle. Washington, D.C.: NPA Press.

Kaboub, F. and Aliriza, F., 2019, 'Modern Monetary Theory: A Tool for the Global South?' Rosa Luxemburg Stiftung, www.rosalux.de/en/publication/id/41284/modern-monetary-theory-a-tool-for-the-global-south

Keynes, J. M., 1933, 'National Self-Sufficiency,' *The Yale Review* 22, no. 4, pp. 755–769.

Kregel, Jan., 2004, 'Two views on the Obstacles to Development,' *Social Research (NSSR)* 71, no. 2, pp. 279–292.

———, 2008, 'Financial Flows and International Imbalances – The Role of Catching up by Late Industrializing Developing Countries,' Levy Economics Institute. Working Paper 528. February.

———, 2010, 'An Alternative Perspective on Global Imbalances and International Reserve Currencies,' Preface by Dimitri Papadimitriou. Levy Economics Institute. Public Policy Brief 116.

———, 2019, 'Globalization, Nationalism and Clearing Systems,' Preface by Dimitri Papadimitriou. Levy Economics Institute. Public Policy Brief 147.

Minsky, Hyman. P., 1965, 'The Role of Employment Policy,' Paper presented at *Poverty in America* national conference held at the University of California, Berkeley (February 1965). *Ending Poverty: Jobs, Not Welfare.* New York: Levy Economics Institute of Bard College, 2013.

———, 1988, 'Schumpeter: Finance and Evolution'. Hyman P. Minsky Archive. 314. https://digitalcommons.bard.edu/hm_archive/314

———, 1989, 'Money Manager Capitalism'. Hyman P. Minsky Archive. 13. https://digitalcommons.bard.edu/hm_archive/13

———, 1993, 'Finance and Stability: The Limits of Capitalism' (1993). Hyman P. Minsky Archive. 43. https://digitalcommons.bard.edu/hm_archive/43

———, 1994a, 'The Debt Deflation Theory of Great Depressions' (1994). Hyman P. Minsky Archive. 159. https://digitalcommons.bard.edu/hm_archive/159

———, 1994b, 'Financial Instability and the Decline (?) of Banking: Public Policy Implications'. Hyman P. Minsky Archive. Paper 88. http://digitalcommons.bard.edu/hm_archive/88
———, 1994c, 'The Financial Instability Hypothesis and Current Common Problems of Rich Capitalist Economies,' Fausto Vicarelli Lecture at the University of Macerata: 1–11.
———, 2008, *Stabilizing an Unstable Economy*, New York: McGraw Hill.
Minsky, Hyman P. and Vaughan, Mark D., 1990, 'Debt and Business Cycles,' Hyman P. Minsky Archive. 202. https://digitalcommons.bard.edu/hm_archive/202
Tymoigne, Eric and Wray, L. Randall., November 2013, 'Modern Money Theory 101: A Reply to Critics,' Levy Economics Institute. Working Paper 778.

5 Estimating economic surplus in Argentina

The neoliberal strategy, its crisis and the neo-developmentalist model (1991–2015)

Leandro Marcelo Bona

5.1 Introduction

The theory of economic surplus (ES) that emerged from the monopolistic version of Marxism (Baran, 1957) pointed out that capitalism was going through a specific stage of its development where there was not a tendency toward a falling rate of profit (Marx's argument) but, on the contrary, there will be an increasing tendency toward ES accumulation by monopoly capital. The ES, unlike Marx's surplus, did not arise exclusively from the exploitation of labor but also from various mechanisms related to the monopolistic formation of prices (Baran, 1953). ES is conceptualized not only by profits, but also by rents, interests and even higher level salaries (from those workers in managerial, marketing and other highly paid activities).

Authors such as Furtado (1978) and Prebisch (1981), both Latin American structuralists,[1] considered that ES accumulation and destination were the axis on which the social stratification of Latin American countries was based. Furtado suggested the calculation of ES as the difference between a cost of social reproduction (CSR; formed mainly by salary remunerations) and the gross domestic product (GDP). This permitted him to identify the trends of living conditions for workers due to changes in the CSR[2] and the simultaneous hoarding of social wealth by the elites, which appropriate the major part of the ES.

The analysis of the ES reached its zenith toward the middle of the last century, when class struggles attained a peak. Since the mid-1970s, with the advent of neoliberalism, numerous critical theories (such as radical structuralism and dependency theories, which emphasized the heterogeneous class structures, power, foreign dominance of the productive structure and unequal appropriation of ES) were displaced within the framework of the defeat of socialist and popular projects and the rise of orthodox economic formation (Harvey, 2005). Recovering these concepts and tools in the present aims to contribute in the field of critical economic thinking, being part of a generalized struggle against mainstream economics, an economic thinking that has served to justify and implement regressive distributive measures such as privatizations, deregulations, fiscal austerity and labor precariousness.

DOI: 10.4324/9781003451990-8

This chapter studies the evolution of Argentina's political economy during convertibility (1991–2001) and Kirchnerist administrations (2002–2015). In order to do so, this work revives the analysis provided by the theory of ES and offers instruments to measure it. The interest in this period arises from the existing controversies regarding the continuities and ruptures between the neoliberal order (of which convertibility was its "superior stage") and the neo-developmental or populist model that was deployed during the Kirchner governments. The study not only investigates the evolution of social wealth and its distribution during both projects, but also aims to combine it with the concept of accumulation regime.[3] Special attention will be given on the crises for each period (1998–2001 and 2012–2015), where social emergencies were tackled with different strategies, leading to different social and economic outputs. ES theory allows us to understand these differences by analyzing the generation, appropriation and uses of social wealth.

To achieve this purpose, the study is organized as follows: after this brief introduction, the first part of Section 5.2 presents the theoretical framework and the methodology – the ES theory, the way to quantify it and the concept of accumulation regime. The second part of Section 5.2 briefly highlights the main characteristics of the accumulation regimes verified in Argentina during the periods of convertibility and the Kirchner administrations. Section 5.3 presents the estimates of the CSR and the ES between 1991 and 2015. Section 5.4 investigates the origins of ES: profits, rents and higher level salaries. Section 5.5 analyses the dynamics of ES destinations. The chapter ends with final remarks.

5.2 Theoretical framework, methodology and the period of interest

5.2.1 Capital, social classes and power: economic surplus theory

Since the studies of classical economists, there has been a special interest in discussing the processes of production and the generation of wealth in modern societies. Coinciding with the need to put the focus of economic debate in the productive sphere, the main authors of that time identified an ES liable to dispute between social classes. According to Smith (1994) and Ricardo (2004), wages fluctuated around a level of equilibrium (natural for the first, of subsistence for the second) that guaranteed the reproduction of workers but did not allow them to accumulate wealth, while the surplus product was divided between capitalists and landowners. Marx (2010) defined wages as the payment corresponding to the labor force, a value determined by historical and moral components (in short, by the dynamics of class struggle). That made possible the social reproduction of the working class, while the capitalists appropriated the surplus generated in the labor process.

During the 20th century, structuralist and Marxist thinkers developed the ES approach, which they defined as the difference between what society produces and what it requires for its reproduction. In order to analyze this concept, Marxist thinkers (Baran and Sweezy, 1966) searched methods to determine a CSR that would represent a parameter to determine the value of the basic living conditions of societies. Once this amount was obtained, they could estimate ES (which resulted from the difference between CSR and total production). The quantification of this variable served as an argument to show the irrationality of the capitalist system, due to the low levels of resources that were used to develop economic productive forces and generate better life conditions for majorities. Instead, military spending, publicity, luxurious consumption, among other uses, absorbed significant proportions of wealth.

From a structuralist perspective, Furtado (1978) proposed the measurement of a CSR, which was defined as an annual income that society requires in order to develop its tasks and guarantees fundamental needs of food, health care, social security and education, among others. To determine this CSR, he took wages from unskilled manual workers (since it referred to the sector of the population that did not benefit from human capital investment) and added basic public expenditure (housing, health, education).

Even during the raise of neoliberalism in the 1980s and 1990s, some authors continued to apply this approach, and used different quantification methods: Lippit (1985) associated the basic income of reproduction to essential consumption (different then from luxury or superfluous consumption); Danielson (1990) proposed as a criterion the sum of the minimum income (subsistence wages paid in agriculture) multiplied by the number of productive workers (from the agricultural sector); Yeldan (1995) measured salaries in small-scale enterprises as representative of the reproductive income (given that the capacity for union organization in large firms would allow workers to appropriate part of the surplus); while Somel (2003) estimated it by calculating the essential consumption from the institutional minimum wage.

For the Argentine case Sbattella (2001), inspired by Furtado's ideas, estimated the CSR (and then the ES) during the period of 1980–2000 using the average income of 5th decile of the population and expanded it to the entire employed population, since it represented unskilled manual worker's income. Later on, in Sbattella, Chena, Palmieri and Bona (2012) these authors adjusted the calculation of the CSR by adding new components. First, they separated total potential workers in activity from those inactive; and then they adjusted the non-salary components of the CSR, provided by the State. As a result, they obtained a wage component, a non-wage and a pension component. The calculation of the wage component was estimated according to the incomes of the unskilled manual workers, averaging between those who belong to the formal and informal sectors (which reaches between 33% and 45% of total labor force in Argentina). In turn, non-wage components were incorporated adding transfers (subsidies to transport and energy, public investment in basic education and health) and subtracting taxes, according to the tax burden on working-class population. Pension component was calculated using minimum pensions.[4]

As a synthesis, the different alternatives examined to estimate the CSR and the ES are presented in Table 5.1.

Table 5.1 Methodological alternatives for economic surplus theory

Author	*Methodology*	*Country and date*
Phillips (in Baran and Sweezy, 1966)	**ES = property income + waste of the productive process + surplus absorption by the State + penetration of sales campaigns** Property income: income from work in non-corporate companies, excessive depreciation expenses, income, interest and others. Waste in the production process: advertising, market research expenses, sales commissions, etc. Absorption of surplus by the State: public expenditure Penetration of sales campaigns: advertising	USA (1949–1963)
Furtado (1978)	**ES = GDP – CSR – capital stock depreciation** CSR: *non-skilled worker's wages*	No estimations
Prebisch (1981)	**ES = increases in productivity that remain in the hands of the wealthy classes of the productive means**	No estimations
Lippit (1985)	**ES = profits + rents + interest + share of worker's income used in nonessential consumption – nonessential consumption** Essential consumption: minimum budget for a family (from USA statistics)	Turkey (1980–1992)
Danielson (1990)	**ES = GDP – subsistence wages from productive workers – capital stock depreciation** Subsistence wage: *agricultural wages* Productive work: *all work in private sector* Unproductive work: *all work in public sector*	Jamaica (1962–1984)
Yeldan (1995)	**ES = GDP – subsistence wages × productive workers – capital stock depreciation** Subsistence wage: *slow scale private industries wages*	Turkey (1980–1992)
Somel (2003)	**ES = GDP – essential consumption** Essential consumption: *official minimum wage*	Turkey (1980–1996)
Sbattella (2001)	**ES = GDP – CSR** CSR: *5th decile income + public expenditure in health, education and social assistance – income taxes*	Argentina (1980–2000)
Sbattella, Chena, Palmieri and Bona (2012)	**ES = GDP – CSR – capital stock depreciation** CSR: *non-skilled worker's wages + minimum pensions + public investment in basic education and health + tariff subsidies on energy and transport – tax pressure*	Argentina (2003–2008)

Source: Prepared by the author.

In the next section, the study follows the Sbattella, Chena, Palmieri and Bona (2012) methodology to estimate the CSR and the ES, which was performed in other opportunities (Bona, 2018a, 2018b). This methodology captures volumes, trends and oscillations in the reproduction conditions of the subaltern classes[5] (expressed in the calculation of the CSR), which are modified by power social relations.

5.2.2 The period in focus: convertibility (1991–2001) and Kirchnerism (2002–2015)

Toward the last decade of the 20th century, a large part of the nations of Latin America intensified the processes of trade liberalization, sectorial deregulation, privatization of public enterprises and labor precariousness, in what has been characterized as the neoliberal period (Guillén, 2007). Then, toward the end of the 1990s and early 2000s, several countries (especially in South America) changed their political sign, motivated by the challenge (partial or radical, depending on the case) of this model, initiating the cycle of neo-developmentalist or leftist governments in the region (Katz, 2016).

Argentina represents one of the clearest examples of this transition between two political and social stages, in the context of transformations in internal (sectorial disputes over the valorization of work and the ES) and external (world market dynamics and strategies) economic conditions, respectively. Inside the State these economic and social changes expressed different class relations and forces (Poulantzas, 1969).

Following this logic, the convertibility (1991–2001), was the "upper stage" of the neoliberal project that had been installed in Argentina since 1976 through the civic-military dictatorship. The main objective of that strategy was to redefine the Argentinian social and civil society, in order to weaken the mobilized working class and the political movements that were contesting the status quo. The dictatorship considered that the industrialized cities were a focus of political activism that was challenging the social system, and decided to reorganize the economic structure through deindustrialization, liberalization, deregulation and reduction in public goods and services (Bona and Páez, 2021).

All these economic policies generated a massive transfer income from labor to capital, and, fundamentally, to the latter's most powerful sector. This scenario was generally the case in the western world (Patnaik and Patnaik, 2020). The consolidation of convertibility in the 1990s would take place at a very particular moment in the international context, during the rise of the Washington Consensus and after the economic breakdown of the Argentinian hyperinflation of 1989/1990, which enabled a social claim for stability by means of introducing austerity measures.

The purpose of the neoliberal project was to redefine the accumulation regime, in order to redistribute the ES by disciplining the working class. This was achieved by the implementation of higher levels of exploitation of the labor force (outsourcing, dismantlement of labor laws and, fundamentally, a new and high unemployment "floor"), the encouragement of "traditional" exports (through new technologies in the agricultural sector such as packages of transgenic seeds, fertilizers, agricultural machinery, installation of multinational production plants for technological packages, new mining and hydrocarbon laws, and so on) and recreation of the cycle of financial valorization[6] based on the dynamics of external indebtedness and capital flight. In order to implement this program, the economic authority fixed exchange rate parity (in addition to enabling the free convertibility of the peso with the US dollar) and a State reform that would initiate a broad process of privatization of public companies (Ferrer, 2008).

In terms of dominant classes, the power bloc[7] during the period was constituted by the biggest corporations of the country (traditionally landowners, but later on, conglomerates that had diversified their investments into construction, services and export-oriented industries) and the foreign capital (especially linked to finances and services). A local-foreign bloc that shared the business of the privatizations and benefited from financial liberalization, which permitted the exteriorization of wealth (Basualdo, 2020).

Like many countries in the region, toward the end of the 1990s, the neoliberal order was severely questioned in Argentina, in a context of a massive capital flight, high external indebtedness and significant social conflicts derived from deindustrialization and the increase in unemployment (Azpiazu and Schorr, 2010). One of the main reasons was the debt-led growth strategy, which started during the *coup d'état* in 1976 but was exacerbated during the 1990s. In order to sustain the currency board,[8] the Argentine government (together with the private sector) took massive loans from private creditors, whereas the economy was increasing its imports and reinforcing its export dependency on raw materials. When credit got expensive, the government appealed to multilateral organizations (World Bank, International Monetary Fund) that conditioned their loans to the implementation of fiscal austerity measures, together with a second wave of structural reforms (such as new labor and tax laws, and privatizations).

Between 1999 and 2001, economic stagnation due to orthodox economic policy packages led to a reduction in public incomes. Austerity measures generated a constant reduction in aggregate demand and consequent decrease in tax revenues, which pushed for more public expenditure reduction that undermines employment and consumption recovery – the classical austerity vicious cycle (Basualdo, 2010). When international creditors anticipated a default (2001), the crisis heated the country profoundly – Argentina reached almost 20% of unemployment and 40% of poverty, a social emergency comparable only with the situation that emerged during the Covid-19 pandemic (and later on) in 2020–2022. With no more international credit, convertibility could no longer continue. The crisis of 2001 was then resolved when decisive steps were taken to abandon the economic foundations of convertibility and start a new accumulation regime (López 2016).

The shift in the accumulation regime was expressed in the main economic decisions that took place in 2002/2003: a sharp devaluation of the local currency, the pesification (conversion of currency foreign deposits into pesos) of previous dollarized commitments for companies, the default on external debt and a generalized system of subsidized tariffs for public services, among other aspects. All these measures quickly generated a massive and unprecedented income transfer from labor to capital[9] and the consequent improvement in the relative position of the tradable good producers (agro-exporters, internal market industries, construction, etc.; Varesi, 2016). As a consequence of pesification of debts and tariffs, foreign companies that operated in the country experienced a significant reduction in wealth and future cash flows. These measures reflected the changes among the power bloc, which became ruled by monopoly domestic corporations and excluded the alliance with foreign capital (Basualdo, 2020). Conditions for an economic takeoff were settled.

During the Kirchner governments (2003–2015) it is necessary to distinguish between two stages, separated by different international and national conditions. The first stage took place between 2003 and 2008, where the new "winners" would have been the sectors producing goods and, within these, those commercially inserted into the world market (benefited by low labor costs, the virtual absence of external competition via the peso depreciation and the rising rhythm of commodity prices). Even so, and as a consequence of the above, subaltern classes gradually improved their relative position in the context of the recovery of wage share, mainly due to "employment effect" (unemployment went from 22% in 2002 to 8% in 2008), and secondly, by "income effect" (raise in wages, although in this case exclusively on behalf of formal workers).

The second period, which runs from 2009 to 2015, is characterized by the strengthening of income redistributive measures that allow the inclusion of Kirchnerism within the group of "populist Latin American" governments. This was due to both the dynamics of the political struggles for the management of agricultural rent (which quickly reorganized the social alliances in power) and the outbreak of the international crisis (in 2008/2009), which were key to understand the national/popular drift in the bosom of the Kirchner administration.

In this stage, there was a decisive increase in public social spending (abandoning the fiscal surplus registered between 2002 and 2010), the strengthening of collective bargaining agreements as vectors of wage improvements (although increasingly hampered by an inflation derived from the distributive bidding[10] (CIFRA, 2015), the nationalization of some of the company's previously privatized (the social security system, the flag airline, the national water company, the biggest oil company), the State appropriation of land rents, the multiplication of income transfers, the establishment of exchange controls (duty measures), among others. The dispute over ES generated capital class responses in the form of high inflation levels (López, 2016).

This "populist shift" reflected the reorganization of the power bloc. After the first period of hegemony of the biggest conglomerates (diversified oligarchy), the second stage expressed the tensions between some of these capital fractions and the subaltern classes (that increased their bargaining power as unemployment was reducing). The national-popular moment of the Kirchner governments was characterized for their confrontations with the landowners, the international financial markets and specific conglomerates (such as the dominant medias or the main industrial exporters; Bona, 2018b). Between 2012 and 2015, however, higher inflation and a reversal in the terms of trade combined with economic stagnation, expressing the limits of this "populist" accumulation regime with no changes in economic structure (Cantamutto, Schorr and Wainer, 2016). Among a considerable reduction on commodity prices, external constraint reduced the possibilities to improve income distribution, but the crisis was managed by augmenting the State control of enterprises, the appropriation of rents and the capital controls, in order to sustain lower incomes (Basualdo, 2017). The economic stagnation of the Kirchner period (2012–2015) was then tackled in a very different way, compared to the austerity measures taken by the end of convertibility. In this sense, fiscal surplus turned into a growing deficit.

The CSR and the ES, as it is about to be shown, reflect these changes and help explain their boom and crises.

5.3 Measuring the cost of social reproduction and the economic surplus

The calculation of the CSR allows (see Table 5A.1) to quantify ES, which is defined as: Economic Surplus = Gross Domestic Product – Cost of Social Reproduction – Capital stock depreciation (K. dep.; Table 5.2).[11]

The obtained results are presented both in constant dollars of 1991[12] and in terms of the participation of each variable in GDP (Figure 5.1). The evolution of each variable shows different phases in ES and CSR between 1991 and 2015.

In the first place, ES grew considerably during the expansive phase (1991–1998) of the convertibility regime, which reflects a strong increase in incomes appropriated by dominant classes. It is a process of successful recovery from

Table 5.2 Evolution of gross domestic product (GDP), cost of social reproduction (CSR), capital stock depreciation (K. dep.) and economic surplus (ES) in Argentina, 1991–2015, US constant dollars (1991)

Year	*GDP*	*CSR*	*K. dep.*	*ES*
1991	166.104	60.133	19.983	85.988
1992	202.146	73.329	22.333	106.484
1993	222.904	84.065	24.883	113.956
1994	236.497	87.305	25.796	123.396
1995	230.572	81.763	25.877	122.932
1996	236.250	77.666	25.432	133.152
1997	248.420	80.882	25.764	141.774
1998	249.722	83.429	27.204	139.089
1999	231.754	82.112	26.387	123.256
2000	224.744	78.788	24.620	121.336
2001	206.661	75.050	22.826	108.784
2002	78.881	22.752	11.659	44.470
2003	94.328	24.659	12.764	56.905
2004	118.883	34.092	14.069	70.721
2005	138.937	41.111	14.412	83.413
2006	157.301	48.510	15.715	93.076
2007	189.085	60.399	18.201	110.485
2008	229.921	74.866	22.423	132.632
2009	212.391	79.701	22.825	109.866
2010	265.225	93.971	27.097	144.157
2011	319.409	117.948	32.393	169.068
2012	343.786	132.529	36.891	174.365
2013	357.413	139.839	39.486	178.088
2014	324.214	122.383	38.477	163.354
2015	363.011	144.534	44.249	174.228

Source: Prepared by the author.

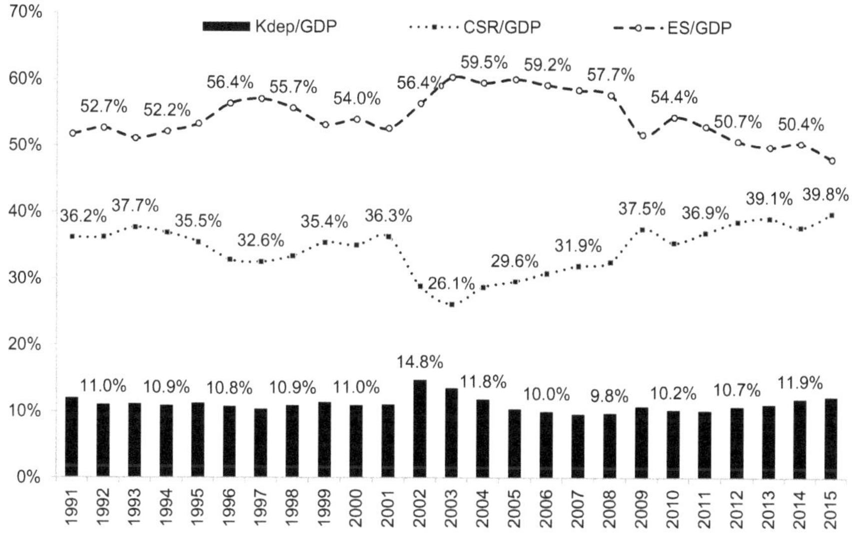

Figure 5.1 Cost of social reproduction (CSR), capital stock depreciation (K. dep.) and economic surplus (ES) as share of GDP, Argentina, 1991–2015.

Source: Adapted from INDEC (Instituto Nacional de Estadística y Censos) (2023). National Accounts (Argentina).

the crisis of the 1980s, when all the economic and activity registers (production, employment, investment) had collapsed, especially during hyperinflation (1989/1990). With this extremely negative background, the neoliberal policies of the 1990s could profit from a quick takeoff.

The ES increased by 44% in constant dollars between 1991 and 1994, as well as a significant recovery in the CSR, which increased by 45% in that period (thanks to price stabilization and salary reparation to levels prior to hyperinflation). However, this process of extremely dynamic economic growth slowed down between 1995 and 1998 (even though the ES continued to increase), once the expansive effects of privatizations (in investment and tax revenues) and postcrisis rebound were overcome. On the other hand, the evolution of each of these variables as a percentage of GDP shows that ES always exceeded 50% of the GDP, which indicates that Argentina is a country with enormous capacity for generating wealth and potentially satisfying its needs. The period that goes from 1991 to 1998 showed a growing process of surplus accumulation in relation to GDP, which reached 55.7% in 1997. This phase was characterized by a double phenomenon: economic growth (with the exception of 1995) with decline of the CSR, which indicates a redistribution of wealth that goes from the subaltern classes (dependent on the income of social reproduction) to the dominant ones, resulting in an increase in unemployment. In fact, these results were logical within the framework of the processes of labor precariousness, commercial openness, deregulation, privatization, etc., that exacerbated wage heterogeneity, punishing especially social classes that were at the base of the distributive pyramid (informal workers and unemployed (Santarcángelo and Schorr, 2001).

This trend was reversed from 1999 to 2001, when the share of ES in the product decreased during economic recession. It could be identified as a "spurious" increase of the CSR/GDP ratio, since it did not reflect better life conditions of subaltern classes or decreases in inequality, but by effects of the greater fall in the GDP. This dynamic intensified the contradictions within civil society, laying the material foundations for the development of the crisis of 2001: the ES accumulation declined and the subaltern classes experienced a systematic reduction on their reproductive levels since 1999. Major local conglomerates pushed for austerity measures and wage reductions as a profit maximization strategy. Leading dominant conglomerates managed to reorganize the power bloc, and abandoned the alliance with foreign capitals by pursuing the devaluation strategy. They prevailed by encouraging the elimination of convertibility in January 2002 (Basualdo, 2010). Effectively, the currency board was a corset that made extremely difficult to reduce nominal (and real) wages, and the Central Bank authority could not execute monetary policy.

After the abandonment of the convertibility regime, the 2002 devaluation depressed the volume of all variables in constant terms, although results were more sensitive for the subaltern classes, CSR: it decreased by 59%. During the first stage of Kirchner governments (2003–2008), there was a substantial increase of all the variables in the context of economic recovery, although CSR expanded the most: GDP and ES multiplied by 2.9 and 3 times respectively, while CSR did it 3.3 times. This situation indicates that wage and retirement income and public social investment in education and health recovered more quickly than profits, rents and benefits (ES components), especially after the 2002/2003 "wage expropriation" due to devaluation. It should be noted that this increase in CSR was more due to "employment effect" (almost 4 million new jobs) than "income effect" (real wages) (Bona, 2018a).

In spite of the above, in terms of the new distributive structure of GDP, it was the period of greatest social regression: in 2003 ES reached its maximum proportion of GDP (60.3%), while only a quarter of it corresponded to social reproduction (26.1%), the lowest record of the entire series under analysis. The ES/GDP average in the first stage of the Kirchner governments (2002–2008) was 58.8% while CSR/GDP only reached 29.8%. During the whole convertibility regime, these values averaged 53.6% and 35.3%, respectively. The regressive situation was the result of 25 years of neoliberal policies.

Finally, internal changes in civil and political society, together with decisive changes in international scenario, are crucial to characterize the second cycle of Kirchner governments. This explains the upward dynamic of CSR in this period, which increased both in constant values as in relation to GDP, reaching a maximum in 2015 (39.8%). In this context, the expansionary public policies in periods of recession (2009, 2012 and 2014) were decisive, since the CSR continued to increase in constant dollars (with the exception of 2014). This soothed crisis effects among subaltern classes thanks to social protection system (not only a growth in public spending, also an expansion of State employment, consumption promotion programs, renovation household equipment possibilities, income education incentives, etc.). Instead of austerity measures in a context of the reversal of the terms of trade, expansive measures served to improve income distribution.

Complementarily, the dynamics of ES entered into a terrain of relative stagnation between 2012 and 2015: in 2015, total ES (in dollars) was only 9.1% higher than in 2012, and its participation in GDP fell to 48%, the lowest record in the entire series under analysis. These results express the limits for expanding this type of "populist" accumulation regime when a set of conditions are combined: the surplus sources diminish (terms of trade reversal), economic structure has reinforced its dependency on raw materials with lack of value added and wage levels progressively reduce the mass of profits (through exchange rate appreciation effect).

5.4 Origins of economic surplus: profits, rents and higher level salaries

The analysis of the origins of ES requires identifying its sources. Based on available information and the methodology followed in Bona (2020),[13] this section presents the distribution of ES between profits, rents and higher level salaries.[14]

Figure 5.2 shows several aspects to be highlighted. The first one is that the greater proportion of ES is constituted by profits (between 65% and 90% between 1991 and 2015). However, the dynamics of ES distribution among the four identified variables is extremely instable. Rents had, during convertibility, a stable

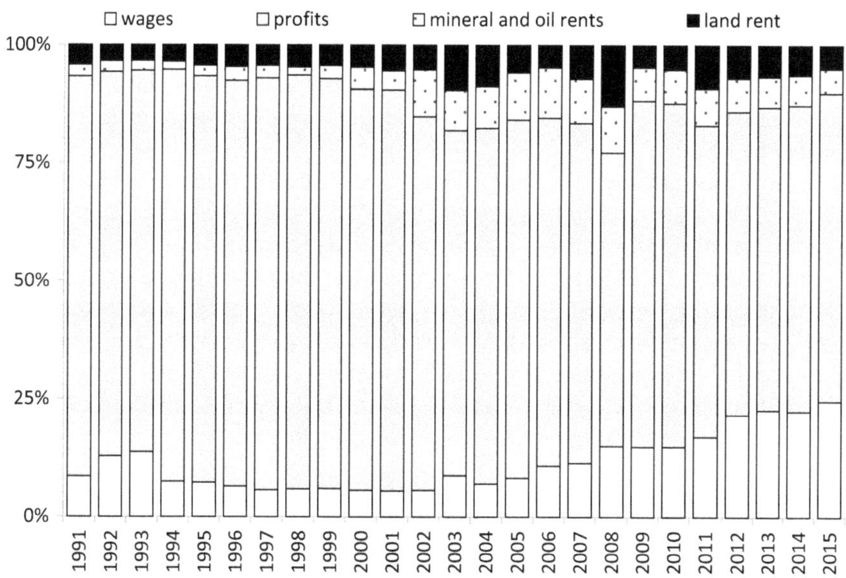

Figure 5.2 Distribution of economic surplus between wages, profits and rents (land, mineral and oil). As share (%) of ES, Argentina, 1991–2015.

Source: Prepared by the author.

participation on ES, around 6%, although slightly higher in 2000–2001 (10%) (see Table 5B.1).

Later on, during the Kirchner governments, the weight of those rents grew to reach 23% (2008) and then declined due to the effects of the growth in the share of land rent as well as higher level salaries (higher from that of reproductive income levels). In effect, land rent, which was displaced during the 1990s (between 3% and 5% of ES), grew to 6%–10% after devaluation and then, between 2008 and 2015, moved over 5%–9% of ES. Both phenomena show the increase in export commodity prices (until 2012), as well as the new set of relative prices after convertibility. This change operated quickly, by transferring income from low wage workers to rentier sectors.

Another issue to be mentioned is the movement registered in higher level salaries over this period. These workers increasingly appropriated ES during the first tranche of convertibility (1991–1993, reaching 14%) and then lost relevance until 2005, when they remained between 6% and 7%. From then on, higher income workers managed to appropriate a greater part of ES, reaching 25% in 2015, its highest record in the entire period under analysis.

The political economy is these results ratify the political differential nature of the projects implemented between 1991 and 2001 and 2002 and 2015. In the 1990s, profits, especially explained by the weight of services (privatized and financial sector) and part of the most dynamic productive capital (inserted in tradable sectors), were the axis of appropriation of ES. In as much, rents (traditional sources of wealth in periphery countries like Argentina) did not expand their weight in ES, while higher paid workers had a relatively stable proportion on ES.

On the other hand, as a result of changes in the internal capital accumulation conditions, together with the movements in world market prices since 2002, the prominence of rents grew considerably and higher salaries managed to appropriate much more ES.

Among this picture, the State played a differential behavior during both periods.[15] During the Kirchner governments, even if rents grew significantly, the introduction of export tariffs (on oil, mineral and land sectors since 2002) captured a significant portion of those incomes.[16] As part of the redistributive strategy, the State fixed export taxes (35% on soy exports) in order to: (a) disconnect local from international food prices, (b) reduce landowners appropriation of rents and (c) finance public expenditure programs. These tariffs operated as part of a multiple exchange rate model, had different exchange rates and were established depending on the sector (Chena, Panigo, Wahren and Bona, 2018).

5.5 Economic surplus destinations

According to Paul Baran and Celso Furtado, the analysis of ES destinations has a central importance since it expresses the modalities of development by setting the orientation of resources in productive or unproductive uses. These theorists indicate that, as long as ES uses remain unproductive, the condition of underdevelopment tends to perpetuate itself, reinforcing the center-periphery system.

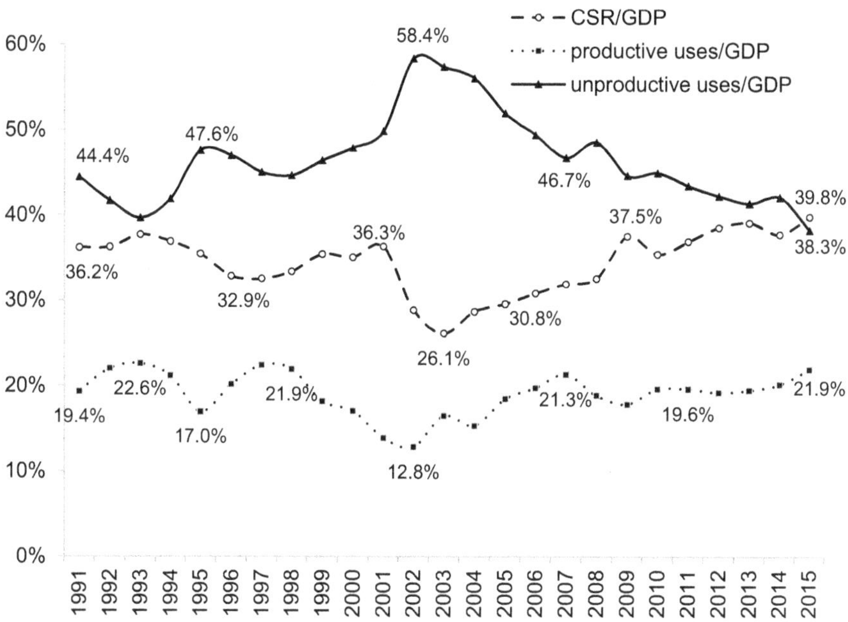

Figure 5.3 Evolution of the cost of social reproduction (CSR), productive and unproductive uses of economic surplus and capital stock depreciation as share of GDP, Argentina, 1991–2015.

Source: Prepared by the author.

In order to discriminate ES destinations, Figure 5.3 presents a distinction between productive (investment and internal savings) and unproductive (capital flight, imported consumer goods, sumptuary residential construction and non-essential consumption) uses of ES for development.

Results indicate that in Argentina the ES destinations underwent important transformations along the two accumulation regimes under analysis. In this regard, although the first stage of convertibility (1991–1996) was characterized by an important growth (in constant dollars per capita) of all the variables under study, the one that did the most is the one that compiles the unproductive uses of ES and permitted its increase as share of GDP. In absolute terms, productive destinations increased considerably (5.8% cumulative annual growth rate [c.a.g.r.]), while CSR registered a much lower rate of growth (3.8% c.a.g.r.). Consequently, during the "golden" stage of the convertibility period (1991–1996), although material conditions of subaltern classes were recovered, they did so as a result of post-hyperinflation recovery, while ES grew significantly more.

Productive investment increased in the same period due to the effects of privatizations and the dynamics of residential construction and the sustained expansion of savings (derived from exchange rate stability and currency appreciation).

On the other hand, imported consumption, sumptuary construction and nonessential consumption were the most dynamic uses among unproductive destinations of ES, while capital flight only erupted around 1994–1996, when capital inflows decreased due to the sale of State assets.

The regressive tendencies noticed in the described first stage of the convertibility regime, even in the context of the significant growth of GDP, multiplied toward the period of crisis (1999–2001), when there was a collapse of the productive uses of ES: productive investment and savings fell at a cumulative annual rate of 13%. The unproductive uses of the ES decreased in constant values as well as the reproductive income (−2.3 and −2.2%, respectively). These results express the exhaustion of the convertibility regime for both the subaltern and dominant classes, since (although they fell in constant terms) the unproductive destinations gained participation in GDP and capital flight turned out to be the "escape valve" of wealth (unproductive uses of ES grew systematically between 1998 and 2002; Figure 5.3).

The 2002 devaluation opened a new scenario, especially negative for subaltern classes and beneficial for the power bloc that hegemonized the first stage of the post-convertibility cycle: productive capital scored a substantial growth that allowed a vertiginous increase of the productive investment (+22% c.a.g.r. in constant dollars per capita) as well as the always predominant unproductive ES destinations (+13% c.a.g.r). The CSR, after an "expropriation" derived from the devaluation in 2002, also scored significant improvements (+17% c.a.g.r.), although it only came after an unprecedented regressive income redistribution that would only be altered during the second cycle of Kirchner governments. The unproductive uses of ES between 2002 and 2008 averaged 47.5% of GDP, CSR 33.8% and productive destinations only 18.6%. This accumulation regime was not prone to enable distributive improvements, and this became clear after the political events of 2008/2009 (the conflict between the government and the landowners) that modified the power bloc.

The second cycle of Kirchner governments (2009–2015) expresses the disputes to forge a new accumulation regime that promoted improvements on reproductive incomes and progressive income transfers. CSR/GDP then expanded more than any other variable (due to the by the increase in wages, retirement and public social investment components) and unproductive ES destinations fell. For this reason, between 2009 and 2015, CSR/GDP climbed to its highest average in comparison with the other stages, reaching 37.9%, while unproductive destinations represented 42.4%.

Even in spite of the above, the (Productive Investment + Savings)/GDP figure averaged 19.7% in this period, in a context of economic stagnation. This evidence is a result of the absence of major changes in the Argentine productive structure, inherited from the neoliberal project. The possibilities of improving income distribution and guarantee human rights (education, health) for the majorities face clear limits for peripheral countries, due to external constraint problems and the persistent resistance of the traditional power bloc to resign to increasing proportions of the ES (Cantamutto, Schorr and Wainer, 2016).

5.6 Conclusions, lessons and proposals

This study examines the evolution of the Argentine political economy between 1991 and 2015, period in which two accumulation regimes were set in motion: the neoliberal project under convertibility model (currency board, 1991–2001) and the populist stage under the Kirchner governments (2002–2015). In order to do so, this chapter recovered the ES theory and presented a methodological proposition to measure it.

Results indicate that the volume of the ES generated in Argentina is relatively high (in terms of mass of profits and rents), which means that the country generates much more wealth than needed in order to reproduce its population in decent conditions. In both accumulation regimes the economy managed to take off after two very deep crises: hyperinflation in 1989/1990 and the convertibility collapse (and later devaluation) in 1999/2002. The ES/GDP share, which oscillated between 48% (2015) and 60.3% (2003) throughout the series, illustrates the significant wealth created in this whole period and the high potentialities to redistribute it, refuting classical *spillover theory* ("first grow and then distribute"). But redistribution of wealth depends on different social alliances that push for their own interests.

The origins of the ES in the Argentinian case underwent important transformations throughout this period. During convertibility, profits generated between 65% and 90% of ES, while the evolution of international prices allowed a significant increase in rents (mining, oil and land rents) toward 2002–2015 (15%–25%). This massive wealth generation resulted in important sociopolitical disputes over its appropriation. In turn, wages also absorbed a significant portion of surplus in the second period of the Kirchner governments (2008–2015). In this context, the action (or omission) of the State played a decisive role in the appropriation of the ES and its redistribution: while during the neoliberal model the State pursued to transfer incomes from labor to capital, by reducing progressive taxes, deregulating labor laws and reducing public investment, between 2002 and 2015 the State increased its ES appropriation by augmenting taxes and tariffs and then financed income transfers and public investments.

Evidence shows that ES unproductive destinations always are higher than productive ones, and the former oscillate between 38% and 58% of GDP. During convertibility, unproductive destinations of ES tended to growth in the context of an increasing appropriation of ES by elites, meanwhile between 2002 and 2015, they experienced a countertendency due to the State interventions and the recovery of subaltern classes organization and politic capacity. Even so, during the Kirchner administrations the CSR grew more than investment and saving, limiting income redistribution and long-term progressive alliances and economic policies. This provides evidence that the challenge is to focus not only on ES appropriation and uses, but also on its generation.

The way the country managed the convertibility crisis (1998–2001) and the external constraint during the Kirchner administrations (2012–2015) shows important differences and opposite results. While during the convertibility crisis austerity measures reinforced stagnation and regressive income distribution, during the populist cycle, the State implemented a different approach, based on capital controls, tax increase, fiscal expansion and State control of productive sectors, combined with income transfers for the subaltern classes. While in the convertibility crisis unemployment and income distribution deteriorated, in the second case both remained constant or even improved (of course, this situation generated new social struggles for the appropriation of ES, expressed for example on higher inflation levels). These differential outcomes give important lessons for the analysis of the pandemic and post-pandemic context; austerity measures and income concentration have generated poor economic results and, most importantly, dramatic social consequences.

The rising power of the capitalist classes among the world during the last decades (Picketty, 2019) and the concentration of incomes during the pandemic (World Bank, 2022) signals the irrationality of the contemporary economic system. ES theory, used in the Argentine case in this chapter, shows that State appropriation of wealth and redirection among its uses could generate considerable social improvements. In Argentina, unproductive uses of ES, such as capital flight, reduce potential productive investment by 15%–20% of its total value. With the reduction of a quarter part of profits appropriated by capitalists, the country could increase by 50% its health and education CSR. The changes among appropriation and uses of ES depend on political struggles, generally arising during critical times such as the post-2008 crisis and the Covid-19 pandemic.

As Baran and Sweezy pointed out in the past century, ES approach keeps its significance for analyzing, comprehending and discussing capitalism in present days. For that purpose, this work aims not only to recover the tradition of ES theory, but also to provide actualized tools to tackle present challenges.

Acknowledgement

The author wants to thank the comments and suggestions made by Jon Mulberg to a previous version of this chapter. Nevertheless, he is excluded from any mistakes or omissions, which are responsibility of the author.

Notes

1 Latin American structuralism is an economic school of thought created in the 1940s mainly in the Economic Commission for Latin America and the Caribbean of the United Nations. One of the main contributions was the distinction between core and peripheral countries for the analysis of underdevelopment.
2 Cost of social reproduction reflects the historical and material conditions of reproduction of the working classes (Furtado, 1978).
3 "The accumulation regime describes growth models in the long run … Its typical parameters essentially result from two institutional forms: the salary relation and the form of competence" (Boyer, 2007, 81–82). In addition to the regulation approach, other authors have gone beyond and considered that "it refers to the articulation of a given operation of the economic variables connected with a defined economic structure, a specific form of State, and clashes between existing social blocs" (Basualdo, 2007, 6).
4 For specific details on the methodology, see Bona (2018a and 2018b).
5 The Gramscian concept of subaltern classes refers to a broad group of popular sectors, an intersectionality of the variations of race, class, gender, culture, religion, etc.

6 Financial valorization has been defined as: the placement of surplus by large firms in several financial assets (securities, bonds, deposits, etc.), in domestic and international markets. This process, which emerges and is predominant in the Argentine economy since the end of the 1970s, expands due to the fact that interest rates, or the relation between them, exceed the profitability of the various economic activities, since the accelerated growth of external indebtedness makes it possible to place local capital abroad by operating as a mass of recoverable surplus and/or by releasing profit for these purposes (Arceo & Basualdo, 1999, 41).

7 "(The power bloc) thus indicates the particular contradictory unity of the ruling classes or class fractions, in their relation to a particular form of the capitalist state. (…) In this sense, the concept of the power bloc refers to the political level, it includes the field of political practices, to the extent that this field concentrates on itself and reflects the articulation of the set of instances and of the levels of class struggle at a given stage. The concept of the bloc in power has here a function analogous to that of the concept of the form of State with regard to the legal-political superstructure" (Poulantzas, 1969: 302–303).

8 A currency board stipulates by law that one Argentine peso was equivalant to one US dollar and ensures this applies.

9 Due to currency depreciation and its pass through to prices, inflation scaled while salaries remained constant. Higher prices and lower wages permitted an increase of the economic surplus appropriation by the capitalist and rental classes. For social consequences of devaluation in peripheral countries, see Díaz Alejandro (1963).

10 After a period of practically 0% inflation rates during convertibility, currency depreciation in 2002 generated the reintroduction on inflation among Argentine economy. Between 2003 and 2006 annual rates averaged 7%, but between 2007 and 2015 it registered approximately 25%. Beyond an inflationary international context (due to the increase in commodity food prices) in the 2000s, rises in local wages (after a period of wage reduction previously commented) had, as a response, increases in prices, as a way to dispute the income appropriation. For a discussion on the inflation levels and income disputes in Argentina during the period, see CIFRA (2015).

11 See Appendix 5A.

12 By measuring in US constant dollars of 1991 the information is presented in real terms. The problem among statistics in Argentina between 2007 and 2015 made it difficult to use constant pesos. For more about the problem of inflation and GDP statistics in Argentina during this period see CIFRA (2015).

13 See Appendix 5B.

14 Higher level salaries are those salaries above the defined cost of social reproduction level. Here, we consider the part of the wage which is higher than the benchmark.

15 In this sense, profits are taxed on 35% according to Argentinian legislation (however there is a high proportion of tax evasion), and higher level salaries also pay progressive taxes.

16 Even so, tax structure did not change decisively between both periods (Gaggero and Rossignolo, 2012).

17 All of them are multiplied 13 times considering extra wage at the end of the year.

References

Arceo, E. and Basualdo, E. (1999). Las tendencias a la centralización del capital y la concentración del ingreso en la economía argentina durante la década del noventa. *Cuadernos Del Sur*, 29, 39–68.

Azpiazu, D. and Schorr, M. (2010). *Hecho en Argentina: Industria y economía, 1976–2007.* Buenos Aires: Siglo XXI.

Baran, P. (1953). Economic progress and economic surplus. *Science & Society* 17(4), 289–317.

Baran, P. (1957). *Political economy of growth.* New York: Montlhy Review Press.

Baran, P. and Sweezy, P. (1966). *Monopoly capital.* New York: Monthly Review Press.

Basualdo, E. (2007). Acerca del concepto de patrón o régimen de acumulación y conformación estructural de la economía. Buenos Aires: AEyT FLACSO.

Basualdo, E. (2010). *Estudios de historia económica argentina. Desde mediados del siglo XX a la actualidad.* Buenos Aires: Siglo XXI.

Basualdo, E. (ed.) (2017). *Endeudar y fugar. Un análisis de la historia económica argentina de Martínez de Hoz a Macri.* Buenos Aires: Siglo XXI.

Basualdo, E. (ed.) (2020). *Endeudar y fugar. Un análisis de la historia económica argentina, desde Martínez de Hoz hasta Macri.* Buenos Aires: Siglo XXI.

Bona, L. (2018a). Costo de reproducción social en Argentina. Evolución durante los periodos de convertibilidad (1991–2001) y posconvertibilidad (2002–2015). *Sociedad Y Economía* (34). https://doi.org/10.25100/sye.v0i34.6476

Bona, L. (2018b). El excedente económico en Argentina. La etapa neoliberal (1991–2001) versus la neodesarrollista (2002–2015). *Apuntes del CENES*, 37(66), 93–128.

Bona, L. (2020). *El excedente económico en la Argentina contemporánea. Los sectores generadores de rentas y beneficios, la fuga de capitales y sus implicancias en materia de desarrollo (1991-2015).* PhD thesis. Universidad Nacional de Quilmes, Bernal, Argentina. Available at RIDAA-UNQ Repositorio Institucional Digital de Acceso Abierto de la Universidad Nacional de Quilmes http://ridaa.unq.edu.ar/handle/20.500.11807/2997.

Bona, L. M. and Páez, S. M. (2021). Fases, similitudes y diferencias entre los casos de las dictaduras y economía política en Argentina, 1966-1973 y 1976-1983, y Brasil, 1964-1985. *América Latina en la historia económica*, 27(2), 1–24.

Boyer, R. (2007). *Crisis y regímenes de crecimiento.* Buenos Aires: Miño y Dávila.

Cantamutto, F., Schorr, M. and Wainer, A. (2016). El sector externo de la economía argentina durante los gobiernos del kirchnerismo (2003-2015). *Realidad Económica*, 304, 41–73.

Centro de Investigación y Formación de la República Argentina (CIFRA) (2015). Principales resultados de pobreza e indigencia 2003-2015. Special review, November 2015, centrocifra.org.ar.

Chena, P., Panigo, D., Wahren, P. and Bona, L. (2018). Argentina (2002-2015): transición neomercantilista, estructuralismo à la Diamand y keynesianismo social con restricción externa. Argentina (2002-2015). *Semestre Económico*, 21(47), 25–59.

Danielson, A. (1990). The concept of surplus and the underdeveloped countries: critique and suggestions. *Review of Radical Political Economics*, 22(2–3), 214–230.

Díaz Alejandro, C. (1963). A note on the impact of devaluation and the redistributive effect. *Journal of Political Economy*, 71(6), 577–580.

Ferrer, A. (2008). *Historia económica argentina, desde sus orígenes a la actualidad.* Buenos Aires: Fondo de Cultura Económica.

Furtado, C. (1978). *Prefacio a una nueva economía política.* Madrid: Siglo XXI.

Gaggero, J. and Rossignolo, D. (2012). Impacto del presupuesto sobre la equidad II. Working paper CEFID-AR 46.

Guillén, A. (2007). La teoría latinoamericana del desarrollo. Reflexiones para una estrategia alternativa frente al neoliberalismo. In Vidal, G. and Guillén, A. (eds.): *Repensar la teoría del desarrollo en un contexto de globalización. Homenaje a* Celso Furtado (pp. 489–518). Buenos Aires: CLACSO.

Harvey, D. (2005). *A brief history of neoliberalism.* Oxford: Oxford University Press.

Katz, C. (2016). *Neoliberalismo, neodesarrollismo, socialismo*. Buenos Aires: Editorial Batalla de Ideas.
Lippit, V. (1985). The concept of the surplus in economic development. *Review of Radical Political Economics*, 17(1–2), 1–19.
López, E. (2016). *Los años post-neoliberales. De la crisis a la consolidación de un nuevo modo de desarrollo en Argentina*. Buenos Aires: Miño y Dávila.
Marx, K. (2010). *Capital*, Vol. I. London: Pacific Publishing Studio.
Patnaik, U. and Patnaik, P. (2020). Imperialism in the era of globalization. *Monthly Review*, 67(3), 68.
Picketty, T. (2019). *Capital and ideology*. Cambridge, MA: Harvard University Press.
Poulantzas, N. (1969). *Political power and social classes*. Chicago: Chicago University Press.
Prebisch, P. (1981). *Capitalismo periférico. Crisis y transformación*. Buenos Aires: Fondo de Cultura Económica.
Ricardo, D. (2004). *On the principles on political economy and taxation*. New York: Dover edition.
Santarcángelo, J. and Schorr, M. (2001). Dinámica laboral en la Argentina durante los años noventa: desocupación, precarización de las condiciones de trabajo y creciente inequidad distributiva. *V Congreso Nacional de Estudios del Trabajo*. Buenos Aires: ASET.
Sbattella, J. (2001). El excedente económico en la República Argentina. *Revista Realidad Económica*, 181, 75–90.
Sbattella, J., Chena, P., Palmieri, P. and Bona, L. (2012). *Origen, apropiación y destino del Excedente Económico en la Argentina de la postconvertibilidad*. Buenos Aires: Ediciones Colihue.
Smith, A. (1994). *The wealth of nations*. London: Modern Library.
Somel, C. (2003). Estimating the surplus in the periphery: An application to Turkey. *Cambridge Journal of Economics*, 6(27), 919–933.
Varesi, G. (2016). La Argentina del kirchnerismo: notas sobre hegemonía, acumulación e integración regional. *VII Jornadas de Sociología de la UNLP*. Sociological Department Facultad de Humanidades y Ciencias de la Educación, La Plata.
World Bank (2022). Stagflation risk rises amid sharp slowdown in growth. A World Bank Group Flagship Report. Washington: World Bank Group.
Yeldan, E. (1995). Surplus creation and extraction under structural adjustment: Turkey, 1980-1992. *Review of Radical Political Economics*, 27(2), 38–72.

Appendix 5A

In order to estimate the CSR, we follow the methodology used in Bona (2018a, 2018b). The calculation will be divided into three modules: wage CSR, retirement CSR and State components:

> *Total CSR = wage CSR + retirement CSR + public expenditure in basic education, health and subsidies to residential users of energy and transport – tax pressure*

To measure the wage CSR, we take families (considering children, men under 65 and women under 60 populations as part of households), estimating it from the average income declared in the Permanent Household Survey (EPH) of INDEC. On the other hand, to contemplate the universe of the unemployed, we assign minimum wage (MW). Given that household surveys only include urban population,

MW will also be computed as reproductive income for rural employees because they are among the lowest paid workers (MTEySS):

Wage CSR = (formal workers average wage × number of formal workers) + [informal workers average wage × number of informal workers (in urban areas)[17]*] + [MW × (unemployed + rural workers)]*

For the retirement CSR the household will not be considered, but a reproductive income per person, since the social security system provides individual pensions. We take minimum retirement pension as CSR reference, which is supposed to guarantee the old men and women reproduction (counted 13 times, as in the wage case):

> *Retirement CSR = minimum retirement × number of elderlies covered by the pension system annually*

Table 5A.1 Cost of social reproduction (CSR), million US constant dollars (1991), Argentina, 1991–2015

Year	*Wage CSR*	*Pension CSR*	*Basic education*	*Health*	*Subsidies on E&T*	*Tax rate*	*Total CSR*	*CSR/GDP*
1991	66.983	5.514	4.394	7.557	-		62.996	36.2%
1992	79.199	5.433	5.203	9.165	-		73.957	36.3%
1993	90.812	5.252	6.091	10.335	-		84.065	37.7%
1994	93.123	5.231	6.555	11.499	-		87.306	36.9%
1995	85.653	5.179	6.445	11.364	-		81.763	35.5%
1996	80.855	5.019	6.310	10.892	-	29,59%	77.666	32.9%
1997	83.975	4.908	7.059	11.241	-		80.881	32.6%
1998	87.318	4.792	7.103	11.471	-		83.429	33.4%
1999	84.408	4.760	7.462	11.867	-		82.112	35.4%
2000	80.879	4.212	7.438	11.437	-		78.788	35.1%
2001	77.015	4.186	7.220	10.657	-		75.050	36.3%
2002	22.847	1.745	2.265	3.511	-		22.379	28.8%
2003	24.788	1.998	2.489	4.080	-		24.651	26.1%
2004	36.412	2.501	3.030	4.714	95		34.109	28.7%
2005	43.089	3.136	3.975	5.687	290		41.158	29.6%
2006	50.442	3.919	4.827	6.510	538		48.573	30.8%
2007	59.793	6.498	6.056	8.195	1.305		60.310	31.9%
2008	72.745	7.635	7.765	10.640	2.252	32,49%	74.921	32.6%
2009	76.426	7.858	8.089	12.463	2.232		79.685	37.5%
2010	89.710	9.223	9.263	15.124	2.853		94.030	35.4%
2011	109.529	11.575	12.129	18.725	5.328		117.940	36.9%
2012	122.928	14.042	13.021	21.616	5.447		132.551	38.5%
2013	128.921	15.048	14.031	23.086	5.450		139.761	39.1%
2014	110.305	12.986	12.492	21.184	5.559		122.469	37.7%
2015	134.009	17.010	16.104	26.832	5.776		150.666	39.9%

Source: Prepared by the author from Treasury, INDEC, ASAP, Labor Ministry and US Bureau of Labor Statistics.

To measure social public transfers that are included in CSR we take primary and secondary education and universal health, and we add subsidies to economic sectors that reduce cost of living for working classes.

Finally, in order to draw up an analysis of the State action in determining the CSR, we subtract tax pressure on 5th decile according to Gaggero and Rossignolo (2012), which represents non-skilled workers income (see Table 5A.1).

Appendix 5B

In order to estimate the distribution of ES's origins, we proceeded to discriminate the components related to rent (oil, mining and land), higher level salaries and profits.

For this purpose, the proportions of GDP corresponding to rents were obtained from World Bank and Bona (2020).

Table 5B.1 Rents (oil, gas, mineral, forestry and land), profits and higher level salaries, million US constant dollars (1991), Argentina, 1991–2015

Year	*Economic surplus*	*Oil rent*	*Land rent*	*Mining rent*	*Higher level salaries*	*Profits*
1991	85,988	2,049	3,626	15	7,305	72,992
1992	106,484	2,424	3,634	18	13,594	86,813
1993	113,956	2,388	3,768	5	15,573	92,222
1994	123,396	2,077	4,376	6	9,185	107,752
1995	122,932	2,733	5,330	4	8,852	106,012
1996	133,152	3,836	6,173	5	8,565	114,572
1997	141,774	3,696	6,123	53	8,053	123,851
1998	139,089	2,224	6,480	132	8,219	122,034
1999	123,256	3,286	5,312	148	7,345	107,165
2000	121,336	5,539	5,648	132	6,839	103,178
2001	108,784	4,317	5,901	131	5,961	92,475
2002	44,470	4,262	2,323	132	2,490	35,264
2003	56,905	4,666	5,436	159	4,961	41,684
2004	70,721	5,927	6,208	288	4,901	53,397
2005	83,413	7,931	4,856	418	6,822	63,387
2006	93,076	8,923	4,441	959	10,006	68,747
2007	110,485	9,310	7,847	1,034	12,587	79,707
2008	132,632	12,043	17,218	977	19,861	82,533
2009	109,866	6,882	5,119	928	16,300	80,636
2010	144,157	8,723	7,395	1,619	21,402	105,018
2011	169,068	11,244	15,442	2,024	28,661	111,697
2012	174,365	10,286	12,227	1,969	37,645	112,238
2013	178,088	9,331	11,863	1,330	40,297	114,461
2014	163,354	8,022	10,321	1,252	36,482	106,117
2015	174,228	2,670	8,576	1,021	42,780	113,837

Source: Prepared by the author.

The calculation of wage share in GDP was taken from the National Institute of Statistics and Census (INDEC), which publishes the functional distribution of income (www.indec.gob.ar/uploads/press reports/cgi_06_16.pdf). We subtract from total wages the CSR and then get higher level salaries bill.

Finally, the calculation of profits was made by subtracting the obtained components from total ES (see Table 5B.1).

6 The commodity character of Marx's theory of money

An assessment of the debate and open problems

Nicolás Aguila

6.1 Introduction

Whenever there is an economic crisis, there is a call for a return to the gold standard. National currencies broke all their remaining formal links to gold when the Bretton Woods international monetary system disintegrated. This triggered a controversy on the character of Marx's theory of money, an aspect of his work that had been understudied before that (Foley, 2005; de Brunhoff, 2015). At the core of the debate is whether Marx proposes a commodity theory of money, that is, if he argues that money is a commodity (in particular, gold) or not, and, in either case, how to explain contemporary monetary forms. This chapter assesses the debate aiming to clarify the problems at stake and what are the open issues that should be coherently addressed by contemporary theorists of money.

Moseley (2005: 14) argues that 'most of the authors agree, with varying degrees of certainty and for different reasons, that money does not have to be a commodity in Marx's theory'. In a nutshell, this heterogeneous group of authors claims that, in Marx's view, money is determined by its social functions and not by the physical commodity which supports it, considering that gold was a historical contingency as money, but not a theoretical or practical necessity (Arthur, 2005; Campbell, 2017; Ivanova, 2013; Lipietz, 1982; Matthews, 1996; Moseley, 2005, 2011; Nelson, 2005; Reuten, 1988, 2005; Benetti, 1990; Williams, 2000).

This perspective is criticized, among other reasons discussed below, because of a lack of textual evidence to back its claims. Germer (2005) shows that there is significant evidence supporting that Marx conceptualizes money as a commodity and little to no evidence to suggest otherwise. As a result, several authors defend that, in Marx's view, money is a commodity. These authors can be divided into two groups. One argues that Marx's commodity theory of money is based on the historical workings of the monetary system in his time, but has since been outdated and thus should be replaced, typically with a credit theory of money, within a Marxist framework (Bellofiore, 1989, 2005; Foley, 2005; Ganssmann, 1998; Graziani, 1997; Kennedy, 2000; Lavoie, 1986).

The other group criticizes them by arguing that their rejection of Marx's theory is largely grounded on the empirical note that metals do not circulate as money anymore. Labrinidis (2014b) argues that, for some authors, the absence of a

DOI: 10.4324/9781003451990-9

monetary role for gold is so self-evident that they do not find it necessary to provide any explanation for the dismissal of a commodity theory of money. Similarly, Weeks (2012: 83) claims that rejecting Marx's theory of money based on merely the empirical observation of the lack of any fixed relation between gold and the U.S. dollar is not 'a serious argument' because there are many aspects that cannot be seen and yet are analytically valid. Moreover, Germer (1997) shows that Marx himself acknowledges the almost complete withdrawal of gold from domestic circulation. This recognition would be incoherent if his analysis of the commodity character of money was based on historical observation.

In this chapter, I show that Marx argues that money is a commodity. Moreover, he not only claims that money is a commodity, but that it must be a commodity. In his view, money is the necessary capitalist solution to the problem of the organization of total social labor in a society in which it is allocated indirectly and conducted by private and independent units, without a social entity that can directly establish the social character of private work. Thus, money has to be a privately produced object with the attribute of revealing the social character of use-values produced by different concrete labours, thereby establishing the unity of social labor. In this way, the only historical assumption (in the sense of empirical observation, albeit one grounded in theoretical reasons) is that the money commodity is gold, but not that money must be a commodity. In other words, his commodity theory of money is based not only on historical observation but crucially also on theoretical necessity. This perspective allows him to coherently respond to key questions such as how can money measure value. The positions that argue that for Marx money is not a commodity, or that money was a commodity in Marx's time but not anymore, either evade the issue or fail to give adequate answers.

However, I also argue that, for Marx, the money commodity appears only ideally, or can be replaced by symbols in the performance of some functions. In this way, the theory is in principle compatible with a world in which gold does not circulate as money. In other words, the fact that metals were replaced does not pose, on its own, the unsurmountable challenge to the commodity theory of money that many Marxist authors seem to suggest. Nevertheless, the post-Bretton Woods monetary order does create theoretical challenges for Marx's theory of money, which are usually not recognized or, when acknowledged, not satisfactorily addressed in the literature, both by the authors who accept the commodity character of money, as well as by those who reject it.

First, the fluctuating quote of gold in terms of dollars in open markets implies either that the unit of account has been constantly changing or that gold has a price. Neither option is consistent with Marx's formulation, raising a problem. In the first case, a unit of account that is not fixed represents a theoretical issue in itself, but there are also empirical problems conciliating the historical rate of inflation with the one that should have resulted from the observed change in gold 'prices'. The second scenario means that the unit of account is no longer a given weight of gold, so it requires explaining what is the unit of account denominating now. Second, Marx argues that world money is the only function in which the money commodity has to be physically present, at least for settling international transactions and as a reserve of (central) banks. This problem receives more attention in the literature but the replacement of gold in that role has not yet been satisfactorily explained.

Far from being an academic debate with little practical consequence, answering these open questions is essential for understanding contemporary phenomena. As recent research shows, Marxist theory can shed light on questions about the monetary character of cryptocurrencies (Rotta & Paraná, 2022), central bank digital currencies (Duque, 2020), shadow banking monies (Vasudevan, 2018), and unconventional monetary policies like quantitative easing (Ivanova, 2020; Vasudevan, 2014). Thus, addressing seemingly obscure theoretical issues in monetary theory can improve the theoretical foundations to provide better answers to contemporary empirical issues.

In this way, my close reading of Marx's arguments, highlighting where I find open issues, does not intend to be an exercise of plain exegesis but rather to assess to what extent –if any – Marx's theory of money can aid us to answer the questions of our time. This is particularly relevant for two reasons. First, the rejection of Marx's monetary theory has not led to its replacement with a more inclusive and coherent explanation. Furthermore, some of the open problems of Marx's theory are shared by some non-Marxist heterodox theories of money, which also struggle to explain what the unit of account denominates and the character of world money. Second, the defence of Marx's theory still leaves unresolved some of the issues criticized by its opponents, many of which have to be seriously dealt with.

The rest of the chapter is organized as follows. In the second section, I examine the ontology of money, showing why money has to be a commodity in Marx's view. In the third section, I present the functions of money, paying particular attention to how the money commodity is only ideally needed in the function of measure of values, and how it can be replaced by symbols of value as means of circulation. Additionally, I point toward the problems that the fall of Bretton Woods raises for Marx's theory of money: how to coherently explain the changing quote of gold in terms of U.S. dollars and how to explain world money when international balances are not settled in gold. The fourth section suggests future lines of research.

6.2 The ontology of money

In capitalism, individual producers are atomized and produce privately and independently from one another, choosing individually and without coordination what, how, and how much to produce. However, as in every other form of organization of human society, individuals are not self-sufficient. Thus, to satisfy their needs, they must acquire use values produced by others. In this historically specific mode of production, they do so in a process mediated by a mercantile exchange. In other words, the products of work adopt the form of commodities. As can be seen, in the capitalist mode of production, mercantile exchange is not a contingency; it is the moment when the social nexus is expressed and the unity between social production and consumption is established (Fleetwood, 2000; Caligaris and Starosta, 2016; Campbell, 2017; Weber, 2019).

Marx argues that commodities have a double character: on the one hand, they are useful objects that satisfy human necessities and, consequently, have *use value*, and, on the other, they have *exchange value*. How can two commodities be equalized in exchange? As evidenced in the popular phrase, a person cannot compare apples and oranges because they are incommensurable as apples and oranges. However, an apple and an orange can be equalized in exchange because the two of them share something *as commodities*. Thus, the exchange value of a commodity must be an expression of a common quality that makes commodities commensurable. Marx discovers that the common property is *value*: the two commodities are embodiments of socially necessary abstract labor produced privately and independently (from now on, simply labor).

If it takes one hour of labor to produce a tomato, then the tomato is worth one hour of labor. However, value cannot express itself immediately as such, for example in an expression like 'one tomato = one hour of labor', because the purely social character of values can only be revealed in the social relation between two commodities, so it must express itself in exchange value.

Thus, Marx turns to the analysis of the *simple, isolated, or accidental form of value*, which is that of the relation between two commodities. In it, one commodity (say, tomatoes) takes the relative position expressing its value on the body of another that acts as the equivalent (e.g. beer). The commodity in the relative form enters the relationship, first of all, to show that it is the result of a socially useful activity performed privately and independently, so its sale (its exchange for the equivalent) acts as an *a posteriori* recognition of the social character of the work that produced it. This implies that the equivalent is a commodity that has the attribute of showing whether or not the relative commodity has value. Because of this, the value character of the equivalent must be presupposed, that is, the equivalent does not have to prove that it possesses value (Iñigo Carrera, 2007). In other words, the equivalent is a directly exchangeable form with three peculiarities: (1) its use value becomes the form of appearance of value; (2) its concrete labor becomes the form of manifestation of abstract labor; and (3) its private labor takes the form of social labor. It is here apparent that the equivalent can only play such a role because it is itself a commodity, given that its three peculiarities stem directly from its commodity character (Germer, 2005).

But the relative commodity has to show that it not only has value but also how much it has. For that, the relative commodity expresses its amount of labor time in the body of the equivalent commodity. Assuming that tomatoes are successful in proving their social character, we can reach the expression:

$$x\,tomatoes = y\ beer$$

However, the simple form is insufficient, embryonic. Here the equivalent is a particular equivalent, not a universal one. Thus, it is superseded by the *total or expanded form of value*, where the value of a commodity is expressed in the body of all the others. The problem here is that every other commodity acts as an equivalent. This is still problematic because it does not solve the issue of establishing the social character of private work. The producer of tomatoes can exchange them for beer but if no other producer is willing to accept beer, the producer of tomatoes would not be able to buy all the commodities they need to satisfy their needs. Thus, the organization of a society based on private labor requires a universal equivalent, accepted by everyone because they know that everyone else will also accept it. Consequently, the total form is superseded by the *general form of value* where one commodity becomes the *general equivalent* of the whole universe of commodities. The general equivalent allows reducing all kinds of different concrete labours to their common substance, becoming the 'visible incarnation, the social chrysalis state, of all human labour' (Marx, 1976: 159). The last step is then to move from the abstract need for a general equivalent to the concrete commodity which, through the historical process and by social custom, conquered the monopoly of the role.

Every private producer would be very happy to have the product of their private labor as the general equivalent. However, the independent and equal character of individuals prevents them from being able to coordinate, concede, or impose any commodity in such a social role (Caligaris and Starosta, 2016). It is only the action of society that can turn a particular commodity into the general equivalent. The universal equivalent attaches itself to different commodities historically, but two circumstances result decisive for it to settle on one kind: the money form attaches itself to the most important articles of exchange from outside or to the object of utility constituting the main element of indigenous wealth. Once exchange breaks the chains of local bonds, the money form transfers to precious metals. This is because the latter are commodities whose materiality possesses the same uniform quality, making them fit to embody abstract and, thus, equal human labor; they are capable of being divisible and assembled back, allowing the money commodity to express the purely quantitative difference between magnitudes of value; and they require relatively a lot of work to produce, so they embody a large amount of value in a low volume of material. With the establishment of gold in that role, we arrive at the *money form*.

Money is thus a privately produced object with the attribute of revealing the social character of use-values produced by different concrete labors. In this way, it is the necessary solution to the problem of the organization of total social labor in a society in which labor is allocated indirectly and conducted by private and independent units, without a social entity that can directly establish the social character of private work.[1]

Based on this understanding of what money is, Marx concludes that money must be a commodity. 'Gold confronts the other commodities as money only because it previously confronted them as a commodity' (Marx, 1976: 162). If this was not the case, commodities could not express their value on it. A longer discussion of why follows below when considering the function of the measure of value. What matters at this point is that the commodity character of money is not an assumption but a theoretical result. The 'assumption' (in the sense of empirical observation, albeit one grounded in theoretical reasons) is only that the money commodity is gold, but not that money must be a commodity. In fact, Marx shows that different commodities performed historically the functions of money (such as salt, cattle, silver, and others) before money attached itself to gold (Marx, 2010).

The value of the money commodity fluctuates like that of any other commodity, based on the time of labor necessary to produce it. However, unlike other commodities, the money commodity does not have a price because, to express it, gold would have to refer to itself as equivalent, which would be a truism. No commodity can express its value in itself, because an expression like 'x gold = x gold' is meaningless. According to Marx, the value of gold was expressed at the moment in which gold producers trade it for other commodities.

Having established the need for money to be a commodity, it is now worth asking whether it needs to be physically present. To answer that, it is necessary to discuss the functions of money. However, before discussing what money does, it was necessary to present what money is, as we have done. A commonplace in the Marxist literature is to start the discussion with Marx's account of the functions of money in chapter III of *Capital Volume I*, skipping the content of chapters I and II. This is a mistake that could lead to falling into the neoclassical perspective which reduces the ontology of money to its functions.

6.3 The functions of money

6.3.1 The measure of values and standard of price

When a commodity expresses its value in money, its exchange value becomes its *price*:

$$1\ tomato = y\ gold$$

Here, money acts as the *measure of value*, allowing the expression of the value of commodities in an amount of the money commodity. As every commodity expresses its value in different quantities of gold, there is a technical necessity for doing so in the same units. It would be worthless to express the value of tomatoes in ounces of gold, that of beers in metres of gold, and so on. The values of the different commodities must be expressed in magnitudes of the same denomination, qualitatively equal and quantitatively comparable.[2] In other words, a *unit of account* or *standard of prices* is needed. The quantity of gold that functions as the unit of account must be fixed, representing the same amount across time and space.

Unlike that of any other commodity, the unit of account of the money commodity cannot be established by any private producer because it requires a social agreement. Because of that, the state imposes and regulates it. By doing so, the state responds to a necessity derived from the indirect form of allocation of social labor. The role of the state is limited to regulating the standard of price but plays no role in the ontology of money or its function as the measure of value (Lapavitsas, 2013). Since the standard is exterior to the content of value, it can be externally imposed upon commodity circulation.

Given that metals had previous standards in their weights (ounces, pounds, etc.) those are the names arbitrarily adopted by the state as the standard of price. Thus, continuing with the previous example and assuming that it takes one hour of labor to produce an ounce of gold, we finally reach an expression like:

$$1\ tomato = 1\ ounce\ of\ gold$$

National units of account get historically divorced from metal. However, the state could only impose the standard of price within its borders: 'But in the world market, where state frontiers disappear, such national features of the standards of money disappear as well and are replaced by measures of weight generally used for metals' (Marx, 2010: 311). This point is further elaborated later on.

The price of commodities is an ideal or notional form; commodities do not need the presence of actual gold to express their value. As a result, it is possible to use 'purely imaginary or ideal' gold for this function (Marx, 1976: 190). It suffices that they have a price tag or that the seller announces their price for the values of all commodities to become imaginary quantities of gold of different magnitudes.

The function of the unit of account is at the centre of the debate on the commodity character of Marx's theory of money. Arthur (2005) argues that, in physics, there are three kinds of measures. First, immediate comparative measures like a beam balance or a ruler, where the instrument and the object of measurement share the same property, which exists before commensuration. For example, when someone places a ruler over a paper, they compare the extension of the paper with that of the ruler. The latter is denominated in fractional units (centimetres) of the established fixed unit of account (metre), so the measurement of the paper is commensurable with others. Second, indirect measures like a scale or a mercury thermometer, where the instrument and the object of measurement do not share the same quality. For example, an electronic balance indirectly measures the mass of a human body by measuring the electric current made when compressing a pressure sensor (the heavier the person, the harder the pressure on the compressor, and the higher the current created). Third, complex dimensions require the measurement of several things at once. For example, work is a function of force moving in space and in time, so it requires measuring the three things to get work units.

It is arguably the case that Marx was thinking in terms of an immediate comparative measure: the value of a commodity is measured by comparing it to the value of the money commodity denominated in fractional units of the unit of account (ounces), like the length of the paper is measured by comparing it to the length of the ruler in centimetres. This is a key reason why money must be a commodity: money can only measure value because it has value itself. Explaining how something without value can measure value is one of the biggest challenges for those who argue that for Marx money is not a commodity or that today it is no longer the case. With few exceptions, so far those authors have overlooked the problem, without engaging with it.

This function is unaffected by the material in circulation because, Marx argues, measurement is an ideal operation. As commodities express their value using only ideal gold, whether gold or an alternative circulates does not alter the problem: the money commodity is still the measure of value. Therefore, in what concerns this function, Marx's theory of money is in principle fully compatible with a world in which gold does not play a physical role.

6.3.2 The means of circulation

As a *means of circulation*, money acts as an agent in the metamorphosis of commodities that mediates the social metabolism. In this role, money must be physically present because, by being alienated, commodities suffer a transformation in their real body as use values. Once commodities are bought, they exit circulation having been replaced by money. Thus, what in reality is the movement of commodities appears as the result of the movement of money which, as means of circulation, always 'haunts' the sphere of circulation.

However, Marx argues that gold, in this function, can be replaced by *symbols of value*. His argument can be divided into two steps, one theoretical and the other practical. On theoretical grounds, gold can be replaced by symbols because, as means of circulation, money is a transient moment in the circulation process – it passes quickly from hand to hand. Therefore, its material is not important: it only needs a symbolic existence. This is possible only because symbols of value like paper money represent gold:

> Paper money is a symbol of gold, a symbol of money. Its relation to the values of commodities consists only in this: they find imaginary expression in certain quantities of gold, and the same quantities are symbolically and physically represented by the paper. Only in so far as paper money represents gold, which like all other commodities has value, is it a symbol of value.
>
> (Marx, 1976: 225)

The practical reason follows from the course of actual circulation as its 'natural and spontaneous tendency' (Marx, 1976: 222). Since money must be physically present in circulation, in the passing from one place to another, coins wear down. Additionally, both individuals and states try to take advantage of this situation by clipping and debasing coins (Marx, 2010). Finally, the production of gold is part of the *faux frais of production* that capital tries to get rid of, replacing it with the production of something cheaper. As a result, the nominal and real content progressively divorce from each other, and coins become tokens or symbols of their official metallic content. Therefore,

> In its form of existence as coins, gold becomes completely divorced from the substance of its value. Relatively valueless objects, therefore, such as paper notes, can serve as coins in the place of gold. This purely symbolic character

> of the currency is still somewhat disguised in the case of metal tokens. In paper money it stands out plainly.
>
> (Marx, 1976: 223–224)

It can be seen that Marx was aware that gold could be replaced in circulation, so his commodity theory does not rest on metals actually circulating. Here, Marx repeatedly introduces the state externally to emphasize that the symbol (whether coin or paper) needs to have an objective social validity which, as a mere symbol, could only be granted by the representative of total social capital. However, the role of the state is limited to internal circulation:

> One thing is necessary, however: the symbol of money must have its own objective social validity. The paper acquires this by its forced currency. The state's compulsion can only be of any effect within that internal sphere of circulation which is circumscribed by the boundaries of a given community, but it is also only within that sphere that money is completely absorbed in its function as medium of circulation, and is therefore able to receive, in the form of paper money, a purely functional mode of existence in which it is externally separated from its metallic substance.
>
> (Marx, 1976: 226–227)

With coinage, the purely conventional character of the unit of account becomes even clearer. The original metal names (e.g. ounces) become subdivided into aliquot parts that are given their own legal names like pounds and dollars, which are in turn subdivided into other parts with their own names like shillings and cents. This can be perfectly done because the name of a thing is external to it. In the pre-Bretton Woods era, the name of national currencies was arguably established as a certain fraction of an ounce of gold. For long periods between the eighteenth and twentieth centuries, an ounce of gold was determined to be equal to 3 pounds sterling 17 shillings and 10 ½ pence or 20 U.S. dollars and 67 cents. Except in times of war, these values were stable (de Brunhoff and Foley, 2006). During the Bretton Woods system, the name of the dollar was established in terms of gold at 35 dollars per ounce and the name of all the other currencies in terms of dollars (Weeks, 2012).

The adoption of national currencies leads to a new standard of prices based on their names. For example, if 20 dollars is the name of an ounce of gold, then prices are no longer expressed as:

$$1\, tomato = 1\, ounce\, of\ gold$$

And become expressed as:

$$1\, tomato = 20\, dollars$$

In this way, commodities become denominated in dollars, and money loses its link to metals in its name. However, Marx insists that a definite weight of gold remains the standard of price, regardless of how it is called as national currencies are just a name that a given fixed weight of metal adopts in the internal circulation.

This is consistent with Marx's analysis of the quantitative determination of paper symbols of value. According to him, injecting into circulation symbols in excess of the amount of gold that would have been in circulation in the absence of symbols would lead to a fall in the symbol's capacity to represent value (i.e. inflation). This is analogous to changing the unit of account:

> If the quantity of paper money represents twice the amount of gold available, then in practice £1 will be the money-name not of 1/4 of an ounce of gold, but 1/8 of an ounce. The effect is the same as if an alteration had taken place in the function of gold as the standard of price. The values previously expressed by the price of £1 would now be expressed by the price of £2.
>
> (Marx, 1976: 225)[3]

It is worth emphasizing that Marx's understanding of the laws of circulation is quite different when central banknotes (as opposed to symbols of value directly issued by the state) are the medium of exchange and it has profound differences with the quantitative theory (de Brunhoff, 2015; Lapavitsas, 2017a).

In any case, the symbol emerges spontaneously out of commodity money in circulation, and its unit of account is just a name given to a fraction of metal. Consequently, understanding the symbol would be impossible without first having discussed the nature and functions of money in its commodity character. Conversely, Marx's theory of money, while requiring money to be a commodity, shows how gold can be replaced as a means of circulation for 'symbols of value'. Therefore, the recognition that gold does not circulate internally anymore or that prices are not denominated in ounces of gold is not sufficient to challenge his theory.

6.3.3 Open issues

However, the fall of the Bretton Woods system creates a problem for the Marxist theory of money. Based on what I presented so far, 'dollars' is a name given to a fixed quantity of gold and the money commodity does not have a price. This was consistent until the end of 1969 when gold was quoted at 35 dollars per ounce. Since then, the quote increased permanently, surpassing 1800 dollars at the end of 2021 (World Gold Council, 2022). The fluctuating quote of gold in terms of dollars in markets implies either that the unit of account has changed or that gold has a price.

The first option is simply to say that now the name 'dollar' denominates a different weight of metal than before. This would require changes in the prices of all the other commodities (Foley, 1983; Friedenthal, 2013). If the length of a metre changes, then everyone's heights have to be consequently adjusted. For example, if before:

$$1\ tomato = 1\ ounce\ of\ gold$$

$$1\ ounce\ of\ gold = 20\ dollars$$

$$1\ tomato = 20\ dollars$$

And now the unit of account changes to:

$$1\ ounce\ of\ gold = 40\ dollars$$

Then,

$$1\ tomato = 40\ dollars$$

However, this was not the case. From December 1969 to January 2022, gold 'prices' increased by 5000% while the consumer price index in the United States increased by 646% (World Gold Council, 2022). Not only has the 'price' of gold increased more but also the correlation is low because it displays much higher volatility. Thus, this solution seems to be problematic.

The argument could be saved by saying that the low correlation between the consumer price index in the United States and the 'price' of gold is due to a change in the value of commodities and/or gold. As gold is a commodity, its value can change if the quantity of labor required to produce it changes. For example, if the productivity in the production of gold doubles, then producing a given quantity of gold (say, an ounce) would now take half the time as before. Knowing this, with the information that we have, we can implicitly derive how much the productivity in the production of gold would have to have increased relative to the U.S. economy for the argument to hold. Using numbers that reflect the historical experience (World Gold Council, 2022), in December 1978 the relationship was:

$$1\ average\ commodity = 1\ ounces\ of\ gold$$

$$1\ ounce\ of\ gold = 100\ dollars$$

$$1\ average\ commodity = 100\ dollars$$

Then, in January 2022, multiplying the 'price' of gold and that of an average commodity by the increase in gold prices and inflation respectively, those numbers are:

$$1\ ounce\ of\ gold = 5100\ dollars$$

$$1 \textit{ average commodity} = 746 \textit{ dollars}$$

This would tell us that now:

$$1 \textit{ average commodity} = 6.8 \textit{ ounces of gold}$$

In other words, from December 1969 to January 2022, the productivity in the production of gold would have to have risen seven times more than that of the U.S. economy. Due to a lack of data availability on the worldwide productivity in the production of gold, it is hard to check if that was the case (Weeks, 2012), but it seems unlikely the evolution of the productivity of gold grew seven times more than that of the U.S. economy.

Moreover, there is a second problem with this argument, of a theoretical nature: it would mean that the unit of account is no longer fixed. This is a central quality of units of account, and it is not clear how it could fulfil its purpose if it were flexible.[4] Just imagine what would happen if the length that a metre denominates was variable: heights would have to be constantly adjusted!

The second option is to argue that gold does have a price. One way to do so would be to say that, when coins fulfil monetary functions, they are the specific form of gold that has use value as money. Gold has always had a use value as a precious metal (e.g. in the form of jewellery), and another as money. In the first case, it is satisfying a need of persons, while in the second it is satisfying a need of personifications. That is, people do not need money because it satisfies a human need but only due to the specific form under which the products of labor are allocated in capitalism, namely, the circulation of commodities. As a consequence, it acquires a formal use value derived from its social function. Following the line of reasoning, golden rings fulfil human necessities, but they cannot be used as money, so they always had a price. When gold was used as money, it did not have a price, but when it stopped acting as world money, a price naturally appeared as it became a commodity like any other.

The consequence of this argument is a rejection that a definite weight of gold remains the standard of price. This is because the price of an ounce of gold cannot be expressed in ounces of gold ('1 ounce of gold = 1 ounce of gold' is meaningless), or in dollars, if they are just a name for a fixed quantity of gold. Then, to express the price of ounces of gold, dollars can no longer be denominating a definite weight of gold. So what would the unit of account be denominating now?

Some authors propose that the unit of account is directly denominating quantities of value. They emphasize the role of social convention in the functions of money and argue that the acceptance by commodity owners of something (e.g. paper) is enough for that to become the measure of value, and that acceptance is guaranteed by the state (Lavoie, 1986; Matthews, 1996; Moseley, 2005). According to this perspective, money itself is a 'symbol of value'.

This interpretation has an echo of what Marx (2010: 314) criticizes as the 'doctrine of the ideal standard of money' ('nominal standard' in other translations) that sustains the view that 'the terms pound, shilling, pence, thaler, franc, etc. denote ideal particles of value but not weights of gold or silver or any form of objectified labour'. First, these theories confuse the measure of value with the standard of price (Nelson, 2005). Second, social convention can explain why something without value is accepted, but not how it measures value, and they do not provide a satisfactory answer to how something without value measures value. Third, if value can be directly expressed and measured, it is then not clear why capitalism would need money or prices at all. In other words, why would money require another unit instead of directly being denominated in labor time? Why would 'prices' not be expressed in labor times? In this regard, Marx criticized the 'Ricardian socialist economists' who ignore the necessary character of the value form, that is, that a commodity's value can only express itself in exchange-value, and attempt to directly measure labor time or propose to replace money with labor chits (Saad-Filho, 1993). This could only be possible in a society with a social agreement or authority with the capacity to establish both the socially useful character of the products of labor, as well as their value character. To be able to express their substance immediately, commodities should be the product of a directly socially organized labor. But this will make superfluous the problem that the commodity form came to solve, that is, establishing the social character of labor (Iñigo Carrera, 2007).

To sum up, the fall of the Bretton Woods system, and particularly the changing quote of gold, does pose problems to Marx's theory of money as it implies either that the unit of account is changing, or that gold has a price, two things that are incompatible with Marx's original formulation. In addition, there is a second problem: the commodity character of world money. To get there, we need to finish the review of the functions of money.

6.3.4 Money

Marx only devotes one paragraph to introduce the section 'Money' in chapter 3 of *Capital Volume I* and it is not clear why the following functions characterize money as money. What is he trying to differentiate it from? Commodity money as opposed to symbols? Money as money as opposed to money as capital? As opposed to credit? Or to point out functions that money only has in capitalism as opposed to functions that it also had before? I will follow Marx's original presentation without discussing that issue, although I think that pointing out the ambiguity is worthwhile.

Hoarding: The direct exchangeability of gold makes it the expression of wealth in general. As a result, there is a need and desire to freeze the product of the first metamorphosis and take it out of circulation, transforming it into a *hoard*. By doing that, at least potentially, people can buy commodities without having to sell or, more precisely, having already sold. In this way, money can be privately appropriated, and its social power becomes a source of private power, acting as a measure of the social wealth of its owner. Once gold enters back into circulation, it loses its power, becoming a particular expression of wealth, a non-directly exchangeable commodity.

Given that the necessary amount of money in circulation varies, reserves of money play an important role in regulating it. Hoards adjust themselves to allow for the expansion (providing additional supply) and contraction (absorbing the excess) of the quantity of money in circulation.

Itoh and Lapavitsas (1999) argue that only commodity money can function as a hoard because fiat money does not possess value in its own body. However, they show that hoards can be deposited in exchange for certificates. As a result, the hoarder now only has a title representing their property over the reserves, instead of the actual money. These certificates circulate alongside coins, considered just as good based on their convertibility. Consequently, they also reduce the amount of gold needed as a means of circulation.

Means of payment: With the development of commodity circulation, a commodity changes hands before being sold, that is, its alienation becomes separated in time from the realization of its price. In this process, the seller becomes a creditor, and the buyer a debtor. This change in the metamorphosis of commodities implies a transformation in the function of money: it becomes a *means of payment*. Credit emerges out of this function of money. Gold is replaced by credit instruments in the function of means of circulation, further reducing the physical need for it.

Additionally, the balancing of payments with each other reduces the amount of money in circulation required at any moment in time. At the same time, the concentration of means of payment in one place engenders institutions to economize them through clearing balances. To the extent to which payments balance each other, money functions only ideally, as an accounting operation.

All things considered, as a means of payment money does not need to be bodily present all the time. However, as soon as this mechanism stops working, people demand payments in physical money, which could lead to a monetary crisis.[5] When the demand for money originates in domestic circulation, as an 'internal drain', money can be replaced as a means of payment even during a crisis. Marx argues that: 'The monetary famine remains whether payments have to be made in gold or in credit-money, such as bank-notes' (Marx, 1976: 237). Nevertheless, when the demand for money originates from the need to make payments abroad, money is needed physically as gold.

World money: Marx argues that outside the domestic sphere of circulation, money loses its local functions and returns to its original form as a precious metal. This is because, in the world market, money must be the commodity whose natural form is also the directly social form of abstract labor. *World money* serves as the universal means of payment, as the universal means of purchase, and as the absolute social materialization of wealth.

In this function, Marx insists on the commodity character of world money: 'In this latter role it is always the genuine money-commodity, gold, and silver in their physical shape, which is required' (Marx, 1976: 243). Moreover, in Volume III, Marx makes clear that world money is the *only* function where gold is physically needed (Evans, 1997; Germer, 1997; Ganssmann, 1998; Ivanova, 2013):

> The entire history of modern industry shows that metal would indeed be required only for the balancing of international commerce, whenever its equilibrium is momentarily disturbed, if only domestic production were organized. That the domestic market does not need any metal even now is shown by the suspension of the cash payments of the so-called national banks, which resort to this expedient in all extreme cases as the sole relief.
>
> (Marx, 1999: 371)

Marx emphasizes that metals are not required for every international transaction. In his view, gold is necessary only when credits and debits do not net, so its role was relegated to the balancing of international commerce. Consequently, he argues that countries, typically at the central bank, must accumulate a reserve fund of metallic reserves to settle those balances when due. The ability to hoard depends on a country's position in the international division of labor and in the financial system, and acts as a measure of political power between nations (de Brunhoff, 2005; Foley, 2005; Vasudevan, 2009).

Even when most central banks still have reserves of gold, they are only used to settle international balances in exceptional circumstances (Labrinidis, 2014a). Gold was replaced by different national currencies, above all, the U.S. dollar as means of international settlement. As a result, the largest part of international reserves is also composed of foreign currency. This presents a second challenge to Marx's theory of money, requiring to explain why the physical presence of gold is no longer required for that. In relation to this issue, contemporary Marxist monetary theory has been far more advanced than in the previous problem, with several important contributions trying to provide a Marxist understanding of contemporary world money (de Brunhoff and Foley, 2006; Vasudevan, 2009; Ivanova, 2013; Labrinidis, 2014b; Lapavitsas, 2017b). However, the discussion is still incipient, with important open questions.

6.4 Conclusion

This article shows that in Marx's theory, money must be a commodity. However, gold is only ideally needed or can be replaced by symbols in some functions, so the theory is in principle compatible with a world in which gold does not circulate, contrary to the claims of many scholars who reject it. However, the fall of the Bretton Woods system does present challenges to the theory, which are often overlooked. First, the changing quote of gold implies either that the unit of account is no longer fixed or that gold has a price. Second, Marx argues that gold was still needed as world money, at least for settling international balances and as a reserve fund.

These two problems have not received the same amount of interest in the literature. On the one hand, the issue of world money has attracted a good deal of attention both from those who reject and from those who accept the commodity character of Marx's theory of money, giving rise to many competing explanations. Even when there are still unresolved issues, I believe that Marxist theories of credit money, recovering several insights that Marx leaves in *Capital Volume III*, have made important contributions to updating the theory of world money to understand how could gold be replaced by a national currency in settling international balances and as central bank reserves. On the other, the problem of the fluctuating quote of gold has passed almost unnoticed by the literature, and the few existing answers have not been satisfactory. This issue should be addressed for the logical coherence of the Marxist theory of money.

To conclude, we live in times where there are important and pressing unresolved monetary problems. Marx's theory of money has still valuable insights to address them, while alternative heterodox theories of money have not been able to provide a more inclusive and coherent explanation and also struggle with the character of the unit of account and world money. I hope this chapter contributes to channelling the debate toward the open issues to advance in answers to the questions of our time.

Acknowledgements

I thank Magalí Brosio, Eurydice Fotopoulou, Juan M. Graña, Rubén Lo Vuolo, Jon Mulberg, Joel Rabinovich, Cecilia Rikap, Alfredo Saad-Filho, and the attendees to the 22nd Annual Conference of the Association for Heterodox Economics, where a previous version of this paper received the Early Career Prize for Best Conference Paper, for valuable comments on previous versions of this article. All remaining errors are my own.

Notes

1 Here, I differ with de Brunhoff's argument that '(…) a theory of money applicable to the capitalist system must be subsumed under a theory of money in general, valid for every monetary economy; in other words, a general theory of money' (2015: 19). For a critique of her position in this regard, see Campbell (2017). In a nutshell, this chapter argues that money is a specifically capitalist thing. Previous societies had units of account and means of circulation, but they cannot be properly understood as 'money'.

2 However, this is not to say that money makes commodities commensurable. Commodities are commensurable as values, while money is the way in which they express their quantitative relation (de Brunhoff, 2015; Campbell, 2017; Weber, 2019). In this regard, Backhaus says:

> no physicist would ever make the absurd claim that the Parisian *mètre des archives* or any other measure of length has the 'function' to make what is to be measured commensurable. The dimension of size is a priori common to heterogeneous things. The dimension of size is the precondition, not the result of measuring.
>
> (1997: 351, quoted in Weber [2019: 1472–1473])

3 For a longer discussion on Marx's view and formalizations of them, see Moseley (2011) and Shaikh (2016).

4 Marx was aware that the unit of account could change, but he pointed that out as a historical remark, without stating how that affected the function.

> As a result of an historical process … the names of particular weights were retained for constantly changing and diminishing weights of precious metals functioning as the standard of price. Thus the English pound sterling denotes less than one-third of its original weight … Historical development thus led to a separation of the money names of certain weights of metals from the common names of these weights.
>
> (Marx, 2010: 310)

5 Consequently, Marx argues that in crisis the credit system collapsed back to its monetary base. This is one of the points of contention from those who challenge the commodity character of money. See, for example Ganssmann (1998) and Lipietz (1982).

References

Arthur, C. J. (2005) 'Value and money', in Moseley, F. (ed.) *Marx's theory of money: Modern appraisals*. New York: Palgrave Macmillan, pp. 111–123.

Bellofiore, R. (1989) 'A monetary labour theory of value', *Review of Radical Political Economics*, 21(1–2), pp. 1–25.

Bellofiore, R. (2005) 'The monetary aspects of the capitalist process in the Marxian system: An investigation from the point of view of the theory of the monetary circuit', in Moseley, F. (ed.) *Marx's theory of money: Modern appraisals*. New York: Palgrave Macmillan, pp. 124–139.

Benetti, C. (1990) *Moneda y teoría del valor*. México: Universidad Autónoma Metropolitana y Fondo de Cultura Económica.

de Brunhoff, S. (2005) 'Marx's contribution to the search for a theory of money', in Moseley, F. (ed.) *Marx's theory of money: Modern appraisals*. New York: Palgrave Macmillan, pp. 209–221.

de Brunhoff, S. (2015) *Marx on money*. London and New York: Verso.

de Brunhoff, S. and Foley, D. (2006) 'Karl Marx's theory of money and credit', in Arestis, P. and Sawyer, M. (eds.) *A handbook of alternative monetary economics*. Cheltenham, UK and Northampton, MA: Edward Elgar, pp. 188–204.

Caligaris, G. and Starosta, G. (2016) 'Explicación sistemática y análisis histórico en la crítica de la economía política. Un aporte metodológico a la controversia sobre la naturaleza mercantil del dinero', in Escorcia Romo, R. and Robles Báez, M. L. (eds.) *Dinero y capital. Hacia una reconstrucción de la teoría de Marx sobre el dinero*. Ciudad de México: Universidad Autónoma Metropolitana-Unidad Xochimilco y Editorial Itaca, pp. 123–158.

Campbell, M. (2017) 'Marx's transition to money with no intrinsic value in capital, Chapter 3', *Continental Thought & Theory: A Journal of Intellectual Freedom*, 1(4), pp. 207–230.

Duque, J. J. (2020) 'State involvement in cryptocurrencies. A potential world money?', *Japanese Political Economy*, 46(1), pp. 65–82. doi: 10.1080/2329194X.2020.1763185

Evans, T. (1997) 'Marxian theories of credit money and capital', *International Journal of Political Economy*, 27(1), pp. 7–42.

Fleetwood, S. (2000) 'A Marxist theory of commodity money revisited', in Smithin, J. (ed.) *What is money?* London and New York: Routledge, pp. 174–193.

Foley, D. (1983) 'On Marx's theory of money', *Social Concept*, 1(1), pp. 5–19.

Foley, D. (2005) 'Marx's theory of money in historical perspective', in Moseley, F. (ed.) *Marx's theory of money: Modern appraisals*. New York: Palgrave Macmillan, pp. 36–49.

Friedenthal, T. (2013) 'El dinero: naturaleza, génesis y funciones, un estudio de los fundamentos para su conocimiento presente en el capital de Marx'. PhD thesis, Universidad de Buenos Aires. Facultad de Ciencias Económicas, Buenos Aires.

Ganssmann, H. (1998) 'The emergence of credit money', in *Marxian economics: A reappraisal essays on volume III of capital. Volume 1: Method, value and money*. London and New York: Macmillan Press, pp. 145–156.

Germer, C. (1997) 'Credit money and the functions of money in capitalism', *International Journal of Political Economy*, 27(1), pp. 43–72.

Germer, C. (2005) 'the commodity nature of money in Marx's theory', in Moseley, F. (ed.) *Marx's theory of money: Modern appraisals*. New York: Palgrave Macmillan, pp. 21–35.

Graziani, A. (1997) 'The Marxist theory of money', *International Journal of Political Economy*, 27(2), pp. 26–50.

Iñigo Carrera, J. (2007) *Conocer el capital hoy. Usar criticamente El capital*. Buenos Aires: Imago Mundi.

Itoh, M. and Lapavitsas, C. (1999) *Political economy of money and finance*. New York: Palgrave Macmillan.

Ivanova, M. N. (2013) 'The dollar as world money', *Science & Society*, 77(1), pp. 44–71.

Ivanova, M. N. (2020) 'Marx's theory of money: A reappraisal in the light of unconventional monetary policy', *Review of Radical Political Economics*, 51(1), pp. 137–151. https://doi.org/10.1177/0486613419856727

Kennedy, P. (2000) 'A Marxist account of the relationship between commodity money and symbolic money in the context of contemporary capitalist development', in Smithin, J. (ed.) *What is money?* London and New York: Routledge, pp. 194–216.

Labrinidis, G. (2014a) 'International reserves in the era of quasi-world money', *Research on Money and Finance Discussion Papers*, (46). Accessed at: https://mpra.ub.uni-muenchen.de/59963/1/RMF-46-Labrinidis.pdf.

Labrinidis, G. (2014b) 'The forms of world money', *Research on Money and Finance Discussion Papers*, (45). Accessed at: https://mpra.ub.uni-muenchen.de/59962/1/RMF-45-Labrinidis.pdf

Lapavitsas, C. (2013) *Profiting without producing. How finance exploits us all*. London and New York: Verso.

Lapavitsas, C. (2017a) 'Money and the analysis of capitalism: The significance of commodity money', in Marxist *monetary theory: Collected papers of Costas Lapavitsas*. Leiden and Boston: Brill, pp. 94–121.

Lapavitsas, C. (2017b) 'The theory of credit money: A structural analysis', in *Marxist monetary theory: Collected papers of Costas Lapavitsas*. Leiden and Boston: Brill, pp. 23–50.

Lavoie, D. (1986) 'Marx, the quantity theory, and the theory of value', *History of Political Economy*, 18(1), pp. 155–170.

Lipietz, A. (1982) 'Credit money: A condition permitting inflationary crisis', *Review of Radical Political Economics*, 14(2), pp. 49–57.

Marx, K. (1976) *Capital. A critique of political economy. Volume I*. London: Penguin.

Marx, K. (1999) *Capital. A critique of political economy. Volume III*. Accessed at: www.marxists.org/archive/marx/works/1850/pol-econ/index.htm.

Marx, K. (2010) *Marx and Engels collected works. Volume 29, Marx, 1857-61*. Lawrence Wishart. Accessed at: www.hekmatist.com/Marx%20Engles/Marx%20&%20Engels%20Collected%20Works%20Volume%2029_%20M%20-%20Karl%20Marx.pdf

Matthews, P. H. (1996) 'The modern foundations of Marx's monetary economics', *European Journal of the History of Economic Thought*, 3(1), pp. 61–83.

Moseley, F. (2005) 'Introduction', in Moseley, F. (ed.) *Marx's theory of money: Modern appraisals*. New York: Palgrave Macmillan, pp. 1–18.
Moseley, F. (2011) 'The determination of the "monetary expression of labour time" ("MELT") in the case of non-commodity money', *Review of Radical Political Economics*, 43(1), pp. 95–105.
Nelson, A. (2005) 'Marx's objections to credit theories of money', in Moseley, F. (ed.) *Marx's theory of money: Modern appraisals*. New York: Palgrave Macmillan, pp. 65–77.
Reuten, G. (1988) 'The money expression of value and the credit system: A value-form theoretic outline', *Capital & Class*, 12(2), pp. 121–141.
Reuten, G. (2005) 'Money as constituent of value', in Moseley, F. (ed.) *Marx's theory of money: Modern appraisals*. New York: Palgrave Macmillan, pp. 78–92.
Rotta, T. and Paraná, E. (2022) 'Bitcoin as a digital commodity', *New Political Economy*, 27(6), pp. 1046–1061. https://doi.org/10.1080/13563467.2022.2054966
Saad-Filho, A. (1993) 'Labor, money, and 'labour-money': A review of Marx's critique of John Gray's monetary analysis', *History of Political Economy*, 25(1), pp. 65–84.
Shaikh, A. (2016) *Capitalism: Competition, conflict, crises*. Oxford and New York: Oxford University Press.
Vasudevan, R. (2009) 'From the gold standard to the floating dollar standard: an appraisal in the light of Marx's theory of money', *Review of Radical Political Economics*, 41(4), pp. 473–491.
Vasudevan, R. (2014) 'Quantitative easing through the prism of the Barings crisis in 1890: Central banks and the international money market', *Journal of Post Keynesian Economics*, 37(1), pp. 91–114. https://doi.org/10.2753/PKE0160-3477370107
Vasudevan, R. (2018) 'Shadow money in the 19th century: Is Marx relevant for understanding contemporary shadow money?', *Review of Political Economy*, 30(3), pp. 461–483. doi: 10.1080/09538259.2018.1478509
Weber, I. M. (2019) 'On the necessity of money in an exchange-constituted economy: The cases of Smith and Marx', *Cambridge Journal of Economics*, 43(6), pp. 1459–1483.
Weeks, J. (2012) 'The theory and empirical credibility of commodity money', *Science & Society*, 76(1), pp. 66–94.
Williams, M. (2000) 'Why Marx neither has nor needs a commodity theory of money', *Review of Political Economy*, 12(4), pp. 435–451.
World Gold Council. (2022) *Gold outlook 2022*. Accessed at: www.gold.org/goldhub/research/gold-outlook-2022

Section 3

Economics Education and Change

7 Qualitative Economics and the Opportunity to Push for Heterodoxy in the Classroom

Juan David Parra

Introduction

Pluralism as Methodological Integration

As the Cambridge economist Ha Joon Chang reminds us in his best-selling book *Economics: The User's Guide,* "[there] is no such thing as one theory that can explain everything better than others" (Chang, 2014, p. 69). During an academic conference in northern Colombia back in 2020, the influential heterodox thinker had the opportunity to expand his view on the necessity of *pluralism* in research in economics. He first suggested that using theories to explain social events should respond to the problem at stake, given the thematic focus of (or the issues addressed by) the intellectual traditions that gave them birth in the first place. For instance, he argued that the neoclassical school of economics does a good job exploring individual decisions in simple markets but might not be genuinely relevant to inform studies on industrial innovation. He also claimed that alternative theoretical constructs respond to different assumptions – or ontologies[1] – and advised young scholars to engage with exploratory fieldwork before defining what theories to use to make sense of the empirical world.

My reflection in this chapter elaborates on the following question: What accounts for an acceptable educational strategy to strengthen the analytical skills of economics students to (prepare them to) follow Chang's advice? This inquiry seems to be a relevant one, considering contemporary voices arguing the importance of enforcing pluralism in the curriculum at universities to counterbalance the public-policy mainstream mindset that has contributed to shaping recent world financial crises (Mearman, Berger & Guizzo, 2022; Decker, Elsner & Flechtner, 2018; Raworth, 2017). However, researchers warn also of the pedagogical challenge this entails because of the risk of overwhelming students and deterring them from learning about non-mainstream economic traditions (Obeng-Odoom, 2019; Fine, 2019; Mearman et al., 2011). Mearman et al. (2011) therefore suggest that learners should not be "exposed to concepts too far outside their *zone of proximal development*, [as] (…) trying to understand the contrast between, say, mainstream and radical viewpoints may be too difficult" (p. 54. *Original emphasis*).

DOI: 10.4324/9781003451990-11

One natural benchmark model for the type of educational strategy this chapter sets to reflect upon is the popular *Curriculum Open-access Resources in Economics* project, or CORE, which has arguably contributed to reshaping mainstream curricular designs of more than 300 universities worldwide (Bowles & Carlin, 2020). Leading exponents of this model share the belief in the urgency of amplifying the exposure of students to different economic theories in the classroom but also warn about the risk of overexposing them to rich accounts of alternative schools of thought. In their case, they raise such a concern based on a more instrumental than a per se pedagogical argument, in the sense that they focus more on *what* students should learn – for example, to be competent in analysing certain economic phenomena – instead of asking how to engage them in inspecting and contrasting theoretical accounts. Consequently, they see it essential to avoid "[reducing] the study of economics to a kind of paradigm tournament, conveying little or no common analytical core concepts" (Bowles & Carlin, 2020, p. 208). Their teaching alternative consists in attempting *pluralism by integration.* It involves "integrating insights of differing schools of thought and (…) other disciplines *into a coherent paradigm* (…) [to] give students analytical tools (…) to *do economics rather than simply to talk about it*" (p. Ibid. *Emphasis added*).

It is hard to deny the merits of CORE for its potential to foster "gradual, significant change in the teaching and application of economics" (Mearman, Guizzo & Berger, 2018, p. 13). At a certain level, the mere fact that this proposal contributes to introducing heterodox thinking (plainly understood as any positions challenging the mainstream) in academic training deserves celebrating. However, I think some emerging comments (and critiques) on the pedagogical nature of this benchmark model also deserve equal consideration. For example, as Mearman, Guizzo and Berger (2018) have noted, "CORE claims to abandon canonical teaching and prioritise data to promote an empirical approach to economics" (p. 252). This last comment unveils its *top-down pedagogical* approach, which seems not to invite students to reflect on different theories as much as to seek to endow them with skills to analyse data using a pre-given theoretical apparatus (or *coherent paradigm*). Sheehan, Embery and Morgan (2015) provide indicative evidence of this when they assert that "[t]he material is not set up to enable them to look at a problem from multiple points of view and to genuinely question the grounds on which an analysis proceeds" (p. 216).

As Mearman, Guizzo and Berger (2018) further contend in their detailed analysis of CORE's teaching proposal, the critiques mentioned earlier reflect, in the end, a poor commitment to dealing seriously with alternative theory building and exploration. As they put it,

> CORE does not treat [alternative] schools [of thought] as having live research programmes. Instead, [these] are either treated as defunct bodies of theory confined to the history of economic thought or their critiques are superficially co-opted, with no injunction to engage meaningfully with them.
>
> (p. 249)

I hence see this benchmark methodological proposal (problematically) falling in what Stilwell (2019) has identified as the same *monist trap* of many mainstream economists of simply pushing their *own barrow* –"by espousing only their own preferred [theoretical] alternative to the orthodoxy" (p. 41). That orientation is contrary to responding to Chang's (2014) invitation to motivate to engage in the contrast of possible theoretical explanations for specific economic events. Furthermore, it might even limit the scope of the CORE project itself, vis-à-vis the goal set by its exponents of securing the provision of proper skills in students for doing real-life economics. As Sheila Dow (2003), the influential pluralist economist, reminds us, *the real social world* "does not lend itself to representation by a singular, deductive axiomatic system" (p. 20), meaning that even if students master one (alternative) theory, that will never be enough to equip them to make sense of (many) economic realities.[2]

Interestingly Dow (2019) herself has also reflected more recently on the education of economists debate – and from the awareness that the kind of monism criticised above "is all the more insidious in that it discourages critical thinking [in students]" (p. 25). I interpret her work in that area as decidedly moving away from the teaching principle of pluralism *by theoretical integration* (in the vein of the CORE project's proposal) to favour more instead the notion of pluralism by *methodological integration.* Consider, for instance, the following excerpt of her authorship where she further develops this idea:

> Even more fundamental is that a pluralist curriculum includes material on the methodology of economics. Differences between schools of thought are associated with methodological differences, so students need some understanding of how to appraise different methodologies (as well as economic theories). The capacity and skills for critical thinking need to be learnt for application to methodology. But, further, an understanding of methodology is fundamental to understanding the whole rationale for a pluralist curriculum, and how it can be applied during subsequent careers. As future practising economists, students will need to be equipped to make their own choice of approach. This requires understanding what each approach involves, but also why one approach may come more naturally than another (because of otherwise unacknowledged ontology and epistemology). They will also need to be equipped to justify their choice of approach and engage in debate with others. All of this requires methodological awareness, something more evident in the other social sciences but increasingly absent in economics.
>
> (p. 26)

The teaching strategy I present in this chapter – thinking about how to answer the research question I previously announced – borrows or incorporates many of the elements suggested by Dow (2019) in this last quote. Consequently, it will distance from alternatives, such as the CORE project, in the sense that I emphasise –as Dow suggests – understanding the methodological foundations of different economic theories before considering using them instrumentally to analyse empirical data. It also builds on the idea that what makes a future economist competent to explore and make sense of economic realities is not the knowledge per se of various theories or approaches but rather the analytical skills to understand their internal consistency and real-life applications. Arguably these principles in thinking on a course design to encourage students to engage with schools of thought beyond the mainstream cohere with Sheehan, Embery and Morgan's (2015) general invitation to "[give] students something to think about, rather than telling them what to think" (p. 230).

Begin by Teaching Qualitative Methods to Economists

Dow's (2019) reflection mentioned earlier includes one additional message I think we should not ignore if we want to see success in any education strategy in creating awareness in young students on the importance of embracing heterodoxy. In the last sentence of the quote, she reaffirms the critique also raised by others [e.g. Fine (2019) and Raworth (2017)] on how the professional economists' guilds tend to dismiss these methodological discussions, sponsoring a discourse that there exists *only one correct way* of doing economics. Consequently, many students might feel that exploring heterodox thinking (seriously) is a waste of time (or, using a more formal expression, has a *high opportunity cost*; Lenger, 2019), also deterring them from wanting to deviate from the mainstream economic mindset.

Hence, the importance I see in exploring learning theory and the invitation of some scholars to conceive teaching at this level as an *act of persuasion* –or as rejecting "the assumption that all students will accept whatever information is introduced into the learning environment fully or in part" (Murphy, 2001, p. 224). For philosophers of education, this translates into the argument that the disposition to learn (e.g. new theories) emerges from the learners' internal deliberations and practical demands for new or specific knowledge (Parra, 2018; Kahn, 2014). Harackiewicz, Smith and Priniski's (2016) overview of relevant literature from the field of behavioural and brain sciences concurs with that idea by placing a focus on the importance of promoting interest in education:

> From an interest theory perspective, problem-based learning provides a learning environment that can trigger and maintain situational interest. First, the problem presented to students highlights a lack of critical knowledge needed to solve the problem, which can trigger situational interest. Second, the search for answers to the problem stimulates curiosity questions—self-generated questions that can promote the development of deeper interest—while requiring students to acquire and organise new knowledge about the topic, which can promote both interest and learning.
>
> (p. 224)

Overall, these principles point to the centrality of triggering the situational interests of students as a pre-condition to encourage them to explore alternative economic traditions or thinking. Said differently, one effective strategy to motivate young economists to explore alternative visions in their discipline departs from *not trying* to address these alternatives *explicitly* in the first place. I instead suggest beginning that quest by first triggering the student's interest in a particular research problem and then providing them with tools to assess (perhaps) mainstream popularised explanations about the topic vis-à-vis what it offers to understand the issue at hand. Based on the realisation that they require more knowledge to find satisfactory answers, such a strategy could help incept the thought that exploring alternative accounts is a good idea.[3]

That way, I have concluded the main argument for the (out-of-the-box, I believe) proposal I will present in the rest of this chapter (which I already outlined in the title): I will start by teaching qualitative methods to economics students. I support that decision in the generally accepted view that qualitative thinking and skills invite people "framing the obvious and looking for traces of that which is less visible or vanishing. It involves becoming consciously aware of ways of thinking that we take for granted and to challenge areas rarely considered" (Swaminathan & Mulvihill, 2018, p. 43). I will further develop this argument during the chapter. I will also reflect upon another act of persuasion I have to consider in my overall teaching strategy, which entails addressing the reluctance of (at least mainstream) economists towards qualitative approaches to economic inquiry (Lenger, 2019; Starr, 2014).

The narrative I present in the rest of the chapter emulates the messages I convey to students throughout the course modules of my class. It includes (i) a justification of the topic (why learning qualitative methods), (ii) the introduction of a methodological framework to situate qualitative research designs in economics research, and (iii) the presentation of a class project inviting students to pose research questions about a topic of their interest. I decided to use that structure – in opposition to one in which each section deals with specific theoretical or methodological discussions – because I intend to inspire detailed class designs to teach qualitative methods to economics students.[4]

Conveying the Role of Qualitative Thinking in Economics

Some Opening Arguments to Spark Interest in Students of Economics

As mentioned earlier, before arriving at specific methodological orientations on the *mechanics* of analysing the world qualitatively, it is crucial to persuade students of the benefits of learning these particular skills. That is the case because, according to Starr (2014), there exists a tendency within the economics profession "to associate 'good' research qualities (representativeness, rigour, objectivity, explanation) with quantitative data and methods, and corresponding 'bad' ones (un-representativeness, informality, subjectivity, description) with the qualitative" (p. 240). Consequently, I argue that the challenge of unleashing the pedagogical principles outlined earlier about profiting from the teaching of qualitative thinking to (eventually) spark the interest in students in exploring different theoretical traditions in their discipline begins with this first act of persuasion.

Starr's (2014) paper published in the prestigious *Journal of Economic Surveys* summarises common arguments cited by scholars in that field to advocate for mixed methods research, hence representing a valuable pedagogical source for this purpose.[5] In her account, consulting qualitative sources is justified in some of the following situations:

> (a) when very little is known about the topic, so that broad exploratory research is needed to identify its basic characteristics; (b) when there has already been a lot of quantitative research on the subject, but key questions remain unresolved; (c) when back-and-forth with an interviewer is thought to be needed to help elicit full and accurate information; (d) when the topic under investigation has some inherent complexities the researcher wants to be able to capture.
>
> (pp. 240–241)

Jha, Rao and Woolcock (2007)'s paper, also published in a widely read journal by mainstream economists, helps expand Starr's (2014) overall argument and, in my view, pushes it even further:

> The quantitative analysis of survey data has the advantage of making generalisable statements about large populations, but it is disadvantaged by an unwieldy apparatus that tends to limit what it reveals to hypotheses that circulate within academic or policy circles (…). Informed by potentially dated secondary literatures, these [analyses] run the risk of overlooking the current reality of the subjects under study (…). Our paper goes a step further by (…) integrating participatory appraisals, focus group discussions, in-depth interviews, and participant observation with quantitative data from representative surveys. The survey instruments emerge from the qualitative investigation, drawing on insights from the field to define the topics of interest and identify the appropriate methods of measurement.
>
> (Jha, Rao & Woolcock, 2007, p. 231)

These quotes are straightforward in suggesting to students in faculties of economics that the knowledge of at least some qualitative research skills might improve the usefulness of the toolbox of their discipline. In a nutshell, qualitative inquiry can motivate new research questions, might inform the building of surveys to analyse econometrically and perhaps, more importantly, can assist in unravelling complex explanations behind events we observe through variations in metrics and social indicators. Moreover, as the second quote emphasises, qualitative inquiry opens a potential scope for innovation in economics research by allowing researchers to question existing explanations that are perhaps insufficient for specific topics. In line with this chapter's introductory reflection, this last idea is already anticipating part of the argument on the usefulness of looking for alternative viewpoints (or theories) to do better research in economics.

Here I also find it helpful to quote Gertler et al.'s (2016) influential manual on impact evaluation – a topic that has gained momentum in recent years as fundamental in the training of economists. These authors acknowledge explicitly that qualitative inquiry has a role in informing researchers and policymakers about the underlying social processes that help explain why econometric models show or not statistically significant results about the effects of policy interventions:

> Qualitative data provide context and explanations for the quantitative results (…). In this way, qualitative work can help explain why certain results are observed in the quantitative analysis and can be used to get inside the "black box" of what happened in the program.
>
> (p. 16)

These arguments on the potential contribution of qualitative analysis in economic research resemble the ones contained in the previously cited articles, particularly vis-à-vis the need to explore the inherent complexities behind economic (or policy) events. Still, the elements in Gertler et al.'s (2016) narrative sound (somehow) less abstract as they present them in the context of *practical* discussions on how to use public resources efficiently (e.g. employing *evidence-based* policy). In such a way, I show students that scholars within the same (mainstream) discipline open some space for other approaches (or methodologies) to complement their work. They even recognise that such knowledge might help improve their analytical skills and competencies to act as *good economists*. I argue that in this phase of the study plan, an opportunity arises to suggest specific methods from qualitative traditions that might fit this overall narrative.

Introducing Qualitative Economics

One central element in the training of economists is the use of models to describe and predict the behaviour of economic agents (Mearman, Berger & Guizzo, 2022). These models often rely upon assumptions of rational and hence predetermined (or fixed) social preferences (Bowles & Carlin, 2020). Experienced heterodox educators like Fine (2019) not only confirm this reality but express surprise that the rigour in the teaching of sophisticated mathematical and statistical techniques frequently occurs "without simultaneously having developed conceptual understandings and a keen sense of what is important or not" (p. 81). While we could further elaborate on this critique with students, my course's rhetoric instead – and strategically – emphasises that mainstream economists are ready to accept the value of doing (some) qualitative work to understand social interactions underlying their mathematical and statistical models.

This raises the question: How can we rationalise qualitative analysis's role in economics research, again, without exposing students to concepts too far from their comfort zone? In preparing the class materials, I found a plausible answer in Woodrow & Fast's (2019) work in *qualitative economics* (as they have baptised it). These authors' narrative departs from problematising contemporary economic thought's objectivist and rationalistic methodological foundations. Their approach focuses instead "upon the [subjective] economic actions of people, groups, and their networks in everyday (…) life and how they are trying to make sense of the present and construct the future" (p. 2). The point I highlight here (with students) is not the critique of mainstream economics, per se, but instead on their invitation to study "the dynamics of human change within society" (p. 22). Such an approach arguably responds to economists' demand (cited before) to get inside the *black box* of quantitative analyses. As Starr (2014) puts it, guilds of economists are willing to recognise that "bringing the perceptions, experiences and understandings of research subjects into discussions of economic issues and topics that concern them can yield unexpected and highly valuable insights" (p. 258).

The proponents of this tradition see the analysis of business economics as a case in point of their discourse applied to real-world economic events. For instance, the proposal of rephrasing classical economic dilemmas – like the neoclassical theory of the firm – using *Symbolic Interactionism*[6] – serves the purpose of conveying to analysts of the economy the importance of focusing not only on measuring inputs and outputs but on exploring meaning and interpretation in the human processes involved.[7] To see it, consider their following assertion:

> The firm should be understood as the actions and meaning knowledge of the individual actor and of the actors' collective actions over time (…). In this organising, intersubjective moving pictures of what the firm and the environment are will be created among the actors and create a view of seeing, both on themselves and of the context. The firm and its development come from interpretation and understanding of the situation by those actors who are involved in their organisational actions.
>
> (Woodrow & Fast, 2019, p. 212)

While arguably, this view of a firm's activity entails departing from the neoclassical paradigm of profit-maximising behaviour, the intention here is to convey to students the message that the notion of causal inquiry in economic research requires asking questions centred on how agents interact in specific contexts or environments (Downward & Mearman, 2007; Dow, 2003). Therefore I discuss with them the importance of anticipating that in any economic study, the people involved "have to live with and exist with uncertainty and ambiguity", and consequently, they are "exposed to many different interpretations and understandings" (Fast & Woodrow, 2012, p. 167). At that moment, I can start bridging the scope of their potential academic research interests as economists (e.g. understanding why X happens) and the value qualitative analytic skills portray. That is the case because, precisely, according to Maxwell (2013), one of the central intellectual goals of the latter is to contribute to "[u]nderstanding the meaning, for participants in the study, of the events, situations, experiences, and actions they are involved with or engage in" (p. 30).

An Overall Methodology to Teach Qualitative Reasoning

Qualitative Inquiry Is Not (or Should Not Be) that Messy

Despite the openness of (at least some) mainstream economists to explore the inclusion of qualitative methods in their research toolbox, I argue that doing so also entails pedagogical (and rhetorical) considerations. A common belief exists in the profession that non-quantitative inquiry is messy (or unstructured) and too subjective (Starr, 2014). Lenger's (2019) survey study among professors, journal editors and even economics postdoctoral students in Germany confirms the existence of a "methodological criticism of the open question structure [perceived as one distinctive feature of qualitative research], which was classified as 'too ambiguous'" (p. 958). He, therefore, interprets that "[t]here is a desire for clarification and definition (…) to reduce uncertainty and facilitate greater control (…) with regard to the data being generated" (p. 958).

As I have argued elsewhere, I do agree with the general feeling (of, perhaps, mainstream economists) that some orientations (or approaches) to qualitative research are indeed excessively (and unjustifiably) unstructured (Parra, Said-Hung & Montoya-Vargas, 2021). In my view, shared by others (Emmel, 2013; Pawson, 1996), there exists a variety of commitments among qualitative-oriented researchers to the plausibility of generating causal knowledge[8] in social studies, which explains the preference among many of them for open-ended data collection and analysis techniques.[9] However, authors like Maxwell (2013) argue that qualitative inquiry does have a central role in the development of causal explanations of "how x plays a role in causing y" (p. 52). Arguably, this entails a need for bringing some systematicity to qualitative research designs, which is consistent with the economists' view of rigorous economic research (Downward & Mearman, 2007). My point in making this argument to students – again, without overwhelming them at this stage with the epistemological details of this discussion – is to address their possible internalised belief that qualitative research is simply messy and, hence, of little use to inform rigorous empirical work.

Maxwell (2013) himself – and in the same line as other authors sharing his epistemic orientation – presents theory-based research designs as providing a rationale for a kind of qualitative inquiry able to answer the type of causal questions he has in mind [see, e.g. Brouselle & Burejeya (2018)]. He writes that using preliminary theory to inform data collection and analysis plans "illuminates what you see. It draws your attention to particular events or phenomena, and sheds light on relationships that might otherwise go unnoticed or misunderstood" (Maxwell, 2013, p. 75). Before rationalising this argument to students, I suggest a class exercise to illustrate how it is plausible and reasonable to resort to specific principles to use qualitative information to test theories in the field. Here I am particularly interested in persuading them how such a logic potentially answers many of the concerns of (perhaps mainstream) economists about the messiness of non-quantitative applied methods. I use *edutainment* – or instructional uses of television, videos or films – tools to assist me in making that (abstract) argument because of their potential "to generate enthusiasm, engage students with the content, and clarify new conceptual information" (Saldaña, 2008, p. 248).

The dialogue in Extract 1 is an excerpt from a video clip of a well-known TV series I present to students during class.

Extract 1

Setting: Jonathan and Nancy have a conversation in Nancy's bedroom. They are worried about their friend Barbara who, they believe, was kidnapped by a monster from another dimension.

"My mom said she talked to Will. If he is alive, there is a chance Barbara is, too."

"That means that she is trapped… in that place. We have to find it again."

"You wanna go back out there?"

"Maybe we don't have to. When I saw him, he was feeding on that deer. Meaning it's … it's a predator, right?"

"One sec… Sharks can detect blood in one part per million. That is one drop of blood in a million. And they can smell it from a quarter-mile away."

"So, you are saying it can detect blood?"

[Softly] "It is just a theory."

"We could test it. But if it works…"

"At least we'll know it's coming…"

Post scene: In chapter 8 of that same season of the tv series, they test their theory. They meet at Jonathan's house and prepare themselves for the arrival of the monster by placing some traps around the place. After deliberately cutting themselves across the palms of their hand, the blood of the wound made the monster appear. [10]

The second dialogue (Extract 2) of a videoclip, which I also present during the class, is from a classic film from the late 1990s.

Extract 2

Setting: three scientists in a laboratory, Dr. Eleanor Arroway, Fisher and Willie discovered a radio signal that is apparently arriving from a star system called Vega. They try to make sense of the pulsing noise.

"All right, let me hear it.

(PULSING)

Listen to that…It could be AWACS out of Kirtland jamming us. But I'm doubting it."

"Whatever it is, it ain't local. – Position?"

"[…] Somewhere in Lyra, I think. Vega?"

"Can't be"

[…]

"Vega. I scanned it a bunch of times at Arecibo. It was negative results, always."

[…]

All right, it's restarting.
Wait a minute. Those are numbers.
That was a three, the one before it was a two.
Base-10 numbers. Just start counting now, see how far can we get.
One.

"Seven."

"Seven. Those are primes.

2, 3, 5, 7, those are all prime numbers. There's no way that's a natural phenomenon.

…

Let's just calm down and pull up the star file on Vega."

"It doesn't make any sense. The system is too young...
so it can't have a planetary system ...
let alone life or a technological civilization."

"Maybe they didn't grow up there. Maybe they're visiting."

"Spacecraft? This system is full of debris.
It would get clobbered."

"Well, not if they used their laser blasters and photon torpedoes."

"That's not funny."

"How else are we gonna explain it?"

"Willie's right. If we go public with this and we're wrong, that's it. It's over. We're cooked."[11]

In my course's rhetoric, the first extract represents *good* practice in (causal) qualitative inquiry, while the second does not. They both have in common that the story's characters are trying to solve a problem. I argue that debating some contrasts in the alternative strategies used to seek an answer constitutes a pedagogical opportunity to convey central messages about the logic of qualitative reasoning in research to students (again, at least from the research paradigm I employ in my class).

Which strategy effectively assisted the characters in each situation to solve their query? By placing this question to students, I intend to start pointing out and inviting them to consider different elements involved in each scene, such as, for instance, the use of previous knowledge to build explanatory hypotheses or the specific role of theories in designing research strategies. These are elements that, as I will explain in more detail afterwards, constitute methodological pieces of a semi-structured approach to applied qualitative inquiry. From Extract 1 I highlight how the path towards solving the mystery of finding the monster involved a creative process of considering alternative explanations, which even drew Nancy and Jonathan to imagine the mystic creature *as if* it were a shark (e.g. a predator attracted by blood). In the case of Extract 2 the scientists failed to answer their dilemma even if they were experts in their field. That happened after several attempts to derive explanations directly from data.[12] It was probably the case because, in contrast to what happened in scene one, the protagonists could not anticipate potential explanatory hypotheses to assist them in interpreting observable events. In my view, one can express that same idea using specialised terminology from the theory-based approach or tradition informing qualitative inquiry (which shows the relevance of the methodological arguments expounded earlier):

> The most important thing to understand about your conceptual framework is that it is primarily a conception or model of what is out there that you plan to study, and of what is going on with these things and why—a tentative *theory* of the phenomena that you are investigating. The function of this theory is to inform the rest of your design—to help you to assess and refine your goals, develop realistic and relevant research questions, select appropriate methods, and identify potential validity threats to your conclusions.
>
> (Maxwell, 2013, pp. 39–40, *emphasis in original*)

At this point, citing to Emmel's (2013) work on qualitative sampling techniques intends to reinforce the idea that qualitative inquiry is about verifying and refining potential explanations (or preliminary theories) brought to researchers before fieldwork. It also serves to clarify to students more practical implications entailed in that qualitative research rationale:

> A scientific realist sampling strategy is driven through sets of ideas (or theories) about the social world we seek to investigate in a particular context. This theoretical understanding is invariably expressed in the early part of the research as research questions, which describe particular theoretical assumptions to be tested and refined. These frame the choices made about who or what to sample in the research.
>
> (p. 79)

At the end of this class module, I tell students a more formal way of outlining these overall reflections to frame these research principles using the notions of abductive and retroductive inference. As Jagosh (2020) presents them, "[w]hereas retroduction is inference to theorise and test hidden mechanisms [or, as I put it to students, the explanations we are aiming for], abduction is the inventive thinking required to imagine the existence of such mechanisms" (p. 122). The key point here is the notion of complexity in studying social interactions. As considered in the discussion of Woodrow and Fast's (2019) proposal on qualitative economics above, empirical events (or that observable economic phenome, like variations in price indexes or unemployment rates), result from people's interactions in specific contexts. To the extent that many of those interactions are unpredictable, linear reasoning (e.g. every time X happens, Y follows)[13] is logically flawed when explaining economic phenomena (Downward & Mearman, 2007; Wuisman, 2005). An alternative is to endorse iterative thinking to frame research designs. That is, thinking in advance – and based on available evidence – about potential and contextual relevant explanations (abduction) and choosing the most credible one (based on new evidence collected) vis-à-vis the phenomena we seek to explain (retroduction). In my view, Extract 1 illustrates that mode of abductive and retroductive reasoning combined, which is part of the rationale behind its selection among my class materials.

To reiterate my point, I make these last arguments to students partly responding to the assumption that economists often feel uncomfortable with the lack of structure they perceive as a typical characteristic of non-quantitative research. However, I believe the above reasoning endorses an (at least) semi-structured logic to introduce qualitative thinking in economic inquiry. Therefore, integrating (at least implicitly) the principles of abduction and retroduction to theorise economic phenomena is part of the pedagogical arsenal I bring to the class not only to persuade students about the benefits of exploring qualitative methods. It also intends to motivate them to start appropriating the logic of exploring alternative explanations as a good practice in social research.

The Class Project

For Vicent and Wapshott (2014), the theory-based research rationale expounded so far represents a cornerstone of the scientific approach to knowledge accumulation in social inquiry. "Where existing theory fails to explain what is observed", they write, "there is an opportunity to *abduct* and *retroduct* new forms of understanding" (p. 155. *Emphasis added*). Under this worldview, the research process "is not typically a linear progression" and, therefore – precisely because of complexity in the social word – "is likely to involve false starts as the researcher oscillates between exploring *what we know* (…) and considering that *which is 'out there'* but inadequately explained" (Ibid., *Emphases added*).

The final class project, consisting of making a research design incorporating qualitative methods to address each student's master's degree thesis topic, finds justification in the last methodological rationale. On the one hand, this exercise – that I explain below – will draw on the principle of departing research designs from *what we know* instead of, for instance, asking students to modify in advance their assumptions of reality expressed in alternative literature to the one they tend to consult. However, the discussion in the last section (regarding abduction and uncertainty) should have conveyed that these initial theories are necessarily provisional, meaning they need to be tested and refined in the field to explain specific economic events (Maxwell, 2013).[14] Therefore, the class project will also invite students to problematise their preliminary theoretical preferences based on (some) empirical data.

Notably, at this point in the course design, I have not mentioned class discussions on particular qualitative data collection or analysis tools or anything concerning technical issues like sampling specific strategies or validating (qualitative) findings. For Swaminathan and Mulvihill (2018), it seems pedagogically sound to deal with such topics in the advanced stages of the course. In reflecting on their vast experience in teaching qualitative research methods skills, they write that "we [should] not approach skill-building as separate from the emotional work that qualitative research involves" (p. 7). The final class project I present below responds to such a pedagogical principle by inviting students to reflect upon their master's degree project – to work on an issue I assume interests them. One main goal here is for them to develop, in the way, some qualitative data collection and analysis techniques to help them open the black box of their researched phenomena.

Phase 1: Thinking Critically about Dominant Explanations

During phase one of the final class assessment, I ask students to introduce their theoretical framework – whichever they decided to use in their thesis – to engage in a first abductive process or exercise. Again, the goal here is to start identifying assumptions (behind their preferred theory) of how different agents in their study interact to make different outcomes possible. To assist them in that first activity, we discuss a published study that, in my view, illustrates quite well the research principles outlined so far. To see how that is the case, it suffices to quote an excerpt of how its authors introduce their research problem (concerning the functioning of market incentives in education systems) and comment upon their general methodological rationale to address it:

> Existing research on quasi-markets, vouchers, and school competition has not reached clear conclusions concerning the costs and benefits of these policies, although it usually raises education equity concerns (…). Our main objective in this article is to explain how quasi-markets work in the education sector and to assess the extent to which related policies in fact generate new educational opportunities for the poor. (…) A key step in [our research design] lies in systematically articulating the main theoretical assumptions on which the policy to be analysed is grounded (…). To a great extent, the theoretical roots of [quasi-markets] in education can be traced to public choice theory, which is why we dedicate the second section of this article to identifying the main premises in this theory.
>
> (Verger, Bonal & Zancajo, 2016, pp. 225–225)

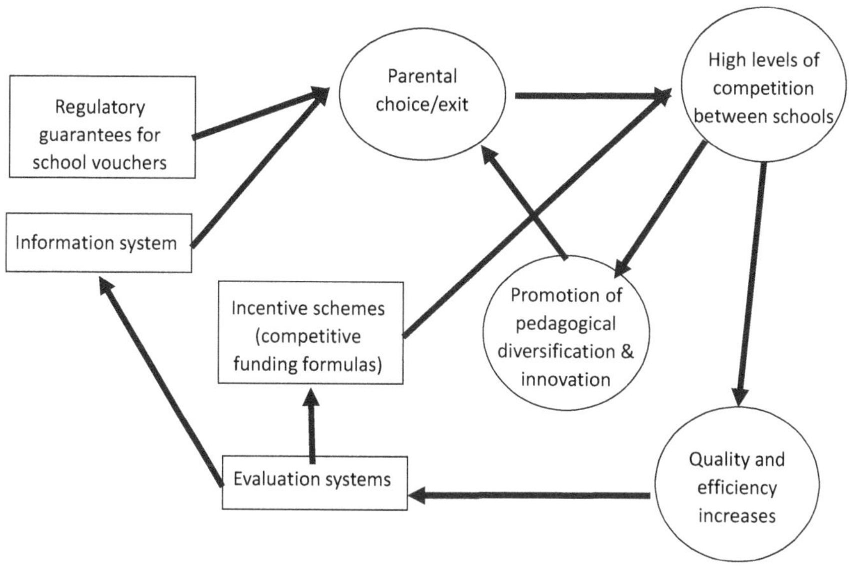

Figure 7.1 Example of a conceptual map: representation of the public choice theory in education.

Source: Adapted from Verger, Bonal and Zancajo (2016).

Figures 7.1 and 7.2, the first one from the cited paper and the second one built based on its content, summarise the results of the initial study's phases described earlier. Presenting the first one to students has the additional purpose of suggesting how to proceed with the first exercise of elucidating their initial research theories with the assistance of concept maps to pull together and make visible their implications (e.g. processes, inputs, outputs; Maxwell, 2013). Here it is worth noting that the paper's authors engaged in that exercise by calling the assumptions of a mainstream theoretical framework – public choice theory – in their field of study (see Figure 7.2), which is a way of departing their inquiry from *what we know*. As they discuss it, that worldview assumes rationalistic behaviour shaping interactions of educational agents to explain (potentially) why introducing market incentives (e.g. fostering school competition) should increase the efficiency (e.g. increase school innovation) of education systems.

Inspired by Verger, Bonal and Zancajo (2016)'s exercise – and before delving into other debates on how to start problematising (mainstream) theoretical frameworks using qualitative data – the students must prepare a class presentation. For that, they should generate a concept map (similar to Figure 7.1) and identify some underlying assumptions – based, for instance, on literature reviews they have already engaged with for the master's degree research – of the theories informing their thesis project (similar to Figure 7.2). Here they are allowed and encouraged to use their common

About families

...well informed family choices are the main trigger of school competition. According to market theory in education, access to objective and transparent information about the quality of the different providers are necessary for consumers to make accurate decisions. A voucher system needs to promote access to information on school quality to allow families to behave as competent consumers (...) Market advocates tend to think of families as "benefit maximisers" or as educational actors, whose decisions are guided exclusively by instrumental nationality.

About directors and educators

Schools in question will treat maximising children's learning outcomes as the clear priority; in fact, schools often have other interests and agendas that may be concealed from their "clients" (...). Economic theory identifies "asymmetric information" as the main factor underlying the principal – agent problem in school choice – the agent may know distinctly more about the possible transactions, trade-offs, and outcomes involved than the principal, and so be much better placed to give an appearance of compliance with the terms of the agreement, while in fact putting its own interests first.

Competition in the provision of the service.

The theory of education markets posits that it is providers' response in the competition to satisfy consumers' demand that ensures the highest level of market efficiency. There are two sides to this assumption. The first is encapsulated in the assertion that "school competition generates higher levels of efficiency and quality"; the second concerns the assumed levels of innovation and diversification associated with higher levels of competition (...) Under market theory one expects that numerous providers of the same service operating in the same territory will guarantee vibrant competition.

Figure 7.2 Main assumptions of public choice theory in education.

Source: Adapted from Verger, Bonal and Zancajo (2016).

sense (and hence, implicitly, their former knowledge of the subject matter) to ask what must be the case for X to become Y (throughout different stages of a theory of change represented in their map). For Maxwell (2013), these *thought experiments*, which are "regularly used in social sciences such as economics" (p. 68), are central in qualitative research as "they encourage creativity (…) to make explicit the experiential knowledge that [researchers] already possess" (p. 69).

The next phase of the class invites students to question those assumptions (of their initial abduction) more systematically by collecting and analysing some qualitative information to test and discard potential explanations. That exercise evokes retroduction. As I argue below, at this moment, class participants might start becoming aware of the potential advantages of exploring alternative (perhaps heterodox) theories to equip their research designs better.

The Class Project (Phase 2) – Doing Some Qualitative Data Collection and Analysis

To rationalise more technical matters to students – to prepare them for the final class assessment – I continue building upon Verger, Bonal and Zancajo's (2016) work (as an exemplar of how economists can approach applied qualitative inquiry), where they argue the following:

> To achieve [our research] objective, we focus on the case of Chile, the country that has embraced quasi-markets in education for the longest period and on the largest scale (…). [The] qualitative data of the study come from a sample of 10 schools in a socially mixed neighbourhood of the city of Valparaíso (…) Two public schools, seven private subsidised schools, and one fully private school composed the sample—a distribution of providers types is very similar to the average distribution prevailing in Chile and particularly representative of the school system in Valparaiso. In total, we interviewed 10 principals, 64 families, and 20 teachers. The interviews aimed at capturing the different logics of action and strategies on both the demand and the supply sides of the phenomenon. Results were analysed using categories that had been identified through review of [the public choice] literature on quasi-markets in education conducted prior to the field study.
>
> (pp. 224, 233)

In my view, this quote alone encapsulates essential intuitions for deploying the qualitative research approach endorsed in the course. First, the authors suggest that they have chosen the Chilean case to explore *different logics of action and strategies* of people, accounting for the various processes and connections outlined in Figure 7.1. That means that the selection of setting for their inquiry aimed to seek a specific context that made it possible to study central aspects of (or, as we put it before, social actions and interactions associated with) their preliminary theoretical hypotheses. They also clarify their use of interviews as their primary qualitative research method to collect information from a (relatively) small sample of schools (N=10) that, again, fits into specific characteristics that seem relevant to exploring the premises of the schooling quasi-market model. Finally, they tell readers how they have relied on the information gathered in their previous exploration of the literature to read and interpret their data. Altogether, I argue that this whole methodological argument clearly illustrates the implications of applied abduction and retroduction, as suggested before in the chapter.

Based on these premises, phase two of the class project consists of conducting an interview with an expert in the specific area of the student's research project and analysing it. Because this is a class exercise, I allow students to seek the best possible key informant they can have access to promptly – e.g. a professor from the university. I insist them, however, that during an actual case research scenario, they should justify that selection with their preliminary theories in mind.[15] Manzano's (2016) work is valuable at this stage of the course by providing a detailed guide on types of questions and suggestions about their specific sequencing during a conversation that researchers could adapt to explore previous theoretical constructs in the field. That means that in line with the qualitative research methodology expounded so far, she motivates researchers to make explicit efforts to test explanatory theories when conversing with experts. Using her words:

> The subject matter of the interview is the researcher's theory and interviewees are there to confirm, falsify and, basically, refine the theory. (…) It starts with teaching the interviewee 'the particular (…) theory under test' and then 'the respondent (…) is able to teach the [researcher] about those components (…) in a particularly informed way' (…). [Therefore] participant views are explored through conversations (and not ticking boxes).
>
> (Manzano, 2016, p. 355)

Notably, such a rationalisation of interviewing unveils a preference for semi-structured interview protocols [see also Pawson (1996)]. It also suggests to researchers what they should try doing during conversations – teaching and learning theories – and that (preliminary) theoretical constructs act as heuristic devices to maintain focus in the conversation and represent a point of reference to start interpreting/validating findings. Again, I assume that sharing these arguments with young economics should address their potential prejudgments about *extreme* subjectivity in qualitative inquiry.

Once the course participants have conducted their interviews, we meet in the classroom to discuss and apply data analysis. I ask them to bring their interview notes to the session and search for an opinion piece published in a national or local newspaper written by an expert on their topic of interest (to have an additional source to analyse). I then provide them with a printed version of the format in Table 7.1. As one can infer, this template attempts to recreate the logic behind an actual coding exercise (that many researchers engage in using computer-assisted qualitative data analysis software). In column A they must type an identifier for the social actor they interviewed/or read, and column B invites students to write down, in their own words, how this person reacted to each theory or hypothesis shared with them. In the case of the newspaper piece, I ask them to emulate a similar logic by relating excerpts of the columnist's analysis to potential answers to questions in the interview protocol. Column C then asks to identify relevant quotes from each source to back up the content included in column B. As I clarify to students in class, the point here is not to extract excerpts from conversations only to support

Table 7.1 Format to assist in the analysis of information

Interviewee/source (A)	*Findings that talk explicitly to different hypotheses (B)*	*Add quotes that support your finding (C)*	*Additional ideas and quotes (D)*
	1		
	2		
	3		
	1		
	2		
	3		

specific (and, in some cases, even arbitrary) interpretations of qualitative sources in the writing of research reports. On the contrary, such an exercise – of verifying that direct quotations do indeed illustrate specific arguments emerging from the student's analysis – "helps ensure that [the interpretation of an informants point] is fair and accurate" (Graff & Birkenstein, 2017, p. 42), hence contributing rigour and transparency in qualitative inquiry.

Finally, column D allows adding information that students felt was relevant to their discussion but could not figure out where to place it. Such possibility is essential in qualitative analysis because unexpected findings (vis-a-vis the theoretical background work) might contain analytical elements to invite new questions about potential causal drivers behind the analysed phenomena – which, once again, speaks to the logic of abduction (Gibbs, 2018).

The last session of the class focuses on the presentation of preliminary findings. Part of that reflection consists of conveying individual learnings of the interview process (e.g. what worked and what I would do differently in a future interview) and sharing thoughts about the potential value-added of qualitative inquiry in the participant's master's degree dissertation process. A pivotal moment regarding the general theme of this chapter on how to motivate students to explore heterodox schools of thought occurs when they reflect (responding to one of the indications to prepare that activity) on the extent to which the conversation with an expert validated preliminary explanations inspired in their original theoretical framework, and why. Because of the seminar's scope, we do not enter into details about those alternatives. However, I argue that when they realise that their initial theoretical preference is incapable of fully answering their research questions, that opens a potential demand for exploring heterodox literature in their research projects.

Closing Remarks

In this chapter, I addressed the teaching of economics debate regarding appropriate pedagogical strategies to motivate the exploration of alternative economic theories and traditions to the ones dominating the economics curriculum. Drawing on principles from psychological and learning theory in higher education, I suggest that one preliminary step to achieving that goal consists of persuading students of the benefits of deviating from the mainstream academic scholarship to build solid analytical foundations to study real-world economics. In that vein, I argue that teaching young economists some qualitative research skills and what it entails – for example motivating creativity in thinking about potential explanations to specific economic phenomena – represents a possible avenue to increase their demand for exploring heterodox economics.

Based on that premise, I presented some key features and steps into a pedagogical strategy I designed to introduce qualitative inquiry in an economics master's degree programme (in Colombia). The activities and assignments I outlined were thought anticipating prejudgments that (at least some) economists might have regarding the messiness of non-quantitative research strategies to collect and analyse information. I believe that doing otherwise – that is, using more traditional takes to teaching qualitative methods based on the contrast and critique of research epistemologies and paradigms – would obfuscate the ultimate goal of my course. Therefore, the ideas and arguments expounded above are relevant to the chapter's purpose – inviting ways to introduce heterodoxy in the training of economics – but might also inspire qualitative course designs in general.

Notes

1 A (perhaps) standard definition of ontology, useful for social scientists, describes it as "as a theory or set of assumptions concerning what 'exists' and thus what is and what is 'knowable'?" (Sumner & Tribe, 2008, p. 55). For instance, Verger Bonal and Zancajo (2016) assert that, from an ontological perspective, "Public choice theorists assume that human beings are rational and self-interested utility-maximizers and, on the basis of this core concept, construct the models that explain what they consider to be governmental failure in service provision" (p. 227). By contrast, Watson (2005) notes that if one alternatively decides to endorse an ontology from another school of thought, like old institutionalism, the assumptions about individual and social behaviour from which social theories emerge would differ. For instance, "Veblen's political economy is an attempt to understand the way in which the individual act through first understanding the social pressures that are brought to bear upon the individual to think and identify themselves in a particular way" (p. 96). In this economic theory framework, people do not behave and take decisions as isolated atoms –as in the public choice underlying ontology – but instead follow some habituated actions shaped by pre-existing social norms and values.

2 The author draws this conclusion by endorsing the philosophical tenets of Critical Realism, a research orientation philosophy that questions theoretical determinism in causal academic inquiry. Critical realists argue that the social world is an *open system* "subject to outside influences which cannot be anticipated (…) and evolution and interaction within the system which also cannot be anticipated" (Dow, 2003, p. 16). Therefore, they question the suitability of deduction in social inquiry – or the use of predefined theories "to explain and predict particular empirical phenomena (…) from a set of propositions about general regularities or universal laws" (Wuisman, 2005, p. 367) –, because that logic of research endorses a *closed-system* (or deterministic) ontology. The teaching proposal I present in this chapter departs from this same philosophical orientation.

3 The steps into the teaching strategy I will describe suit, I contend, the principles of an *immanent critique*, which is at the core of a realist approach to social research. It coheres, following Bhaskar (2016) with the idea of persuasion – as a goal of higher education – mentioned before: Immanent critique

> specifies that criticism of an idea or a system should be internal, that is, involve something intrinsic to what (or the person who) is being criticised. It typically identifies a theory/practice inconsistency, showing that the position being disputed involves a claim or analysis that would undermine the point, values or substance of the position (…). A moment's reflection shows indeed that this is the only way an argument can ever ultimately be won. Merely to assert what one believes will get nowhere unless it impinges in some way on what one's opponent believes.
>
> (pp. 2–3)

4 University instructors usually split their classes into modules and sessions. Each of those sessions introduces specific literature and theoretical references as they progress in students' learning process. Therefore, the structure of the chapter seeks to assist teachers in splitting their messages to students as they walk towards the ultimate learning goals of the whole seminar.

5 One could make such an argument by discussing alternative paradigms of thought and their preferred methodological stands. However, because of the points made before about the identity of economists, that strategy might result in a dead-end to motivate students to explore alternative methods.

6 They define this concept or approach as "the study of collective action between groups or organisations (…) through the symbols (and meaning of) involved in the interaction" (Woodrow & Fast, 2019, p. 26).

7 Some readers interested in the field of philosophy of knowledge might point out a potential contradiction in the rhetoric presented so far by arguing the incompatibility of symbolic interactionism – a strand of postmodernism – and the critical realist approach that I claim inspires my course design. However, I stand closer to Maxwell's (2012) interpretation of the critical realist tradition in that debate. In his view,

> Critical realism is also compatible with some of the assumptions and implications of postmodernism (…) [including] their [same] rejection of a unitary, objectivist concept of truth, and their affirmation of grounding of accounts in perspectives that are inevitable local rather than universal.
>
> (pp. 9, 67)

My point here is that endorsing some tenets of Woodrow and Fast's (2019) approach to qualitative economics does not entail that I am neglecting the possibility of finding plausible explanations for economic phenomena – given the postmodern stance against the plausibility of explanations at all. Instead, I recognise the centrality of the postmodern insight on the central role of studying various perspectives as an entry point to build a better understanding of real-life economics.

8 My reasoning, in this case, draws on the consideration that one distinctive feature of economists is their belief and endorsement of *causality* in their work, whether they identify as orthodoxy or heterodox, or despite differences in their approaches to study it (Lainà, 2018; Dopfer, 1986). Given different research paradigms' commitment to specific ontologies, not all social scientists (and qualitative researchers, in particular) believe in the possibility of building fallible causal knowledge about society Maxwell, 2013; Dow, 2003). Therefore, I argue that economics students might find more comfort with qualitative approaches – and rationales – that endorse causation as a central goal of applied research (Downward & Mearman, 2007).

9 For example to grasp multiple perceptions of reality in people's minds, which is the scope of research they attribute to qualitative methods.

10 Extract from 8flix.com (n.d.).

11 Extract from scriptslug.com (n.d.).

12 Deriving theory, or explanation, directly from data is consistent with the methodology of Grounded Theory. Implicitly, I am suggesting that such a tradition does not represent a best practice in causal-oriented qualitative research (Downward & Mearman, 2007).

13 Implicitly, here I am dealing with the methodological critique in the literature to pure induction as adequate inferential logics to frame causal research (Harman & Kulkarni, 2006; Wuisman, 2005).

14 As Maxwell's (2013) text also helps to clarify, that is an essential step into the quest for relevant answers to research puzzles because "[t]rying to fit your insights into established framework can deform your argument [and] weakening its logic" (p. 51).

15 Such an argument is consistent with the theory-testing qualitative research framework described earlier. As Manzano (2016) puts it,

> [s]ince the unit of analysis is not the person, but the events and processes around them (...) the importance is not on 'how many' people we talk to but on 'who', 'why' and 'how'. We are trying to understand how our interviewees understand and have experienced [the phenomena under research] and compare those experiences with our hypotheses.
>
> (pp. 348–349)

With such reasoning, I am implicitly answering another significant concern of (mainstream) economists, which is the issue of sampling in qualitative analysis. Indeed, Starr (2014) sees as a problem that "with economists schooled in the idea that 'more n is better', sample sizes considered to be sufficient in other fields (...) are usually viewed as too small to be informative by economists" (p. 244). The idea of purposive sampling – a sample relevant enough to explore a particular theoretical construct – that derives from the theory-based research framework that guides my teaching strategy might, therefore, contribute to answering concerns in the minds of economics students regarding the relevance of relatively small samples informing qualitative inquiry..

References

88flix.com (n.d.). *Stranger Things*, available at https://8flix.com/transcripts/stranger-things-season-1-dialogue/

Bhaskar, R. (2016). *Enlightened Common Sense: The Philosophy of Critical Realism.* London and New York: Routledge.

Bowles, S., & Carlin, W. (2020). What students learn in economics 101: Time for a change. *Journal of Economic Literature, 58*(1), 176–214.

Brouselle, A., & Burejeya, J.-M. (2018). Theory-based evaluations: Framing the existence of the new theory evaluation and the rise of the 5th generation. *Evaluation, 24*(2), 153–168.

Chang, H.-J. (2014). *Economics: The User's Guide.* London: Pelican Books.

Decker, S., Elsner, W., & Flechtner, S. (2018). Economics and its teaching at a critical juncture. In S. Decker, W. Elsner, & S. Flechtner, *Advancing Pluralism in Teaching Economics: International Perspectives on a Textbook Science* (pp. 1–10). London: Routledge.

Dopfer, K. (1986). Causality and consciousness in economics: Concepts of change in orthodox and heterodox economics. *Journal of Economic Issues, 20*(2), 509–523

Dow, S. (2003). Critical realism and economics. In P. Downward, *Applied Economics and the Critical Realist Critique* (pp. 12–26). London: Routledge.

Dow, S. (2019). Pluralist economics: Is it scientific? In S. Decker, W. Elsner, & S. Flechtner, *Advancing Pluralism in Teaching Economics: International Perspectives on a Textbook Science* (pp. 13–30). London: Routledge.

Downward, P., & Mearman, A. (2007). Retroduction as mixed-methods triangulation in economic research: Reorienting economics into social science. *Cambridge Journal of Economics, 31*, 77–99.

Edwards, P., O'Mahoney, J., & Vicent, S. (2014). Critical realism as an empirical project: A beginner's guide. In P. Edwards, J. O'Mahoney, & S. Vicent, *Studying Organizations Using Critical Realism: A Practical Guide* (pp. 1–20). Oxford: Oxford University Press.

Emmel, N. (2013). *Sampling and Choosing Cases in Qualitative Research: A Realist Approach.* London, Thousand Oaks, New Delhi, Singapore: Sage.

Fast, M., & Woodrow, C. I. (2012). Qualitative economics: A perspective on organization and economic science. *Theoretical Economics Letters, 2*(2), 162–164.

Fine, B. (2019). In and against orthodoxy: Teaching economics in the Neoliberal Era. In S. Decker, W. Elsner, & S. Flechtner, *Advancing Pluralism in Teaching Economics: International Perspectives on a Textbook Science* (pp. 78–94). London: Routledge.

Gertler, P. J., Martínez, S., Premand, P., Rawlings, L. B., & Vermeersch, C. M. (2016). *Impact Evaluation in Practice* (2nd ed.). Washington, DC: The World Bank.

Gibbs, G. (2018). *Analysing Qualitative Data* (2nd ed.). London: SAGE.

Graff, G., & Birkenstein, C. (2017). "They say / I say": *The Moves that Matter in Academic Writing* (3rd ed.). New York and London: W. W. Norton.

Harackiewicz, J., Smith, J., & Priniski, S. (2016). Interest matters: The importance of promoting interest in education. *Policy Insights from the Behavioral and Brain Sciences, 3*(2), 220–227.

Harman, G., & Kulkarni, S. (2006). The problem of induction. *Philosophy and Phenomenological Research, 72*(3), 559–575.

Isaksen, R. (2018). Without foundation or neutral standpoint: Using immanent critique to guide a literature review. *Journal of Critical Realism, 17*(2), 97–117.

Jagosh, J. (2020). Retroductive theorizing in Pawson and Tilley's applied scientific realism. *Journal of Critical Realism, 19*(2), 121–130.

Jha, S., Rao, V., & Woolcock, M. (2007). Governance in the gullies: Democratic responsiveness and leadership in Delhi's slums. *World Development, 35*(2), 230–246.

Kahn, P. (2014). Theorising student engagement in higher education. *British Educational Research Journal, 40*(6), 1005–1018.

Lainà, P. (2018). Meta-theory as a uniting framework for economics and global political economy. *Journal of Critical Realism, 17*(3), 221–232.

Lenger, A. (2019). The rejection of qualitative research methods in economics. *Journal of Economic Issues, 53*(4), 946–965.

Manzano, A. (2016). The craft of interviewing in realist evaluation. *Evaluation, 22*(3), 342–360.

Maxwell, J. (2012). *A Realist Approach for Qualitative Research.* London: SAGE.

Maxwell, J. (2013). *Qualitative Research Design: An Interactive Approach* (3rd ed.). Los Angeles, London, New York: SAGE.

Mearman, A., Berger, S., & Guizzo, D. (2022). How different is heterodox economists' thinking on teaching? A contrastive evaluation of interview data. *Review of Political Economy, 34*(1), 45–68.

Mearman, A., Guizzo, D., & Berger, S. (2018). Whither political economy? Evaluating the CORE Project as a response to calls for change in economics teaching. *Review of Political Economy, 30*(2), 241–259.

Mearman, A., Wakeley, T., Shoib, G., & Webber, D. (2011). Does pluralism in economics education make better educated, happier students? A qualitative analysis. *International Review of Economics Education, 10*(2201), 50–62.

Murphy, K. (2001). Teaching as persuasion: A new metaphor for a new decade. *Theory into Practice, 40*(2), 224–227.

Obeng-Odoom, F. (2019). Pedagogical pluralism in undergraduate urban economics education. *International Review of Economics Education, 31*, 100158

Parra, J. (2018). People, personal projects and the challenging of social structures: A contribution to the reflection on the challenges of teaching development studies. *Third World Quarterly, 39*(11), 2188–2202.

Parra, J., Said-Hung, E., & Montoya-Vargas, J. (2021). (Re)introducing critical realism as a paradigm to inform qualitative content analysis in causal educational research. *International Journal of Qualitative Studies in Education, 34*(2), 168–182.

Pawson, R. (1996). Theorizing the interview. *The British Journal of Sociology, 47*(2), 295–314.

Raworth, K. (2017). *Doughnut Economics: Seven Ways to Think Like a 21st-Century Economist.* Vermont: Chelsea Green Publishing.

Saldaña, J. (2008). Popular film as an instructional strategy in qualitative research methods courses. *Qualitative Inquiry, 15*(1), 247–261.

Scriptslug (n.d.). *Contact*, available at https://assets.scriptslug.com/live/pdf/scripts/contact-1997.pdf

Sheehan, B., Embery, J., & Morgan, J. (2015). Give them something to think about, don't tell them what to think: A constructive heterodox alternative to the core project. *Journal of Australian Political Economy, 75*(Winter), 211–231.

Starr, M. (2014). Qualitative and mixed-methods research in economics: Surprising growth, promising future. *Journal of Economic Surveys, 28*(2), 238–264.

Stilwell, F. (2019). From economics to political economy: Contradictions, challenge, and change. *American Journal of Economics and Sociology, 78*(1), 35–62.

Sumner, A., & Tribe, M. (2008). *International Development Studies: Theories and Methods in Research and Practice.* Los Angeles, London, New Delhi and Singapore: Sage.

Swaminathan, R., & Mulvihill, T. (2018). *Teaching Qualitative Research: Strategies for Engaging Emerging Scholars.* New York and London: Guildford Press.

Verger, A., Bonal, X., & Zancajo, A. (2016). What are the role and impact of public-private partnerships in education? A realist evaluation of the Chilean Education Quasi-Market. *Comparative Education Review, 60*(2), 223–248.

Vincent, S., & Wapshott, R. (2014). Critical realism and the organizational case study: A guide to discovering institutional mechanisms. In P. Edwards, J. O'Mahoney, & S. Vicent, *Studying Organizations Using Critical Realism: A Practical Guide* (pp. 148–167). Oxford: Oxford University Press.

Watson, M. (2005). *Foundations of International Political Economy.* New York: Palgrave.

Woodrow W, C. I., & Fast, M. (2019). *Qualitative Economics: The Science of Economics.* Switzerland: Springer Nature.

Wuisman, J. (2005). The logic of scientific discovery in critical realist social scientific research. *Journal of Critical Realism, 4*(2), 366–394.

8 Conclusion

"Crisis of What?" "Crisis for Whom?"

Jon Mulberg and Thoralf Dassler

Crisis? Which Crisis?

There have been a plethora of crises, both proceeding and during the writing of this volume. There was the financial crisis of 2008, which began in the housing market and affected businesses and economies worldwide. This was followed by formal declarations of an environmental emergency (the terminology – an emergency rather than a crisis – is notable) which had, as we know, actually existed for many years beforehand. Of course, we have also had an (ongoing) Covid crisis. Most economies now face an inflation crisis, and are facing or planning for an energy crisis. In the UK there was an exchange rate crisis linked to a government debt crisis, which, in turn caused a pension fund liquidity crisis. There is also presently an ongoing healthcare crisis.

It could be the case that these crises are all independent, but this is a long list for it all to be coincidental. This chapter considers some of the linkages between these crises. Indeed, the Secretary-General of the United Nations, António Guterres, claimed in 2020, that the pandemic was a "dress rehearsal for the world of challenges to come" (United Nations 2020). One of these challenges was the climate crisis.

The Secretary-General was correct to try and warn of the effects of climate change – if the pandemic was bad, the coming environmental catastrophe will be far worse. It is possible we will have both widespread flooding and droughts leading to disruption of food chains, which will be affected also by lack of biodiversity, plastic pollution in marine environments, and by crop damage due to extreme weather events, salt-water flooding or lack of irrigation. There is also likely to be widespread deterioration in air quality and lack of drinking water security. Much of this is already beginning to show itself, but on present trajectories, we will enter a phase of the crisis, which, unlike the pandemic lockdowns, will never end.

Interestingly, the Secretary-General's address also outlined many of the concerns that have driven both heterodox political economy in general and the research positions outlined in the previous chapters – economic "calamity" and unemployment; loss of human rights; inequality; social fragmentation and poverty – but he also links these to political action, claiming we need leadership that, he believes, is regularly divorced from power (United Nations 2020). The questions of power and

DOI: 10.4324/9781003451990-12

governance have been issues within heterodox political economy since its earliest inception.

While the use of state power to intervene in normal social life was evident during the pandemic and has been remarked upon (Lidskog and Standring 2022), probably more remarkable has been the growth of state management over economic activity. Indeed, it could be said that many of the governmental responses to the pandemic have marked a departure in economic governance, which can usefully be compared – and applied – to the environmental crisis. Of particular note is the manner in which economic governance became a question of political economy, in that the locus of the problems is now held to be within government.[1] We argue that this is a new departure, in that the problem is viewed as being a problem for governments that it is their responsibility to address, even if the eventual solution lies in markets or in civil society. The pandemic witnessed unprecedented government involvement within the economy, often involving individual financial support on an unprecedented scale. The political constraints caused by the pandemic showed up the limitations of the current set of market institutions, and demonstrated how the issues were beyond the ability of market systems to handle.

Also noticeable was the centrality of ethical considerations. The discourse has moved away from the Thatcherite claim that there is "no such thing as society", to be replaced by an ethic of equity, as witnessed by the UN Secretary-General referring to social schisms and inequalities as "injustices", which the pandemic "exploited" (United Nations 2020). Even the US Congress debated legislation against profiteering and price gouging, whereas the usual discourse is that all profits are a legitimate part of the capitalist economy.

This ethical parameter, along with the altered notions of economic governance that became evident during the pandemic (and indeed are continuing with current issues surrounding energy costs, interest rates and inflation) chime with much of the debate on ecological economics,[2] and raise fundamental questions concerning the practice of economic "science". As has been outlined in the previous chapters, both the pandemic and environmental issues multiplied existing inequalities along the current fault lines, exacerbating not only class differences but also race and gender inequalities, particularly since women often form the main workforce of informal economies and/or tend to be the major contributors to unpaid care labour (Sultana 2021). Furthermore, these inequalities act as constraints on policy, often resulting in severe limits to market-based interventions – such interventions appear costly, as the price of redistribution adds to the cost of risk amelioration. This in turn results in the need for risks to be "played off" against each other, and risks to life are then pitched against risks to livelihoods. Sultana refers to this as the creation of "sacrifice zones" where "profit is prioritised over people and planetary well-being" (2021, p.2).

The usual response to all forms of risk – economic, medical or environmental – can be described as an example of the "scientisation of politics", whereby decisions are removed from the political sphere, and presented as technical problems to be solved by policy scientists (Habermas 1969). However, these risks remain at their base social and political.[3] They contain unequal and often inequitable distributions of both risk exposure and capabilities of damage mitigation, both nationally and internationally. By defining risks in technical terms, both the understanding and the governability of the risks are decreased. According to Hulme et al., to fully grasp the social nature of a crisis we need to move beyond branding of the problem as technical, and conduct a pluralistic broadening of knowledge applications. This will reveal the nature of the "normative choices". The questions to be asked, they claim, are "a crisis of what" and "a crisis for whom?" (Hulme et al. 2020).

Risks are seldom singular however, they are more often interactive. Real-life decision-making will involve trade-offs between risks with multiple dimensions (Hulme et al. 2020) and "science will not come on a white horse with a solution" (Jasanoff 2020, cited in Hulme et al. 2020, p. 2). Decisions concerning uncertain and interacting risks therefore have a political dimension (Mulberg 2020). This raises the question of a democratisation of the decision-making process regarding policies on risks. As Beck points out, decisions concerning risk are seldom taken by those facing the risks (Beck 1992). The entire point of the scientisation of politics is to create a policy elite, elites which according to Sultana are often privileged, powerful, masculine, and white (Sultana 2021, p.3). They ignore the realities of the "frontline communities" who actually faced the hazards – community is often gender, and racially imbalanced (Sultana 2021). Focus therefore shifts from understanding technical "solutions" to understanding decision-making processes. As Sultana suggests, understanding the "contours of suffering" will involve understanding local social systems and power structures, and also the political economies of interacting crises (Sultana 2021, p.8). That is to say that knowledge of economic, political and social institutions is vital to policy assessment.

This was evident in the discussions of pandemic policy earlier in this volume – often the adjustments were unfair or bypassed women and minorities. The most successful responses were those that were built upon alternative institutional arrangements already in place to support these groups.

Environmental Crises

The response of orthodox economics to the question of environmental degradation illustrates the scientisation of politics well. The orthodox approach subsumes all issues into a market-based framework. Environmental problems are regarded simply as market failures, and the solutions put forward "resemble the solutions to any market failure" (Perry and Primrose 2015, p.134). Environmental degradation is interpreted as an "external cost", and the solution is therefore to internalise the costs, through cap and trade schemes or through taxation (Rosewarne 2010, pp.20–21, Stilwell 2011). In a public letter, signed by just under 50 famous economists and public figures, it was claimed that a carbon tax is the most effective environmental policy since "By correcting a well-known market failure, a carbon tax will send a powerful price signal that harnesses the invisible hand of the marketplace to steer economic actors towards a low-carbon future" and the tax "should increase every year until emissions reductions goals are met". They claim this is preferable to regulation, and will promote investment in alternative energy (Wall Street

Journal 2019). The authors suggest that any revenue derived from this tax should be redistributed as a flat rate rebate, which they claim will exceed any energy price hike (Wall Street Journal 2019).

The other main method of incorporating environmental resources into market mechanisms, ironically initially designed to provide an alternative to taxation, is to install a cap and trade system (sometimes called tradable permits), whereby the resource is effectively commandeered by governments, and then sold. The European Trading Scheme, which trades permits for carbon emissions, is an example of this policy in practice.

The first comment to make on the taxation proposal in the Wall Street Journal is how radical a change in thinking and policy it represents – both environmental degradation, and the issue of distribution is acknowledged by leading economists. This is a massive sea change from the days when, for example, the journal *Ecological Economics* was first published.[4] However, the proposal remains simply a modest reform of the agenda of orthodox economics. It is noticeable, for example, how in both these approaches the environment is regarded as identical to all other resources, apart from the need to correct for market failures. It is also unclear that the redistributional effect which the signatories claim will occur will in fact ensue, or if the rising prices of other commodities will cause inflationary pressure that results in the tax bonus being appropriated, which is what has been seen recently in the United States, Europe, and most other regions. Similarly, tradable permits can cause price hikes, which could require massive distributional policies to alleviate. It is possible that, if taken seriously, a carbon tax or a tradable permits scheme would lead to a crisis of governance (Mulberg 2017).

In fact, the proffered technical solutions – taxation or trading schemes – hide the political nature of the problems, just as they did with the pandemic. The need for social and political decisions on environmental usage, in this case over the level of cap to carbon emissions (termed "emissions reduction goals" in the Wall Street Journal letter), remains the same as before, but simply take on a pecuniary guise (Mulberg 2017, 2020). This becomes clearer if we expand our consideration beyond one single hazard (global warming), and consider all aspects of environmental degradation. These are many and various, including water security, air pollution, plastics pollution, biodiversity, food security, waste and so on. Presumably all of the commodities involved in environmental degradation should be subject to either tax and cap or cap and trade. This would then encompass virtually all of the commodities currently produced.

We would need to make a decision on the quantity of all production, which would in effect turn the economic system into a form of market socialism, whereby governments effectively appropriate resources from corporations, and control supply and price to clear capped markets. Economic governance would be entirely altered.[5] While the present authors would certainly entertain this approach (and would certainly suggest the wholesale overhaul of economic governance is necessary), this is clearly not the aim of the signatories to the Wall Street Journal letter. In common with most of the economics profession, they wish to "avoid debate over the size of government" (Wall Street Journal 2019). However, if environmental protection is taken seriously, it seems unlikely this will be possible.

Further evidence of the political nature of environmental economic policy can be seen in the approach to international trade. Taxation policy cannot be separated from international trade policy, and will require a withdrawal from unfettered international trade. The authors suggest a "border carbon adjustment system" (Wall Street Journal 2019), which we take to mean a targeted import tariff. This is an obvious necessity to enforce national indirect taxation, otherwise cheaper imports would flood the markets. However, this would be a complete about-turn for current international trading policy, and go against current economic orthodoxy.[6]

The other objective of a carbon tax is to generate alternative forms of production and consumption, but many environmentalists believe that because of the emphasis of orthodox economics on 'growth', the conventional, market-based, approach to managing climate change is inherently incompatible with saving the climate, as economic 'growth' requires more and more resources. So far carbon neutrality – a state where CO_2 production balances with its removal – remains unobtainable, not least because the current technologies (such as tidal power, battery storage for intermittent renewable energy production and so on) require further development. Carbon neutrality in production has, in many cases, simply shifted the issue along the supply chain. Just the same as elsewhere, there are diminishing returns in technological development also. At any event, this is not something that the economist can really speculate on. The assumption of orthodox economics that alternatives will always be available is no longer valid.[7]

Crises and Money

This brings us to a discussion of economic 'growth'. This is presented as a technical issue but it has actually provided a political underpinning for limiting management of both the Covid pandemic and environmental degradation. It has been held that economic 'growth' (usually crudely operationalised by the use of gross domestic product figures) is vital for employment and income. This was used to justify limiting and ending pandemic interventions and support (Stewart et al. 2022, p.412).

The feasibility and desirability of constantly increased GDP have long been discussed within the environmental debate. In particular, it is often held that any 'decoupling' of increasing GDP from material and energy use (and the associated increases in waste and emissions) will not be possible (see e.g. Jackson 2009), so any increased GDP will result in the same issues of global warming, pollution, and degradation resource depletion that we mentioned earlier in the chapter. Elsewhere, Mulberg has pointed out how the converse also holds, and how most of the practical measures for environmental protection will involve a lowering of GDP, since by definition it will involve less economic activity (see Mulberg 1995, 1996, 2017). Interestingly enough, this would likely be the case if the carbon tax proposed by the Wall Street Journal signatories was actually enacted.

However, limiting or lowering GDP will have political repercussions. The idea of 'growth' has long been used as a smokescreen for the avoidance of debate on income and wealth distribution. If we get a bigger cake, debates on the proportions of the slices can be avoided. This is, of course, what was behind the famous Kennedy quip that "a rising tide raises all boats"; that we are all better off if the total wealth created rises. However, we are now faced with storms rather than rising tides, and not all boats are equal. Along with the spectre of a flat (or falling) GDP may well be a rising debate on income and wealth.

A variation on this is an assumed link between employment and GDP. However, any such linkage is clearly only temporary. The GDP of the United Kingdom is currently three times higher now than in the year Jon Mulberg (the older of the chapter authors) was born, even after allowing for inflation. However, unemployment has not fallen by an equivalent level.

This belief in the link between employment and GDP partly explains why "growth fetishism" continues (Blackwater 2015a). There might be deeper considerations to take into account, however. In particular, the relationship between GDP and credit needs to be considered. It has been argued that there is a causal relationship between credit and growth; if credit is lent at interest, then GDP will need to increase to repay the debt (Douthwaite 2015; Blackwater 2015a). This has a number of effects. It contributes to the subordination of both social and ecological protection to raising national expenditure (Stuart et al. 2021), which can be witnessed in both pandemic policies (such as the much-ridiculed "eat out to help out" policy of the UK Chancellor, which subsidised restaurant dining at the height of the Covid outbreak), and in the continued lip-service to environmental protection.

It also brings our focus onto money and credit. While Aguila outlined in an earlier chapter the Marxian analysis of money as a commodity, Douthwaite (and other environmentalists) claimed that money in contemporary economies is for the most part bank debt. Money is therefore created for profit by a powerful banking system, but the profit (interest), Douthwaite claims, can only be repaid by an increase in unsustainable rise in production (Douthwaite 2012).

Rosa Luxemburg (writing mainly in the 1910s) offered a similar analysis of the role of money in the imperative to growth. However, she also points out (writing it should be noted, before J.M. Keynes) that – in Marxist terms – capitalist production could not take place without credit. Furthermore, commodities only make profits when they are sold. This meant that there had to be what later became known as "effective demand" for capitalist production to ensue. Luxemburg's analysis – using Marxist terminology – was that for the capitalist class as a whole profits could not come from sales between themselves, but neither could they come from sales to the (wage-earning) working-class – workers cannot spend money they do not have, and no overall profit can be gained from workers spending their wages, since profit is the excess of sales over costs, and in this analysis costs are ultimately wages. The income from sales to the working class would only match the expenditure already incurred in wages.

The function of money and credit is therefore to increase effective demand. This can be focused either internally within developed societies or externally in less developed economies. Luxemburg's concern (preceding the 1920s crash) was on the latter. To obtain a market for sales, debt and effective demand had to come into the system from outside, and new overseas markets needed to be developed. This would not only undermine the non-capitalist economies, but tie in these economies as permanent debtors (Blackwater 2015b).

Luxembourg viewed money as a contemporary form of imperialism, which debt-binds the emerging economies to advance capitalist states. Money and finance, she claimed, have a definite purpose of political and social control. Unlike Dowthwaite, for Luxemburg money does not simply perform technical functions to enable economic activity, but is a social institution, which enables social and political control, and is another site of class struggle. Control of money is a major element of power and freedom (Bagchi 2022).

According to Bagchi, we can see this analysis playing out in the current era. He claims that the dominance of the US dollar subordinates economics in the periphery to the policy decisions of the US Federal reserve, exposing them to sudden reversals of capital flows, speculation and currency volatility. He claims peripheral currencies are also tied to liquidity infrastructures controlled by international financial institutions (Bagchi 2022).

Imperialism therefore, becomes embedded in domestic arrangements through the power of financial organisations, such as the International Monetary Fund, who impose rules, subordinating social and political equality to economic growth. International debt was therefore "a tool of subordination" (Bagchi 2022). We saw in the chapter by Bona how this played out in Argentina. These organisations are often accused of subordinating environmental protection also.

The other sphere of market expansion is internal. Blackwater points to the mass inclusion of women and adolescents into the waged economy, and the subsequent commodification of all aspects of social life (Blackwater 2015a). The chapter from Cihani outlines Minsky's analysis of the fragility of monetary systems, and the increasing role of financial institutions in the functioning of the money and credit system.

However, this economic imperialism and internal expansion, Luxembourg pointed out, was ultimately doomed to failure. In essence, this is a huge debt bubble, whereby debt was repaid by profits from debt (Blackwater 2015a). Keen (and others) have pointed out how the inclusion of personal debt in econometric models could be used to predict the 2008 crash (which began, it should be recalled, with a default within the domestic housing market, a major element in the total commodification of social life; Blackwater 2015b). However, it is held by Luxemburg that the system as a whole is unsustainable. As Blackwater puts it "Growth requires credit which requires growth, and it cannot go on forever" (Blackwater 2015b, p.83).

Crisis of Economics?

The current challenges for governments worldwide came at a time when the discipline of economics is itself in a period of crisis, not least due to the complete failure to foresee the 2008 crash.

This left even HM the Queen of England somewhat bemused. More importantly, it caused an unprecedented protest among students of economics about the relevance of their own discipline. The 2008 crash, exposed and inability to either predict or explain economic phenomena and called into question the entire providence of the discipline.

However, what should the malcontented students be taught? As Parra suggests in his chapter, replacing one set of scientific and technical claims with another is unlikely to be satisfactory. As has been seen throughout this chapter, the responses to the variety of crises, especially regarding environment and the pandemic, have involved disguising political and social decisions as technical issues.

In fact, the trajectory of policy-making, as well as the challenge to expertise from the students of economics, has followed quite well Beck's description of what he referred to as the risk society, an emerging society where the focus is not on the production of goods, but rather the avoidance of bads. The ontology of risk avoidance is, however, different to that of production, and requires a different epistemology of science. Beck claims that the risks now being faced are immense, and transcend time and space, so that 'testing' in the usual meaning of the term is not possible. In this sense, Beck merges this with what is often called uncertainty. Risks, for Beck, involve both objective and subjective components, and comparing risks unnecessarily involves non-objective elements. Both physical and social science are therefore required in risk assessments (Beck 1992).[8]

Applying this to economic 'science' (which, incidentally, Beck does not attempt) suggests the acknowledgement and development of a plurality of approaches, acknowledgement of the political and social character of economic activity and of the political and social character of decisions on personal and environmental safety, and indeed a realisation that economics itself is part of the social world it purports to examine. Parra's employment of qualitative economics in a novel approach to economics education is a good start to this project.

Notes

1 This is part of the analysis of the 'Market Socialism' school. For a discussion see Mulberg (1995). We will return to this issue later.
2 However there are obvious differences in the format of the two crises, which explains the differences in immediate policy response – see van der Ven and Sun (2021), and Lidskog and Standring (2022).
3 For a discussion see Mulberg (1996).
4 For a discussion of some of the tactics used to marginalise ecological economics see Spash (2011).
5 For a similar argument regarding environmental regulation see the debate between Eckersley and Mulberg (Eckersley 1992; Mulberg 1992).
6 For a discussion see Daly and Cobb (1994).
7 For a discussion see Mulberg (2017).
8 Beck's belief in the 'democratisation' of risks, and his belief that these will cut across class divisions is less obviously evidenced. It does seem that the availability of 'escape routes' for the populations of richer nations have been underestimated.

References

Bagchi, K., 2022, Rosa Luxemburg and the Imperialism of Money, *Critical Legal Thinking* 17 Nov (online: https://criticallegalthinking.com/2022/11/17/rosa-luxemburg-and-the-imperialism-of-money/).

Beck, U., 1992, *Risk Society: Towards a New Modernity*, London: Sage.

Blackwater, B., 2015a, *Why do capitalist economies need to grow?*, (pamphlet), Green House Think Tank (online: www.greenhousethinktank.org/) January 2015.

Blackwater, B., 2015b, Rediscovering Rosa Luxemburg. *Renewal: A Journal of Social Democracy*, *23*(3), p.71.

Daly, H. and Cobb, J. B., 1994, *For the Common Good, Redirecting the Economy toward Community, the Environment and a Sustainable Future*, Boston: Beacon Press.

Douthwaite, R., 2012, Degrowth and the Supply of Money in an Energy-Scarce World. *Ecological Economics*, 84, pp.187–193.

Douthwaite, R., 2015, *The Ecology of Money* (Schumacher Briefings Book 4), Cambridge: Green Books.

Eckersley, R., 1992, Green versus Ecosocialist Economic Programmes: The Market Rules OK? *Political Studies, 40*(2), pp.315–333.

Habermas, J., 1969, *Towards a Rational Society*, trans. J. Shapiro, London: Heinemann (translation in 1971).

Hulme, M., Lidskog, R., White, J.M. and Standring, A., 2020, Social Scientific Knowledge in Times of Crisis: What Climate Change Can Learn from Coronavirus (and Vice Versa). *Wiley Interdisciplinary Reviews: Climate Change*, *11*(4), pp.1–5.

Jackson, T., 2009, *Prosperity without Growth*, London: Earthscan.

Lidskog, R. and Standring, A., 2022, COVID-19 and the Environmental Crises: Knowledge, Social Order and Transformative Change, in Brown, P.R. and Zinn, J.O., eds., *Covid-19 and the Sociology of Risk and Uncertainty: Studies of Social Phenomena and Social Theory Across 6 Continents* (pp.267–293), Cham: Springer International Publishing.

Mulberg, J., 1992, Who Rules the Market? Green versus Ecosocialist Economic Programmes: A Response to Eckersley. *Political Studies, 40*(2), pp.334–341.

Mulberg, J., 1995, *Social Limits to Economic Theory* (1st ed.), London: Routledge.

Mulberg, J., 1996, Environmental Planning, Economic Planning and Political Economy. *International Sociology*, *11*(4), pp.441–456.

Mulberg, J., 2017, The Challenge of Environmental Governance: Ecology and the Need for a Heterodox Political Economy. *Journal of Australian Political Economy, 80*, pp.129–154.

Mulberg, J., 2020, 'The Risk Society and the Ontology of Economics' in Hermann A. and Mouatt S., eds., *Contemporary Issues in Heterodox Economics: Implications for Theory and Policy Action* (pp.34–43), London: Routledge.

Perry, N. and Primrose, D., 2015, Heterodox Economics and the Biodiversity Crisis. *Journal of Australian Political Economy*, *75*, pp.133–152.

Rosewarne, S., 2002, Meeting the Challenge of Climate Change: The Poverty of the Dominant Economic Narrative and Market Solutions as Subterfuge. *Journal of Australian Political Economy*, *66*, pp.17–50.

Spash, C.L., 2011, Social Ecological Economics: Understanding the Past to See the Future. *American Journal of Economics and Sociology*, *70*(2), pp.340–375.

Stilwell, F., 2011, Marketising the Environment. *Journal of Australian Political Economy*, *68*, pp.108–127.

Stuart, D., Petersen, B. and Gunderson, R., 2022, Shared Pretenses for Collective Inaction: The Economic Growth Imperative, COVID-19, and Climate Change. *Globalizations*, *19*(3), pp.408–425.

Sultana, F., 2021, Climate Change, COVID-19, and the Co-production of Injustices: A Feminist Reading of Overlapping Crises. *Social & Cultural Geography*, *22*(4), pp.447–460.

United Nations, 2020, 'COVID-19 Dress Rehearsal for World of Challenges to Come, Secretary-General Tells General Assembly', press release 22 September.

van der Ven, H. and Sun, Y., 2021, Varieties of Crises: Comparing the Politics of COVID-19 and Climate Change. *Global Environmental Politics*, *21*(1): 13–22.

Index

Note: Endnotes are indicated by the page number followed by "n" and the note number e.g., 90n3 refers to note 3 on page 90. Page locators in **bold** and *italics* represents tables and figures, respectively.

abduction 130, 131, 132, 134, 135
accumulation regime 76, 90n3
Agarwal, B study 22
alternative accounts 122–3
Alternative Law Forum 29, 36
Amma Canteen 12, 24n1
analysis of information, format assistance 136, **136**
Argentina: austerity measures 79, 80, 84, 89; capital stock depreciation 82, **82**, *83*, *87*; crisis recovery 82–3; currency 80, 91n9; currency board 80, 91n8; debts 80; devaluation 84, 88; economic growth 83; economic recession and recovery 84; economic stagnation 80, 81, 88; economic structure reorganization 79; financial valorization 79, 91n6; gross domestic product (GDP) 82, **82**, *83*, 84, *87*, 95, 96; higher salaries 85, 86, 91n14, 95; hyperinflation 79, 83, 89; income transfer 79, 80, 89; inflation 91n9, 91n10; loans 80; neoliberal policies 79, 80, 83, 84, 89; pesification 80; "populist shift" 81; poverty 80; privatizations 79, 80, 83, 87, 88; production investment 87, 88; power bloc 80, 81, 84, 91n7; public policies 84; raw materials 85; redistribution of wealth 83; regressive tendencies 88; renationalization 81; rents 85–6, 89, 95; sociopolitical disputes 89; taxes 80, 86, 91n15; unemployment 80, 83, 84; wages 81, 91n10, 96; wealth generation 83, 89; working class exploitation 79
Argentina convertibility 76, 79, 80, 87, 89; collapse 89; crisis 89–90; regimes 82, 84, 88
Argentina cost of social reproduction (CSR) 94; calculation 82, **82**, *83*; evolution *87*; and GDP ratio 84, 88; growth 89; recovery 83; upward dynamic 84
Argentina economic surplus (ES): accumulation decline 84; destinations 86–8, 89; distribution 85, *85*, 95; and GDP average 84; increase 83; origins of 85–6; quantifying 82, *83*; uses 86, 87, *87*, 88, 90
Argentina regimes: accumulation 79, 80, 82, 84, 88, 89; *coup d'état* 80; dictatorship 79
Argentina society: conflicts 80; internal changes in 84; protection system 84–5; regression 84; redefining 79
Ashoka University 30
Association for Heterdox Economics 7
austerity policies 2; necessity to discard 60
Azim Premji University (APU) study 29

Bagchi, K 149
bancor surpluses 69
bank accounts, lack of 29, 36
bank check system 63
bank reserves 99
banks, key roles of 61
Beck, U 150, 150n8
Bengaluru: service sector 27; urban female informal workers 30
black box of research 125, 126, 132

Blackwater, B 149
Bogotá: coronavirus cases 48, **48**, 49, **49**; family policies 46; gini coefficient 50; informal economy 49–50; local policies 46; mayors 46
"border carbon adjustment system" 147
bottom-up planning 14
Bretton Woods era 5, 105; after 6, 98, 106, 109; before 105; disintegrated 97

cap and trade system 146
capital asset prices, determination of 64, 65
capitalist system: "casino" 62; commercial 61, 62; fundamental property of 61; importance of finance in 59; inherent instability 59, 62, 63, 64, 67; irrationality of 77; People's Capitalism 62; profits 64; producer independence 99; stages of 61, 62, 63; use of wealth 77
carbon emissions trading 146
carbon neutrality 147
carbon tax 145, 146, 147
casual and self-employed workers 29
Catholic religion 42, 43, 47
Chang, Ha Joong 119
Chile, school system 135
Class Projects 131–2, 134–7
class struggles 75, 76
classic film clip 128–9
climate change: forecast 143; incompatibility with economic growth 147
coins 104, 105
colonial and precolonial families 42
Columbia: air pollution 51; cash programs 50; Catholic Church 47; classification of economic sectors 50; colonial history 46–7; corruption in 51; COVID-19 51–2; democratically elected government 43; development of market economy 47; duty of State 45; elites 47; 'emergency basic rent' 50; family 42–5; gender violence 50, 52; gig economy 46, 50; Gini index **48**; household classification 48–9; inequality 46–8, 49, 50, 51; informal economy 44, 46, 49–50; international trade 44, 47; lower education levels 50; market exchanges 44; monopoly of power 47; national constitution 44; natural resources 46–7; neoliberal policies 44; pandemic spending 51; political parties 43; privatization 44; privileged and under-privileged 47; redistributive policies 44, 51; remote working 50; repression of collective action 51, 52; SISBEN survey 50; social mobility index 48; social protests 52; source of income 44; subsidies 50; support of State 45; taxation 44, 51, 52; trust in government 51; universal basic income proposal 51; vested interests 46–7; vulnerability of people 48; welfare policies 43–4; women at disadvantage 50; working conditions 44
Columbian national family welfare institute (ICBF) 43
commodities 70, 100; as money 101–2; price of 70, 102, 146
community kitchens 14, 16
concept maps 133
concubinage 42–3
construction workers 28, 29, 32, 33, 34, 35; without Jan Dhan accounts 34
cost of social reproduction (CSR) 75, 76–7; estimation 93–5; retirement 93, 94; wage 93–4, 96
COVID -19 (SARS-CoV-2) 11; Bogotá positive cases 48, **48**, 49, **49**; combating *19*; containment (USA) 22; as a dress rehearsal 143; effect on women and girls 19; exit strategy (Kerala) 18; exposing vulnerability of financial system 59; financial and economic crises afterwards 1, 59–60; impact in Columbia 52; injustices exploited 144; job losses 28; policies 148; resilience, comparison of Indian states 20, *21*; state involvement in economy 144; unequal impact of 2
credit 110, 113n5; and growth 148; informal 28
credit cards 62–3
creditors and debtors 110
Creoles 47
criollos 42, 43
crises: management, people-centric 18; and money 147–9; social nature of 145
critical realism 138n2, 139n7
critical thinking 121
crop damage by extreme weather 143
currencies, adoption of 105
currency links with gold, broken 97, 98

current account surplus 66
Curriculum Open-access Resources in Economics project (CORE) 120, 121

Danielson, A 77, **78**
debt: bubble 149; commitments 65; defaults causing 61; deflation 61, 62, 63; in foreign currencies 70, 71; government 62, 66, 143; international 149
Delhi households 29
derivatives 63
developed countries' imposition of trade liberalization 70
developing countries: domestically produced goods and services 71; economic and financial reform strategies 70; economic stagnation and debt 70; inflationary pressures 72
'dollarization' 71
dollars: as international currency 111; and peripheral currencies 149
domestic abuse 17
domestic helpers 29, 30, 32, 33, 34, 35; and food rations 28, 33; with Jan Dhan accounts 35; organizations for 29, 36; seen as infection carriers 36
Donati, P 45
drinking water security 143
Ducque's government program 50

econometric models 125
economic 'growth' 147–9; and climate change, incompatibility 147; and full employment 72; and wealth distribution 148
economic activity: people and groups 126: state management 144
economic agents 125
economic approach, major flaw in 4
economic behavior 41
economic internationalism and peace 69
economic liberalism, Polanyi's critique of 40
economic study 126
economic surplus (ES) 5, 75, 76, 82; estimated 77; theory, alternatives for **78**
Economics students, arguments to interest 120, 123–5
Economics: The User's Guide 119
economies: institutionalization of 40; non-capitalist 149; speculative boom 65; stuck 11
economists 109, 119
education; "asymmetric information" in *134*; behavioural and brain sciences 122; of economists debate 121; lack of access to 21; market theory in 132, 133, *134*; public choice theory 132, 133, *134*, 138n1; quasi-markets in 120, 132, 135
edutainment 127–8
electronic funds 62–3
Emmel, N 130
employment: commitment to 67; definition of tight full 67; equilibrium 64; subsidized 68
environmental crises 145–7; orthodox approach 145
environmental degradation 146, 147; interpreted as costs 145
environmental policy 145–6, 147
environmental problems: hiding political nature of 146; seen as market failure 145
environmental protection, necessitating lower GDP 147
equal opportunities 21
ethical considerations of equity 144
European Trading Scheme 146
exchange rate: crisis 143; regime 71
export-led growth 71
external funds 65, 66

Factories Act 36
factory layoffs 36
family 42; choices *134*; definition 4, 44; descendants 42; evolution 42; juridical protection 45; moral and economic sanctions 42; nonlegal 42, 43, 44; support of 43; types 42, 43
farming, community 16
Federal Reserve Bank 61, 62
femicide 50
fiat money 110
finance: capitalism 62; that creates stability 59; inelastic demand for 66; modern theory 62; and the production process 61–2
financial crisis (2008) 1, 143, 149, 150
Financial Instability Hypothesis (FIH) 4, 59–66; contrast to neoclassical synthesis 63; foundation of 60; and the global financial system 69–70; as a holistic approach 59, 67, 72;

investment and finance theory 63, 64; origins of 60
Financial Instability Hypothesis-Informed Policy Proposals 66–72; income policy 68; increased spending on education 68; objectives to eliminate poverty and unemployment 67; subsidized employment opportunities 68
financial instability, mitigating 59, 60
financial sovereignty 70, 71
financial system, international 68
financial/banking sector, primary roles of 60
financing, permanent 65
Fine, B 125
fiscal stimulus (Government of India) 27–8, 29
food distribution 27–8
food, less for women 33, 36, 37
full employment: and economic growth 72; leading to speculative boom 65
function of money and credit 148–9
Furtado, Celso 75, 77, **78**, 86

garment industry 31, 35
garment workers 29, 30, 31, 32, 34, 35; with no bank accounts 35; with no Jan Dhan accounts 34; with no ration cards 33; protest of 36
Garments Mahila Karmikara Munnade 29, 36
Gaviria, President Cesar 44
gender imbalance 145
gender inequality reduction 14
gender violence, Columbia 50, 52
gender-centric policies 36
Germer, C 97, 98
Gertler, P J 124, 125
Gini index **48**
global financial and commodity markets 70
global imbalances 68, 69
global integration and divergent national policy 68
globalization and the erosion of financial sovereignty 68
gold: convertibility 5, 6, 109–10; fluctuating quote 98, 106, 107–8; imaginary 103, 104; monetary role 97–8; physical presence of 110–11; in production 107–8; replaced by symbols of value 104–5; standard 97; value 102, 105, 106, 108
governance, definition 11
government, decentralized 13
Great Depression (1929) 61, 62, 63
Great Transformation, The 41
Gregory, S 20
gross domestic product (GDP) 75; changes, political repercussions 148; and credit 148; figures, use of 147; increasing 147; link with employment 148; of the UK 148
guest workers 11–12, 13
Gutiérrez, V 42

health care crisis 143
health care workers 50–1
heterodox: economic policies 11; educators 125; perception of high cost 122; thinking 120
high-wage industries 67
household surveys 93
human change dynamics 126
Human Development Index 12
human processes, meaning and interpretation 126, 139n7
Human Rights Watch report 52

immanent critique 138n3
impact evaluation manual 124
imperialism 149
import tariff 147
income of reproduction 77
India: access to food 29; income drop 12; informal employment 27; job losses 29; lack of government responsibility 12; lockdown 11, 12, 27; manufacturing industry 31; Post-COVID studies 29–35; poverty 21; raising working hours 36; ration distribution 27–8, 37n1; relaxing labor laws 36; unemployment 12
industrialization 68–9
inflation 106, 146; crisis 143; psychological component to 67; and unemployment 67
Institute for New Economic Thinking (INET) 7
Inter-American Development Bank (IDB) 44
interest rates: long-term 66; manipulations 72; rise of 62; short-term 66
internal funds 65, 66
International Labour Organization (ILO) 28

International Monetary Fund (IMF) 70, 80; rules 149
international trade policy 147
interview process and protocols 135, 136, 137
investment: boom and inflation 65; borrowers' and lenders' risk 66; as a function of quasi rents 66; theory of money and finance 61
iterative thinking 131

Jagosh, J 130
Jan Dhan accounts 28, 35, 37n2; lack of 34
Job Guarantee program 72
joint liability groups (JLGs) 16, 22
Journal of Economic Surveys 124
Juglar cycles 60
junk bonds 62

Karnataka: food security 33–4; government 28; informal workers 28, 32; lack of benefits and job contracts 32; lack of cash transfers 36; lack of financial security 34–5; loan repayments 34, 35, 36; manufacturing sector 30–1, **31**; rent negotiation 34, 35–6; self-employed workers 32; textile manufacture 31, 32; urban female workforce 28, **31**
Kerala: and COVID-19 13, 16; destitute families 17; feminization of 15; floods (2018) 14, 15; food security 12; governments working with people 13, 18; gross domestic product 12; migration 12; 'model of development' 12; poverty eradication 13, 14; protection gear manufacture 17; redistribution policies 12; relief package 20
Keynes, J M: proposal of a clearinghouse mechanism 69, 70; on self-sufficiency 69
Kirchner governments 76, 81, 84, 86, 88
Kregel, Jan 68, 69
Kudumbashree 13, 14–23; bottom-up planning 14; budget hotels 16; community kitchens 14; community-based organizations 15; and COVID-19 fight 15–18 19, *19*, 24n3; domestic abuse 17; essential supplies 16; mission statement 15; as a model in crisis and resilience 18–20, *19*; neighborhood groups 16; public trust 15; restructuring state's role 14; self-sufficiency 16; set up 14; skill training programs 18; support 17; women farmers 16

labour chits 109
labour value 100
Latin America, neoliberal period 79
law Cecilia 43
lenders' risk 66
Lenger, A (2019) survey study 127
life expectancy 12
Lippit, V 77, **78**
loans, interest-free 18
localization 22, 23
lockdown; disproportionate effect on women 27; in India 11, 12, 27; international 11
Luxemburg, Rosa 148, 149

manufacturing industry and infrastructure 62
Manzano, A: work 135–6, 140n15
market economies, challenges to 71
market expansion 149
market socialism 146
market stability, creating 11
Marx, K 76; challenges 98; commodity theory of money 97–8; criticism of 97, 98, 99
Maxwell, J 126, 127, 130, 134
metals as money 97–8, 101
microcredit 15
microenterprises 22
migrant laborers 11–12, 13
milk distribution 28, 33
minimum wage 68, 72, 77
Minsky, Hyman P 59; assumptions in investment and finance theory 64; and Financial Instability Hypothesis 60–6; proposals to mitigate financial instability 59
monetary sovereignty, giving up ('dollarization') 71
money: as bank debt 148; in circulation 104–6, 110; as a commodity 97, 98, 101, 102, 103; and control 149; as creation 148; credit theory 97; criticism of 97; debt-binding 149; as social functions 97; fiat 110; functions of 102–4, 110; hoarding 109, 110, 111; manager capitalism 62; market funds

63; as a measure of value 102, 108; ontology of 99–102; physical presence of 98, 104; reserves 110; as social and private power 109; as solution to organization of labour 98; supply and debt commitments 65; theory of 101, 112n1; world market 103
Moseley, F 97
mutual funds 62

National Council of Applied Economic Research (NCAER) 29
'National Front' 43
neoliberal capitalist globalization 22

ontologies 119, 138n1
orthodox economics 11; challenging 2; differences from heterodox economics 11; unsustainability of 149
'over indebtedness' 61
'ownership-operation' structure 69

panic of 1907 (Bankers' Crisis) 61
paper money 104–5
parental obligation, lack of 42
Patinkin Resolution of the neoclassical synthesis 64–5
payment, means of 110; international 98, 110, 111, 112
pension funds 62; crisis 143; household ownership 62; state 62
Periodic Labor Force Survey (PLFS) 30–5; monthly wage 32; profile of respondents 32–3
plastic pollution in marine environments 143
pluralism 119, 120, 121
Polanyi, Karl: concept of economy 40, 41
policy elite 145
power and government issues 143–4
Primera línea 52, 52n1
production rise, unsustainable 148
production-financing, short-term 65
profit prioritised 144
public choice theory in education 132, 133, 133, 138n1
public distribution system 27, 28, 30
public resources, use of 125

qualitative data 125, 134–7
qualitative economics 125–6, 131, 139n7
qualitative inquiry 125, 127, 129, 130, 131
qualitative methods, teaching 122–3
qualitative reasoning 123–6, 127–8, 129
qualitative sources 124
quantitative analysis of survey data 124
quantitative easing 99
quasi rents as gross profits 65

racial imbalance 145
ration cards 12, 30, 33, 36; lack of 29, 34
research techniques 127
reserve fund 111; gold 111, 112
retail trade 30
retroduction 130, 131, 134, 135
Ricardo, D 76
risk assessment 150, 150n8
risk avoidance ontology 150
risk society 150
risks: changing notions of 62; interactive 145; response to 144–5; trade-offs 144, 145; unequal 144–5
Robinson, Joan 65

"sacrifice zones" 144
salaries, high level 75
same-sex partners 44, 45
sampling strategy 130
Sbattella, J 77, **78**
school competition 133
schools, concealed interests and agendas *134*
Schumpeter's work on the Business Cycle Theories 60
"scientisation of politics" 144–5
Seattle Conference 70
self-help groups (SHGs) 13, 14
short-term performance, pursuit of 62
single motherhood 42, 43; non-recognition of 45
SISBEN survey 50
Smith, A 76
social capital 20
social order 42, 43
sovereign debt problem 70
spillover theory 89
stagflation 62
Starr, M 123, 124, 126
state power intervention 144
Stranded Workers Action Network (SWAN) 29, 30
structuralists 75, 90n1
subaltern classes 78, 90n5
'Subhiksha Keralam' 16
Sultana, F 144, 145

sustainable development goals (SDGs) 20, 21
Sustainable Development index 20, *21*
Symbolic Interactionism 126, 139n6, 139n7

Tamil Nadu 12
taxes 72, 77, 147
terms of trade 68
top-down approach 120
tradeable permits 146
tv series clip 128

underemployment equilibrium 65
unemployment: in India 12; and inflation 67; market reactions to 65
UNICEF 17
unit of account 99, 102, 103; no longer fixed 108, 113n4; state regulation 102, 103, 105
United Nations Development Programme (UNDP) 21, 22
United Nations Women's Regional Office for Asia and the Pacific 27
urban female informal workers, unheard 36
U.S. Treasury 61

value 100, 101
value-added services and commodities 71
vender's discount 63
video clips 128–9
violence, gender 50, 52

wages 76
Wall Street Journal 146–7
women: disadvantaged 21; empowerment of 14; homecare 28, 45, 50; lockdown, disproportionate effect on 27
working class, social reproduction of 76
World Bank 44, 70, 80
world money 98, 99, 109, 110
World Trade Organization 70
Wuhan, pneumonia in 11

For Product Safety Concerns and Information please contact our EU representative GPSR@taylorandfrancis.com
Taylor & Francis Verlag GmbH, Kaufingerstraße 24, 80331 München, Germany

www.ingramcontent.com/pod-product-compliance
Ingram Content Group UK Ltd.
Pitfield, Milton Keynes, MK11 3LW, UK
UKHW020001200926
475702UK00015B/2420
* 9 7 8 1 0 3 2 5 8 8 9 2 6 *